G000049410

Contents

To Lorenzo, who deserves his
"crown of laurels" for patience.

Introduction

Yes, parents-to-be, the time has come! It has been months since you were first informed of the impending arrival. It has been a time of many changes, physical and emotional, for both of you—a time of much planning with the need to make many decisions about how you will change your life together to include the newcomer.

Now, when all arrangements have been anticipated and most of them completed, the time for making one more important and difficult decision has come—*what will you name the baby?*

This book is designed to assist you in selecting a name worthy of your child.

There can be no denial that our names affect our lives. They are basic to our identity since, in most cases, they become attached at birth. Names have emotional implications that can and do influence our social functioning. Parents today are feeling the need to devote much more time and energy to the selection of names for their children. And many adults are feeling the need to alter their names before they can achieve success. This practice of name-changing, which was once attributed solely to members of the acting profession, has become more widespread.

Naming is a custom that has been performed by every civilization known to mankind. It developed with the advent of speech, and evolved as we began making identifications and distinguishing people from one another with different sounds, usually borrowing these from nature.

As language became more stylized, naming grew in complexity. The sources of these first appellations seem to have been uniform throughout all tribal cultures. A common custom was to give the child a name that related to a circumstance surrounding his birth, either an event that coincided with his arrival in the world or a situation of his parents at this particular time. Nature names were always popular, and it was not unusual for a child to be named after a star, a metal, or some mineral element. Animals served as symbols of desired traits and often a child would receive the name of a certain creature because it possessed a characteristic that his parents wished him to emulate. In most ancient tribes of Western Europe, the raven was the trademark of success in battle, the snake of wisdom and immortality, the wolf of cunning and protection, the bear of strength, and the lion of regal power. The horse denoted sacredness, since in many mythologies it was his task to transport the gods. A common practice was to give a child the name of a characteristic he was thought to possess, or of a virtue his parents wanted him to cultivate. The names of the tribal gods were used frequently with the hope that the deity would be pleased and therefore confer his or her blessing on the offspring.

As the size of a primitive tribe increased and the territory it claimed grew in size according to its need for crops and game, intermingling with other tribal cultures occurred. Among the customs and knowledge that were shared, names were prominent.

Surnames are a relatively recent historical development. During the primitive stages of human evolution, the family as we think of it did not exist. The tribe was the basic functional unit, and it would assume a name to differentiate itself from other bands of hunters and food gatherers. That name sufficed to identify all its members. In the Western world, the Romans were the first to conceive of a need for a hereditary title. Each patrician traced his heritage and gave his clan a name that reflected either a characteristic of the nobleman's ancestors or denoted his own occupation. This title would then be taken by everyone in the household, including the servants.

Although the Romans demonstrated the value of an additional name, surnames have been in general use only for about the past thousand years. In England, the nobles were the first to adopt the custom of last names, and most often the names they chose indicated the locations of their estates. Other surnames reflected a characteristic of the ancestor who was the original owner of the name, the trade in which he was employed, or the office he held.

Trends and recognized practices in the selection of names have been and continue to be, common within cultures and across them. That the influence of the gods, elves, and spirits on men's lives was given credence in many ancient civilizations is evident from the meaning of many of the names. Our "primitive" ancestors were very aware of their dependence upon the whims of nature. Since natural forces were believed to be affected by supernatural beings, various methods of titling were derived from the attitudes of the ancients toward these creatures. An ancient Greek would give his child the name of a god in the hope of securing favorable intervention by this deity in the life of his young one. The Hindu belief that God manifested himself in all things, even the commonest of household items, can be traced to ancient times. This was reflected in the names chosen by Hindu parents for their offspring. Many Hebrew names of old provided an opportunity for parents to reaffirm their faith in divine mediation in human affairs. Christians also demonstrated their loyalty to the Almighty by giving their children Old Testament names.

Other peoples, however, were apprehensive in their dealings with the spirit world. The ancient Romans, concerned about the effects of black magic, were secretive about their first names. The Chinese, known for having some of the most beautiful names in existence, had ancestors who would give their children names of unpleasant sound and meaning to fool the gods of ill will into thinking a child was unloved and therefore not worthy of their vengeance. The Irish once believed that a man's life would be shortened if he gave his name to his son. Giving a child the name of a recently deceased relative is taboo among the Jewish people because of their concern for the afterlife of the departed soul.

Religious practices have often influenced name selection. The medieval Christian church insisted that children be baptized with a saint's name. This was an attempt to purge the last vestiges of what the church fathers considered pagan influences in the culture of Western Europe. Since there was an abundance of saints, finding a name for a child under this rule was not a difficult task. After the Reformation, there was a return to Old Testament names. In the late sixteenth and seventeenth centuries, the Puritans revived these names in an attempt to dissociate themselves from the highly ritualized and hierarchical Anglican church. They also favored naming their children for certain virtures exalted in their strict moral code. Many of them carried these names to the New World, where they were common for two centuries.

Religious attitudes were not the only influence on naming. The ancient Germanic peoples were extremely proud of their prowess in war, and this is evident in the origins of many of their names. References to courage and skill in battle, as well as names derived from the accouterments of battle, are very common. Celtic names often originate from words referring to the color of hair or skin tone. In eighteenth-century England, many children were given the romantic names popularized in the literature of the day. In the twentieth century, a resurgence of pride in their cultural heritage has led the Scots and the Irish to revive names used by their ancient forebears. Similarly, in the Scandinavian countries, there is a move toward the use of more Nordic-sounding titles.

In modern America, sentiment and tradition still seem to be the most dominant considerations in name choice. Informality is increasingly apparent, particularly in the use of names that were once considered nicknames. America has always been a land of ethnic diversity, and parents are turning to ethnic names as well as ecological ones more and more in their search for individuality. In addition, many names that were once considered masculine are now deemed appropriate for either sex.

Parents today have many options in selecting a name for their child, but a few things should be considered. Sound is important. It is often advised that a three-syllable first name be used with a one-syllable or two-syllable last name, and that a one- or two-syllable first name be used with a three-syllable last name. One might have second thoughts about giving a child a one-syllable first name with a one-syllable last name because the effect can be abrupt. Many parents are now giving their children two or three names so that the child, as he or she grows older, can choose. This is often done when a boy has the same first name as his father, in order to avoid the confusion that can result. Some people are concerned about whether a name can be pronounced and spelled easily. Once parents were advised to choose names that unmistakably revealed the sex of the child, but this no longer has to be a major consideration.

Since nicknames are almost inevitable in certain cases, it is wise for parents to select one themselves rather than find one inflicted upon them and their child. One warning—avoid the use of the title Brother or Sister, and should it appear, eliminate it as early as possible. These can be very difficult monickers to shake.

As is evident in the following lists, many names have unpleasant meanings. The disagreeable associations of most of these, however, have disappeared with time and usage and need not be a hindrance if the name appeals for other reasons.

The most important factor in naming a child is your contentment with the decision you have made. This is the most essential element in the final selection, since confidence in your choice will do much to ensure its success! So the last advice for you parents-to-be is to relax and trust your own judgment.

(1)
Names
and
Personality

Each person is endowed with a personality—an intangible yet integral part of oneself. Personality is so intrinsic to one's being that it influences even the attempt to examine its nature. One's self-image is the result of how one perceives one's thoughts and actions, which are, in turn, affected by one's personality and others' perceptions of it.

Contemporary psychology suggests that the idea that personality formation begins *before* birth is quite plausible, and many theoreticians pinpoint conception as the starting point. Still, the child is born with a *quite* undifferentiated character that will be molded by many forces quite beyond his control in the first few years of his life.

The name by which an individual is known is immensely significant becaue everything he knows and feels about himself becomes attached to this label. It is the name that separates him from all the external creatures, and it is under this name that he will expose himself to the world outside. The child's self-image attaches itself to this title and becomes forever inseparable from it. That a name becomes quickly intertwined with its bearer's self-development is evident from studies of severely mentally disturbed persons, particularly those adjudged to exhibit personality defects which make it impossible for them to function in society. It is quite common for these people to refuse to give their names, to forget them, or to create new ones for themselves and others.

People do not choose their names at birth but rather have names imposed upon them by their parents. And the names that parents choose often tell much about them: their personalities, interests, and ambitions— the attitudes which in subtle ways will greatly influence the future of their offspring. When a child receives his name, he unknowingly accepts his parents' image of him, as well as the conscious and unconscious cultural associations of his name. This is his starting point in society.

Psychologists believe that social functioning can be affected by one's name. How the individual views his own name and feels it is received by others, affects peer popularity. Who among us as a child did not witness, or even receive, a rash of teasing by other children, the theme of which, if not suggested by the individual's name, at least included it? Of course, how the target of the abuse (I use the word "abuse" even though much teasing is good-natured and is recognized as such by all parties concerned) copes with it depends to a large extent on his self-image, which is indelibly attached to this name, and his past associations and perceptions. If a child feels he has an undesirable name, then it most certainly will be a handicap for him in his social interactions. But his sense of the undesirability of his name is also determined by the messages he receives from others.

Certainly stereotypes exist for many names, and there is evidence that these stereotypes are learned very early. In one study, kindergarten, third-, and sixth-grade students were questioned as to how they viewed ten uncommon names that had been rated by adults as either active or passive. The older children's reactions matched the adults', but there was no such relationship between the kindergarteners' responses and those of the adults. It can be concluded that, to some degree, stereotyping is learned during early school years.

Studies have found that children with names that teachers have found desirable were good students and appeared well adjusted to the general academic environment. Common names are generally perceived as better, stronger, and more active. Boys and men tend to prefer common names. These sentiments are reflected in the frequent use of a small group of traditional given names for boys, the most common being John, Robert, William, and George (there are sixty-two John Smiths in the Manhattan telephone directory, and one can assume that the name John accounts for a large number of the eighty-one J. Smiths). One group of researchers found a correlation between the intensity of learning and behavior problems of a group of schoolboys and the peculiarity of their names. Girls and women, however, seem more willing to accept unusual names, and in many instances prefer them. Although common female names are prevalent, there is much more variety in feminine given names.

Before it is assumed that I am advocating the conference of only a select few common names, and believe that the world would be full of happy, well-adjusted people if all were named John, Joseph, George, William, Robert, Ann, Mary, Helen, and Elizabeth, let me point out that the roster of high achievers in particular occupations, including the arts, academia, and the military, reveals many quite unusual and imaginative names. Perhaps the child with the uncommon name can realize early the value of individuality, and appreciates the aura of independence created by his or her parents. Such a child may be on the path to leadership and creativity.

(2)
Trends
in
Naming

Studying trends in child naming can give results that are often inconclusive and incomplete at best. The reasons are inherent in the naming process. Factors that affect these patterns are diverse: the geographic locations, social class, and religious convictions of the parents, and most of all, the prevailing goals, attitudes, and interests of society in general at any particular time. Thus the art of naming is in flux, as is much else in our modern world. However, there are trends that can tell us something about what is happening and what has happened in the past.

Common names continue to be the most frequent entries on birth certificates. Wilber Zelinsky made a comparative study of the given names of the male populations of sixteen counties along the East Coast from South Carolina to New Hampshire for the years 1760 and 1968 and found **John, William,** and James heading the list in both periods. Thomas, Joseph, and **George** claimed positions in the top ten in both years, reflecting, it seems, a strong sense of tradition and a certain degree of stability. There was, however, more variety in the names found in the 1968 group. The 1760 names were selected from a reserve of about 300, while the 1968 parents had about 3,000 names from which to choose, a tenfold increase.

The names of relatives, particularly grandparents, are a major source of personal names, most often for boys, especially first- or second-born sons. This pattern is particularly strong among families in localities where people spend their entire life in one town and, naturally, kin influence is strong. A boy often will be named after his father and/or grandfather to perpetuate a family name that has been handed down through many generations. Also the mother's maiden name is found frequently as a son's middle name and occasionally even as a first name. Many of the names now regarded as boys' names were once exclusively last names given by mothers to their sons to preserve the name. With time these names became used by parents with no particular emotional tie to the title.

When a relative's name is conferred, it is usually because of a sense of tradition, intimacy with the adult with the name, or the desire that the child acquire the personal characteristic of the original owner of the name. There is much more opportunity today for the child to know the grandparent after whom he or she has been named because of greater longevity. As social mobility manifests itself in increasing physical mobility, this trend of kin-naming has declined and may continue to do so in America.

In the generation of Americans who experienced the upheavals of the 1960s, there has been surfacing a growing respect and longing for a past that is viewed as less mechanical and impersonal than the present. In naming their children, these parents are not only turning to the more common traditional names but also resurrecting such archaic but beautiful names as Abigail, Amanda, Miriam, Jeremy, Joshua, and Jason.

In a country as immense as the United States where there is great variety in beliefs and lifestyles, it is not surprising that there are many approaches to child-naming. Although boys' names have remained generally traditional, there have been substantial changes in girls' names over the years, reflecting increased willingness to express individuality. This practice seems particularly prevalent in the South and the small towns of the Midwest. Not only are unusual spellings used (such as Earlene, Delaris, Evalyne) and suffixes that are generally considered feminine being added to masculine names (-a, -dean, -elda, -elle, -ella, -ice, -ena, -ine, -eta) to form names such as Clydette, Ulyssia, Lloydine, and Martina, but entirely new names are being created that have no particular meaning, such as Aletrice, Eeardean, Noreline, Zerine, Zeralda, Sylbia, Amaza, Mazine, and Princetta.

A custom that is particularly apparent in the South is the use of diminutives. There one finds many Bobbies, Johnnies, Jimmies, Dannies, Davies, Tommies, and Benjies among both sexes, as well as female Carlies, Collies, and Omies and male Ollies, Obies, Zacks, Zebs, Clems, and Sims. Other diminutives are not derived from an actual given name, but rather the title by which an individual is known. (Buckie, Buddy, Sonny, Buster, and Bunnie).

Some are conferred at birth (former speaker of the House of Representatives, Sam Rayburn); others are adopted from general use (Billy ((William)) Graham and Jimmy ((James Earl)) Carter) and are recognized in formal and official situations. In fact, their appeal is informality and a certain folksiness. Politicians seem particularly amenable to the one-with-the-people feeling such names produce. For women, a diminutive of a male name is often combined with a feminine name, resulting in individuals answering to Mary Jo, Bobby Anne, Jimmy Sue, or Betty Bill. Or, an unquestionably feminine name is combined with a feminine diminutive to produce Mary Lou, Betty Jo, Jeannie May, or Sally Lynn.

In the Midwest and South, names derived from geographical terms are frequently discovered. These include Florida, Dixie, Arizona, America, Miami, Texas, Israel, Troy, Richmond, Salem, and Venetia. The custom of giving a child a name that is a title—royal, occupational, or military—or a political rank occurs to a certain degree in all parts of the country, although, again, most often in the Midwest and South. Deacon, Governor, Colonel, Baron, Kaiser, Page, Mate, and Sailor reflect this trend.

Among nationwide trends, one that is apparent to us all is the growing number of names that are used for individuals of both sexes. Many people, both male and female, including this author, answer to these names: Marion, Carol (also spelled Carroll), Vivian (Vivien), Beverly (Beverley), Lynn, Merle, Lee, and Leslie (Lesley).

Other customs of child-naming that seem to reflect social attitudes gleaned from the experiences of the sixties, are the return to religion, notably fundamentalist in nature, and renewed pride in one's social or ethnic heritage. There has been a resurgence of biblical names that were once generally attributed to those of the Puritan persuasion, as well as a re-emergence of ethnic names that had almost disappeared in America as immigrants attempted to assimilate themselves into a country that was dominated by an English cultural history. Black Americans are using very imaginative African names, with not only pleasant sounds, but quite often very beautiful meanings.

Celebrities, politicians, and statesmen have served as sources of names for the children of admiring parents. No doubt the moniker Robert E. Lee, in some form or other, had its heyday in the South during and after the Civil War. A few Betsy Rosses, Queen Elizabeths, Martin Luthers, George Washingtons, Thomas Jeffersons, Patrick Henrys, Napoleons, and Oliver Cromwells can still be found. And I am sure that countless Theodores, Martins, Johns, Charleses, Elizabeths, Eleanors, Marilyns, and Jacquelines owe their names to Theodore Roosevelt, Martin Luther King, John Fitzgerald Kennedy, Prince Charles, Elizabeth Taylor, Eleanor Roosevelt, Marilyn Monroe, and Jacqueline Kennedy Onassis.

Common words, both nouns and adjectives, have been bestowed as given names. Such names are Beauty, Sunny, Brain, Friend, Luck, Normal, Peace, Lively, Bubble, Fate, Chance, and Happy.

Some names have been popular for no apparent reason, such as Jonathan in New England in the eighteenth century, Elmer in the Midwest in the 1940s, and Waldo in New England during the latter part of the nineteenth century.

Middle names are a fairly recent phenomenon. Two names were infrequent for Americans until the end of the eighteenth century and the beginning of the nineteenth century, and did not become general practice until much later. Increased social activity, as well as a need for more definitive identification and a desire for more distinctive titling, seem to have spurred the development of this practice. The custom did not spread to England until the twentieth century (except among the titled), although it had been known in continental Europe for a few hundred years, where Catholic parents wanted to assure their offspring of the blessings and intercessions of more than one saint.

Let us examine the names of our presidents to gain some insight into the development of middle names in this country. (The parenthesized names are those first and middle names that were used infrequently, if ever, when referring to their bearers during their presidencies.)

George Washington	1789-1797	Chester A. (Alan) Arthur	1881-1885
John Adams	1797-1801	(Stephen) Grover Cleveland	1885-1889
Thomas Jefferson	1801-1809	Benjamin Harrison	1889-1893
James Madison	1809-1817	(Stephen) Grover Cleveland	1893-1897
James Monroe	1817-1825	William McKinley	1897-1901
John Quincy Adams	1825-1829	Theodore Roosevelt	1901-1909
Andrew Jackson	1829-1837	William H. (Howard) Taft	1909-1913
Martin Van Buren	1837-1841	(Thomas) Woodrow Wilson	1913-1921
William Henry Harrison	1841	Warren G. (Gamaliel) Harding	1921-1923
John Tyler	1841-1845	Calvin Coolidge	1923-1929
James K. (Knox) Polk	1845-1849	Herbert C. (Clark) Hoover	1929-1933
Zachary Taylor	1849-1850	Franklin Delano Roosevelt	1933-1945
Millard Fillmore	1850-1853	Harry S Truman	1945-1953
Franklin Pierce	1853-1857	Dwight D. (David) Eisenhower	1953-1961
James Buchanan	1857-1861	John Fitzgerald Kennedy	1961-1963
Abraham Lincoln	1861-1865	Lyndon Baines Johnson	1963-1969
Andrew Johnson	1865-1869	Richard M. (Milhous) Nixon	1969-1974
Ulysses S. (Simpson) Grant	1869-1877	Gerald R. (Rudolph) Ford	1974-1976
Rutherford B. (Birchard) Hayes	1877-1881	(James Earl) Jimmy Carter	1977
James A. (Abram) Garfield	1881		

Only three of the first seventeen presidents had middle names, but Calvin Coolidge was the last president to carry only two names. A trend that has already been mentioned is the use of names that were originally surnames as personal names. Three presidents provide examples of this: Pierce, Hayes, and F. D. Roosevelt. Ten had surnames as middle names (J. Q. Adams, Polk, Grant, Hayes, Cleveland, Hoover, F. D. Roosevelt, Kennedy, Johnson, Nixon); four of the latter were in office during the last thirty-five years. This list also demonstrates the use of initials in signatures to represent the middle name. In fact, in the case of Harry S Truman, the initial was a totally independent agent in his title—it doesn't even stand for a name!

Some well-known threefold names of the nineteenth century are William Cullen Bryant, Ralph Waldo Emerson, Henry Wadsworth Longfellow, John Greenleaf Whittier, and Edgar Allan Poe. Maybe we can attribute the widespread use of middle names in the early twentieth century to the influence of letters and politics, as the practice seemed to filter down from the well-to-do to the middle class, and finally to the general populace.

The trend of giving initials as middle names or using initials as middle names really became popular in this country between the two World Wars. In registering personnel for World War II, the army *assumed* everyone had a middle initial. A soldier without one might find himself listed as John IO Smith or John NMI Smith (the IO means Initial Omitted and NMI means No Middle Initial), and such designations can be seen even on tombstones in Arlington National Cemetery.

The successive waves of immigrants during the course of American history have added to our stock of names, particularly in certain sections of the country. Certain nationalities developed patterns for adapting their names to American life.

When the French settled in Louisiana, they brought with them the common first names of Jacques, Jean, Pierre, Marguerite, Marie, and Anna. These names were replaced in popularity mainly by mythological and classical names, and very English forenames. Of course, Louisiana was also influenced by Southern naming practices such as the use of diminutives, unusual spellings, and unique names. When, in the twentieth century, there was a return to French names, more unusual ones were chosen, such as Eugenie, Renee, Genevieve, Maurice, Emile, and Marcel, although they are often given English pronunciations.

The many German and Scandinavian names that were brought to this country were quickly Americanized, if not by the bearer or his parents, then by immigration officials and school teachers to facilitate their own dealings with these new arrivals. Although new Americans of Italian and Irish descent wished to acculturate themselves as easily as possible, many more of their names survived through the years, perhaps because they were easily pronounceable in English. The Greeks, the Slavs and others whose names were difficult to pronounce by the English-trained tongue, saw their native first names—and often their last names—markedly altered if not totally replaced by common American names.

Oriental immigrants have maintained their surnames; however, they have abandoned their given names for American ones and adopted the Western custom of placing the personal name before the family name.

Hispanic immigrants, the most recent large group of newcomers, have managed to maintain their Latin names with only a few minor alterations. Maria is certainly the most common feminine name in this group, far surpassing any other. It is not unusual for a girl named Maria to be known by her second name and to sign her name M. then her second and last name. There are families in which every female child is named Maria, with no confusion in the household at all.

There are naming patterns also among the diverse religious faiths that exist in this country. Mormons look to the Book of the Mormons for their more unusual names. Catholics, however, no longer feel compelled to name their children after saints and now freely choose from the large stock of names available. Until the advent of Hitler, although they occasionally used Old Testament names, the Jewish people chose for their children from the pool of names that other parents of their nationality would select. Since the Holocaust and the rise of Israel, Jewish parents are selecting for their children more traditionally Hebrew names as one way to demonstrate ethnic and cultural pride.

Urban America is often considered by sociologists the fermenting ground of social change in our country. It is felt that once attitudes are established among city dwellers, they often diffuse throughout the nation. If we accept this, an examination of birth certificates at the Bureau of Health Statistics and Analysis of the City of New York may give us some insight into naming trends of the past and future.

Here is a list of the names that appear most frequently on New York City birth certificates in the years shown:

1898: Mary, Catherine, Margaret, Annie, Rose, Marie, Esther, Sarah, Frances, Ida; John, William, Charles, Joseph, Edward, James, Louis, Francis, Samuel.

1928: Mary, Marie, Annie, Margaret, Catherine, Gloria, Helen, Teresa, Jean, Barbara; John, William, Joseph, James, Richard, Edward, Robert, Thomas, George, Louis.

1948: Linda, Mary, Barbara, Patricia, Susan, Kathleen, Carol, Nancy, Margaret, Diane; Robert, John, James, Michael, William, Richard, Joseph, Thomas, Stephen, David.

1964: Lisa, Deborah, Mary, Susan, Maria, Elizabeth, Donna, Barbara, Patricia, Ann(e), Theresa; Michael, John, Robert, David, Steven, Anthony, William, Joseph, Thomas, Christopher, Richard.

1972: Jennifer, Michelle, Lisa, Elizabeth, Christina, Maria, Nicole, Kimberly, Denise, Amy; Michael, David, Christopher, John, James, Joseph, Robert, Anthony, Richard, Brian.

1975: Jennifer, Michele, Christina, Lisa, Maria, Melissa, Nicole, Elizabeth, Jessica, Erica; Michael, John, Robert, David, Christopher, Anthony, Joseph, Jason, José.

Predicting future trends is hazardous in a society as vast and diverse as our own. It is impossible to pinpoint even the forces that will influence the practice of naming in the years to come. I personally would like to see a continuation of the present mix of the unusual and the traditional, the archaic and the imaginative, the collective and the individual, since diversity is much more interesting than uniformity.

(3)
Oddities,
Curiosities,
and Fun Names

Have you ever wished that your name was unusual, that you possessed a title that was exclusively your own, one that others would not forget once they had heard it? We all like to think of ourselves as unique, and at times behave in ways meant to emphasize this fact to the world at large.

This desire for uniqueness seems to be the motivation of many parents who select odd and curious names for their offspring. Samuel, the Old Testament prophet, said, ". . . as he is called, he is." One can appreciate the frustration felt by the John Smith, who in seeking individuality for his son, chose the original name John 5/8 Smith, or that of the parents who named what they planned to be their last child Finis, only to bring into the world at a later date an Appendix and an Errata.

As we reflect upon our history, we are amused by many of the Puritan names that we find. Their goal was not novelty but an obvious attempt to express faith in the ways of the Lord, and their humiliation before his altar. The first name of one Rhode Island man expresses a basic tenet of the Puritan belief—Through-much-tribulation-we-enter-into-the-kingdom-of-heaven—and another, an apology—Sorry-for-sin. Since children often suffered and died on the arduous sea voyage to the New World, a child who survived might be titled Whom-the-Lord-preserved. Other names, less dramatic, represent statements of human will versus God's. These include the likes of Submit, Mindwell, and Hopestill, as well as Fear-not, Faint-not, Stand-fast, The-Lord-is-near, and Praise-God. Less curious Puritan names, still occasionally in use today, reflect the qualities of faith and moral strength revered by the first settlers: Hope, Charity, Grace, Faith, Chastity, Mercy, Silence, and Peaceful.

Religious fervor in this country was not the sole province of the Puritans and neither was the custom of proclaiming it through naming children. In the 1880s, a Texas farmer bore the following prayerlike first name: Daniel's-wisdom-may-I-know, Stephen's-faith-and-spirit-choose, John's-divine-communion-seal, Moses'-meekness, Joshua's-zeal, win-the-day-and-conquer-all.

The study of odd names reveals a few patterns. Robert M. Rennick cites a great variety of unusual names that come from his personal collection, in his article entitled "The Folklore of Curious and Unusual Names" (*New York Folklore Quarterly*, May 1966). One trend demonstrated is the rhyming of personal and surnames such as Ethel Bethel, Jayne Spain, Walter Salter, and Lucy Pusey. Mr. Rennick tells of two children born into the Burst family of Dayton, Ohio, in the 1940s: Mary May and John Will. (For complete enjoyment, please sound the first two names with the last. One can only begin to imagine the taunts invented by their schoolmates.) We also have the case of the former Governor Hogg of Texas who named his daughter Ima. Mr. Rennick also gives us a lighthearted glimpse of the sometimes ironic connection between names and occupations: Larry Upp, who works in an underground factory; Les Trout, who is a conservation official; Doctor Couch, a psychiatrist; Doctor Coffin, a family physician; Little Worth, a public relations representative; Ronald Drown, a lifeguard; Penny Blood, a butcher; and Storm Field, a television weather forecaster in New York City.

There are parents who measure individuality by length, which accounts for such recent additions to our list as Aletha Beverly Carol Diane Eva Felice Greta Harline Io Joanne Karen Loquita Maurine Naomi Orpha Patricia Queenie Rebecca Shirley Teresa Una Valeeta Wanda Xelia Yolanda Zoe from Michigan, and her comrade of circumstance, Anna Bertha Cecilia Diane Emily Fanny Gertrude Hypatia Inez Jane Kate Louise Maud Nora Ophelia Paula Quince Rebecca Starkey Teresa Ulysis Venus Winifred Xenophon Yetty Zeno, who was a woman from Liverpool, England. (What were they called, you ask? The first was known as Pat, the second as Annie.) Not to be outdone by these two women, we have a young male infant who was named Adolph Blaine Charles David Earl Frederick Gerald Herbert Irvin John Kenneth Lloyd Martin Nero Oliver Paul Quincy Randolph Sherman Thomas Uncas Victor William Xerxes Yancy Zeus. One can only wonder how he signed his name! In addition to these, we have beautiful Hawaiian names, some of the longest recorded on American birth certificates, which translate into very poetic descriptions. One such name is Kananinoheadkuuhomeopuukaimanaalohinokeawea-weulamakaokalani (the beautiful fragrance of my home at sparkling Diamond Hill is carried to the eyes of heaven).

Consider the extreme case of Dr. Gatewood. What is the oddity, you ask? Well, he was never given a personal name and during his lifetime never found time or was concerned enough to devise one for himself. He was content, it seems, to be known formally as Dr. Gatewood Gatewood.

It is not unusual to find families where the same initials or beginning letters of the first, and sometimes middle, names are carried by all members. A well-known case is the family of the late President Johnson, which included himself, Lyndon Baines, his daughters, Lynda Bird and Lucy Baines, and his wife, Claudia Taylor, who was known to all as Lady Bird. Other parents have felt quite clever in developing combinations in naming their families, such as the Parisian music teacher who named her eight children Do, Re, Me, Fa, So, La, Ti, and Octave.

Finally, here is a list of miscellaneous names that seemed to result from either a whim of the parents, a conscious effort to be different, or, as in the case of the child named Hard Times who was born during the Depression, a reflection of the parents' circumstances. To Mr. Rennick I am indebted for the following: Peachy Owings Swicegood, Tempus Fugit, Viva M. Playfoot, Ima June Bugg, Percolator Posey, Dreama Nicely, Fix Ax, and Eureka Garlic. To this we will add the Oklahoma man christened Loyal Lodge No. 269 Knights of Phythias Panca City Oklahoma

Smith. The political feelings of his parents were manifested in the name of States Right Gist, a hero of the Civil War. (Need anyone ask on which side he fought?) I shall mention one more story related by Mr. Rennick from the Associated Press News of April 28, 1968, about a three-year-old boy who, when found by the police in Phoenix, Arizona, insisted his name was Baloney. This was verified by his harried mother, who was quite happy to find her Baloney.

Nicknames have become facts of life for many of us, having been inflicted upon us in much the same way as birth, death, and taxes! I have uncles, all now well over the age of 60, who are generally known as Fluker, Bullard, Bailey, and Polly (at birth, Edward, Martin, William, and John, respectively). The origins of these nicknames bestowed in childhood by friends are as obscure as they are unique. My father's name, Robert, was only reduced to Bobby. He was the youngest, which probably accounts for the absence of originality in his given nickname, but also for the fact that within the family circle he is still referred to as Bobby, even as he approaches his 62nd birthday. I thank heaven that the nickname my parents often used for me as a child did not last. In fact, today if I heard someone call "Doops," it probably wouldn't even occur to me to answer!

Nicknames are fun and can only be construed as cruel when they draw attention to a physical characteristic, such as Tiny, Shorty, Stretch, and Gimp (I have never understood how that title evolved for someone who limped). In fact, many famous people in history, politics, sports, and entertainment are known almost exclusively by nicknames. Would you recognize Dorothea Madison, George Herman Ruth, Harry Lillis Crosby, Hoagland Howard Carmichael, Lawrence Peter Berra, Charles Mantle, or Edmund Brown? (They are Dolly, Babe, Bing, Hoagy, Yogi, Mickey, and Pat, respectively.) Remember Buffalo Bill Cody, Dizzy Dean, and Satchmo Armstrong? And everyone in the fifties knew who answered to the name Ike.

Americans have always enjoyed giving nicknames to their statesmen and men of literature. It can be questioned whether these names originated within the general populace itself or sprang from caricatures of the newspapers and magazines. Consider Boss Tweed (William M. Tweed), Harry Wandsworth Shortfellow (Henry Wordsworth Longfellow), New England's John Bull (John Adams), Laureate of Darkness (Edgar Allan Poe), and Useless Grant (Ulysses S. Grant), just to name a few. Guess who was called Illinois Ape? (Honest Abe is a clue!)

Today there are many Elizabeths who enjoy the title of Liz or Betty, Lawrences known as Larry, Williams as Bill, and Katherines called Kathy or Kate. Parents often confer certain names fully expecting their child to use its diminutive. There are parents, however, who spend long hours devising names which they believe are nickname-less. Joseph Berger in *The New York Times Magazine* of April 16, 1961, tells of one mother who named her son Eric, assuming that the only nickname he could acquire would be Rick. You can imagine her frustration when her son returned from school one day to inform her that his friends had dubbed him Earache.

Although nicknames are usually bestowed by someone else, some people give themselves new titles. One thing I have always found fascinating is the given names of actors and actresses. Did you know that Marion Michael Morrison, Born in Iowa in 1907, went on to become an American institution, the Duke of motion pictures—John Wayne? A very successful name was the one developed for Roy Fitzgerald—Rock Hudson. Bernard Schwartz became Tony Curtis, Arthur Gellen, Tab Hunter, and the life and death of Norma Jean Baker immortalized the name of Marilyn Monroe. One actor's name that has always intrigued me is Rip Torn. I was convinced it was contrived by Hollywood bigwigs but discovered that I was far from correct. Elmore G. Torn was called Rip by his father, Rip, who was called Rip by his father, Rip. Alas, the name is a family tradition.

Pet names are special nicknames, and although they may be the common Dear, Honey, Love, and Baby, they express the intimacy of a very loving and tender relationship. I, myself, have a 200-pound Baby around my house, and to me there is no inconsistency in that statement at all.

Curious names are for enjoyment, so if you think your name is odd, rally your sense of humor and be amused—but give the name you are considering for your child second thought. My final comment about nicknames is that they are best taken in stride. Things struggled against seem to stick all the more tenaciously, and a nickname is no exception. So unless the nickname is unbearably offensive, relax and let your child follow your example.

(4)
Astrology
and Names

The ancients believed that human affairs were affected by the stars and planets in relationship to one another. Interest in the field of astrology has revived recently in the West, and a book written today to assist a young couple in the naming of their child would not be complete without a discussion of astrology.

The Zodiac represents a configuration of the movement of the planets, and an individual's astrological sign is dependent upon the position of these heavenly bodies at the time of his or her birth. It is felt that the force of these planets affects the fortune and personality of the child from the moment of birth.

The occurence of the twelve delineated zodiacal periods as well as their influences on the individuals born during these time periods is as follows:

ARIES—March 21 through April 19

Aries, the first sign of the Zodiac, is represented by the Ram. Its ruling planet is Mars. Aries children are leaders, and being a pure fire sign, are ardent and enthusiastic. They possess great moral strength but can be quite strong-willed. Patience is not one of their virtues and they do not tolerate frustration easily. The Aries person can be very organized, and functions best when in command. He or she is most compatible with people having the signs of Sagittarius or Leo.

TAURUS—April 20 through May 20

Taurus is represented by the symbol of the Bull. Its ruling planet is Venus. The Taurus child is a lover of beauty and tranquility. This individual can be generous and kind, but also dogmatic and stubborn—generally an opinionated soul with a rather conservative view of life. As an earth sign, he or she possesses a practical nature. Taurus people are blessed with intuition and many talents. They are most compatible with people born under the sign Capricorn and Virgo.

GEMINI—May 21 through June 21

The Gemini child is blessed with versatility and craves intellectual pursuits. Gemini is represented by the Twins. Its ruling planet is Mercury. This is a dual sign with many conflicting personality traits. These individuals are curious and have inventive imaginations, but, because Gemini is an air sign, they sometimes appear whimsical and indecisive. It is these last two elements of their characters that they must learn to control in order to achieve success. Geminis are compatible with people under the signs Aquarius and Libra.

CANCER—June 22 through July 22

Cancer people are the lovers of the Zodiac. Cancer is represented by the Crab, and its ruling planet is the Moon. Like the crab, these individuals can appear retiring and moody but are really quite sensitive and sentimental, possess an incredible imagination, and love adventure—though they always return to their home base, where they are most comfortable. Cancer children need encouragement, for they may lack confidence in their abilities. They are most comfortable with people born under the other water signs, Pisces and Scorpio.

LEO—July 23 through August 22

The Leo child is known for an outgoing nature, exuberance, and charm. he or she is well liked and successful. Ruled by the Sun, Leo is represented by the Lion. Leos are proud and can be most vain. They are quite ambitious and can be domineering if allowed to be. People born under this sign are powerful and possess extraordinary vitality, as do those born under the other fire signs, Sagittarius and Aries.

VIRGO—August 23 through September 22

Mercury rules the sign of Virgo and its symbol is the Virgin. People born under this sign are methodical and cautious and can, if not careful, waste a great deal of their energy. These tenacious individuals are very intelligent and at times tend to be very critical. Though they worry about success, they do not feel comfortable in leadership positions. The Virgoan prides himself on his knowledge. Selfishness, however, is a fault that requires great efforts of self-control. Virgo is an earth sign, and these people tremendously enjoy the natural beauties of life, as do those born under the other earth signs, Taurus and Capricorn.

LIBRA—September 23 through October 22

Libra is also ruled by Venus and is a lover of the arts. Libra's concern for justice is symbolized by the Scales. This is a romantic nature. The Libran's sense of justice and extreme sensitivity makes it difficult for him to face the harsher realities of life. The individuals of this sign demonstrate genuine concern for the less fortunate of this world. They are most content when they can surround themselves with artistic beauty—pleasant sights, sounds, shapes, colors, and images. Compatibility is best achieved with the signs Aquarius and Gemini.

SCORPIO—October 23 through November 21

The Scorpio child is fired with a great energy force that comes from the ruling planet Mars. The sign is the Scorpion. Scorpios are seekers of truth and hard-working, though they can easily be diverted. They are believed to be secretive, and it is felt that no one person is ever aware of the many sides of a Scorpio friend, lover, or child. Scorpio children are the most magnetic of all the children of the Zodiac. They want to be loved but must learn to overcome strong jealous tendencies to be happy. Those who possess this water sign love the sea because they identify with its tremendous natural energy. Scorpios are most comfortable with Cancer and Pisces.

SAGITTARIUS—November 22 through December 21

The symbol of the sign of Sagittarius is the Archer and the ruling planet is Jupiter. These intelligent individuals are known as defenders of individual freedom. This trait is very evident in their reasoning, and their thoughts display a methodical and astute mind. Sagittarians are often religious in their approach to life. They are not good judges of others, however, and have to be very careful if they are not to be deceived. They are quite possessive of their loved ones and in speech can be blunt and extremely tactless. They are compatible with Aries and Leo.

CAPRICORN—December 22 through January 19

The ruling planet of Capricorn is Saturn, and its symbol is the Goat. Capricorns are the mediators of the Zodiac. Their manner is reserved. Their musings, however, can cause them to be very slow to respond. These individuals excel in detailed work. A Capricorn child can be quite successful in life if exposed early to positive influences. He or she is most comfortable with Virgoans and Tauruses.

AQUARIUS—January 20 through February 18

The children of this air sign are ethereal in their approach to life. They are extremely faithful and kind, avoiding conflict with others at all cost. Instead of working out a problem, they would rather forget it. The Water Bearer is the sign of Aquarius and the ruling planet is Uranus. These influences make these children the most curious of all the children in the Zodiac. The unknown entices them. They are quite talented and success can come easily because of their many interests. Their easiest relationships are with Gemini and Libra children.

PISCES—February 19 through March 20

The ruling planet of the sign of Pisces is Neptune and the symbol is the Fishes. These people are the mystics of the Zodiac and should devote much time to developing the spiritual side of their nature. Tranquil environs are tantamount to their successful functioning. Because of their extremely truthful and sincere natures, they often have difficulty detecting deception in others. Pisces is a dual sign, reflecting both peaceful elements and a willingness to struggle against the forces of dishonesty and injustice. Those born under Pisces are compatible with the signs Cancer and Scorpio.

(5)
Numerology
and Names

Since ancient times, men have believed that numbers have the power to influence their lives. The sixth century B.C. mathematician, Pythagoras, is credited with the introduction of the study of numerology into the Western world. He numbered the alphabet and demonstrated how the use of names and titles can affect us because of the numbers they represent.

In determining the number of a name, the first, middle, and last names must be considered. With a name in mind, use the following chart and add the number of the letters of that name.

1	2	3	4	5	6	7	8	9
A	B	C	D	E	F	G	H	I
J	K	L	M	N	O	P	Q	R
S	T	U	V	W	X	Y	Z	

The result will probably be a two-digit number. If the addition of these two numerals gives you a one-digit number, that is your name number. If the sum is a two-digit number, these two digits should be added to achieve the name number. For example, a name of 63 would have a name number of 9 (6 plus 3). If the original addition, however, results in a number such as 84, whose addition gives a two-digit answer, these two digits are then added to produce the name number. Thus in the case of 84, the name number is 3 (8 plus 4 equals 12, and 1 plus 2 equals 3).

The following characteristics are attributed to the nine name numbers.

— **1.** These people are creative and intelligent leaders who function best when allowed to be their own bosses. The number one promises success and happiness.

— **2.** These are the anxious people. They enjoy activity and do not like being alone. They form solid friendships because the are warm and affectionate. This is a number that governs public activities.

— **3.** Ambition and devotion to family characterize these individuals. These people are trustworthy and possess independent views on religion and philosophy.

— **4.** This number represents musicians and scientists. These individuals are eccentric and often appear incomprehensible. However, they crave affection and are hurt because they are not understood. They are tenaciously devoted to the people they love.

— **5.** This is the number of the traveler. These people are most adventurous and willing to take chances. Their intuition with regard to others is well developed. They are also quick-minded and quite capable.

— **6.** Six is magnetic. People with this name number are very popular and others find their romantic view of life quite attractive. They enjoy the pleasures of life, especially when they can share them with others.

— **7.** These individuals are industrious about everything they attempt and will push themselves to exhaustion if they are not careful. They have an excitable temperament, but are very helpful to others and remain devoted to their loved ones.

— **8.** These warm people are very successful in business. They are capable risk-takers. People with this number have to control their tendency toward the melancholy.

— **9.** This is the number of great energy. Despite a fiery temper, these individuals are very successful both as marriage partners and parents. Independent and of a philosophical nature, they are quick to take up the fight against injustice.

(6)
Girls' Names

ABA — African. A girl born on Thursday.

ABAGEAL — The Irish form of Abigail.

ABBIE — A nickname for Abigail.

ABBY — A nickname for Abigail.

ABENA — A variation of Abina.

ABIGAIL — Hebrew. "Father (source) of joy."

ABINA — African. A girl born on Tuesday.

ABIRA — Hebrew. "Strong."

ABRA — Hebrew. "Earth mother." One who symbolizes universal motherhood.

ACACIA — Greek. "Thorny." Woody plant that represented everlasting life.

ACCALIA — Latin. Foster mother of the founders of Rome, Romulus and Remus.

ADA — Hebrew. An "ornament." Also derived from the Latin for "of the nobility," or an Old English word meaning "happy."

ADAH — Hebrew. "Crown or ornament." Precious one.

ADALIA — Old German. "Noble."

ADALINE — A variation of Adeline.

ADAMINA — Hebrew. "Of the red earth." Feminine of Adam.

ADAN — A variation of Aidan.

ADAR — Hebrew. "Fire" or "outstanding." Sixth month of the Jewish year.

ADARA — Arabic. "Virgin."

ADDA — A variation of Ada.

ADDY — A nickname for Adelaide and Adelle.

ADELA — The French, German, and Spanish form of Adelle, and a nickname for Adelaide.

ADELAIDA — The Italian and Spanish form of Adelaide.

ADELAIDE — Old German. "Noble and kind."

ADELHEID — The German form of Adelaide.

ADELICE — A variation of Alice.

ADELINA — The French, German, Spanish, and Italian form of Adeline.

ADELINE — A variation of Adelle.

ADELLE — Old German. "Noble."

ADELPHA — Greek. "Sisterly."

ADENA — A variation of Adina.

ADERES — Hebrew. "A cape." One who protects.

ADIA — African. "A gift."

ADIE — Hebrew. An "ornament."

ADINA — Hebrew. "Sensuous." A woman with beauty of form.

ADINE — A variation of Adina.

ADIRA — A variation of Abira.

ADITI — Hindu. "Unrestricted." In folklore, mother of the gods, benefactress of the blessings of nature.

ADOLPHA Old German. "Noble wolf." A brave defender of her home. Feminine of Adolf.

ADONIA — Greek. "Beautiful." One who is a goddess incarnate.

ADORA — Latin. "Gift, renown."

ADORABELLA — Latin-French. "Beautiful gift."

ADOREÉ — French. "Adored one."

ADORNA — Latin. "Adorned one." One upon whom nature has bestowed great beauty.

ADRIA — Latin. "Dark one."

ADRIANA — The Italian form of Adria.

ADRIANE — The German form of Adria.

ADRIENNE — The French form of Adria.

AFINA — Rumanian. "Blueberry."

AFRA — Hebrew. "Young female deer."

AG — A nickname for Agatha or Agnes.

AGACÉ — A French form of Agatha.

AGATA — The Irish and Italian form of Agatha.

AGATHA — Greek. "Good woman."

AGATHE — The French and German form of Agatha.

AGAVE — Greek. "Eminent."

AGGIE — A nickname for Agatha or Agnes.

AGLA — Hebrew. Abbreviation of "Thou are mighty forever, Lord." Once used as a charm to exorcise devils.

AGNA — A nickname for Agnes.

AGNELLA — An Italian form of Agnes.

AGNES — Greek. "Pure." The Latin word "angus" means lamb."

AGNESE — An Italian form of Agnes.

AGNETA — The Scandinavian form of Agnes.

AGNOLA — An Italian form of Agnes.

AGUEDA — The Spanish form of Agatha.

AHAVA — Hebrew. "Beloved."

AHIMSA — Hindu. One who is nonviolent in word, thought, and deed.

AH LAM — Chinese. "Flowerlike."

AHUAA — A variation of Ahava.

AHUDA — A variation of Ahava.

AIDA — A variation of Ada.

AIDAN — Gaelic. "Little fire." Symbol of purity.

AILA — A Finnish variation of Aileen.

AILEEN — Gaelic. "Light-bearer." One who is knowledgeable about truth and beauty. An Irish form of Helen.

AILENE — A variation of Aileen.

AILIS — The Irish form of Alice.

AILISA — Old German. "Cheerful and noble."

AIM — A nickname for Amy.

AIMÉE — A French form of Amy.

AIMIL — A Scottish form of Emily.

AINDREA — The Irish form of Andrea.

AIRLIA — Greek. "Ethereal." One who possess unusual delicacy and refinement.

AISLINN — Gaelic. "Inspiration."

AITHNE — Gaelic. "Little fire." A fairy queen.

AJA — Hindu. "Goat." Zodiacal sign Capricorn.

AKAKO — Japanese. "Red." Magical significance as a cure-all.

AKASMA — Turkish. "White climbing rose." One whose purity radiates.

AKELA — The Hawaiian form of Adelle.

AKI — Japanese. A girl born in the autumn.

AKILAH — Arabic. "Accomplished intellectually."

AKOSUA — African. A child born on Sunday.

ALAINE — A variation of Alanna.

ALALA — Greek. "War goddess." Association with Mars makes name suitable for astrological signs Aries and Scorpio.

ALANE — A variation of Alanna.

ALANNA — Gaelic. "Fair and beautiful." Feminine of Alan.

ALARCIA — A variation of Alarice.

ALARICE — Old German. "Ruler over all." Feminine form of Alaric.

ALAUDA — French. "Lark."

ALBANIA — Latin. "Blond, white." A beautiful, fair maiden.

ALBERTA — Old English. "Noble and bright." Feminine of Albert.

ALBERTINE — A variation of Alberta.

ALBINA — A variation of Albania.

ALBINKA — The Polish variation of Albania.

ALCINA — Greek. "Strong-willed." Feminine form of Alcinous.

ALDA — Old German. "Rich in age and wisdom."

ALDEA — A variation of Aldo.

ALDERCY — Old English. "Prince." One who is worthy of a royal station.

ALDIS — Old English. "From the old house." A woman of the traditional virtues.

ALDORA — Old English. "Of superior rank." Or from the Greek meaning "winged gift."

ALEEN — A variation of Aileen.

ALEEZA — Hebrew. "Joy." A child of joy.

ALEITHIA — A variation of Althea.

ALEJANDRA — A Spanish form of Alexandra.

ALEJANDRINA — A Spanish form of Alexandra.

ALERIA — Latin. "Like an eagle." Swift and brave.

ALESSANDRA — The Italian form of Alexandra.

ALETA — A variation of Althea or Alida.

ALETEA — The Spanish and Italian form of Alethea.

ALETHEA — Greek. "Truthful."

ALETJA — A variation of Alethea or Alida.

ALEX — A nickname for Alexandra.

ALEXA — A nickname for Alexandra.

ALEXANDRA — Greek. "Helper and defender of mankind." Feminine form of Alexander.

ALEXANDRINA — The French form of Alexandra.

ALEXINE — A nickname for Alexandra.

ALFA — A variation of Alfreda.

ALFIE — A nickname for Alfreda.

ALFONSINE — Old German. "Noble and ready." The feminine of Alfonso.

ALFREDA — Old English. "Wise counselor." One who is knowledgeable about life. Feminine of Alfred.

ALHENA — Arabic. "A ring." Star in the constellation of Gemini, astrological sign of the Twins.

ALICE — Greek. "Truthful." A child blessed with sincerity. Also a version of Adelaide.

ALICIA — The Italian, Spanish, and Swedish form of Alice.

ALIDA — Latin. "Little winged one."

ALIKA — The Hawaiian form of Alice.

ALIMA — Arabic. "Musical." One who brings rhythm and harmony.

ALINA — Celtic. "Fair and beautiful." Also see Alanna.

ALINE — A variation of Adeline.

ALISON — Old German. "Famous among the gods." Also considered a diminutive of Alice.

ALISSA — A variation of Alice.

ALITA — A nickname for Adelle or Alida.

ALITZA — A variation of Aliza.

ALIZA — A variation of Aleeza.

ALIZAH — A variation of Aleeza.

ALKA — Polish. "Brilliant."

ALLA — A nickname for Alexandra or Alice

ALLEEN — A variation of Alanna.

ALLEGRA — Latin. "Exuberantly cheerful." One who is a joy of life.

ALLENE — A variation of Alanna.

ALLIE — A nickname for Alberta, Alice, or Alison.

ALLISON — A variation of Alison.

ALMA — Arabic. "Learned." Also Italian for "soul" and Latin for "nourishing."

ALMETA — Latin. "Industrious." One with burning ambition.

ALMIRA — Arabic. "Fulfillment of the Word." Or Hindustani for "clothes basket." In India, God is considered part of everything, even household items.

ALODIE — Old English. "Prosperous." A woman destined for success.

ALONA — Hebrew. "Oak tree." A sturdy one. Feminine for Alon.

ALONZA — A variation of Alfonsine.

ALOYS — A nickname for Aloysia.

ALOYSIA — Old German. "Fierce warrior." See *Louise*.

ALPHA — Greek. "First one." First letter of the Greek alphabet.

ALPHONSINE — A variation of Alfonsine.

ALTA — Latin. "High." A woman with lofty ambition.

ALTHEA — Greek. "Wholesome and healing." Another name for "The Rose of Sharon."

ALUDRA — Greek. "Virgin." A symbol of purity. Astrological name for a girl born under the sign of Virgo.

ALULA — Latin. "Winged one." Also Arabic for "the first." Quick of mind and body.

ALURA — Old English. "Counsel from God." Inspirational.

ALVERTA — The Greek form of Alberta.

ALVINA — A variation of Albania.

ALVINIA — Old English. "Noble friend." One who is loyal and loved by all. Feminine of Alvin.

ALYCE — A variation of Alice.

ALYS — A variation of Alice.

ALYSIA — A variation of Alice.

ALYSSA — Greek. "Logical one." Alyssum, a plant with small yellow flowers.

ALZENA — Arabic. "The woman." A personification of womanly virtues.

ALZUBRA — Arabic. A star in the constellation of Leo, the Lion. Astrologically appropriate for a child born under this sign.

AM — Vietnamese. "Lunar" or "female energy." In Oriental philosophy, one of the two original sources of energy from which the world was created.

AMA — African. Name for a girl born on Saturday.

AMABEL — Latin. "Lovable." Fair, soft, and beautiful.

AMABELLE — A variation of Amabel.

AMADEA — Latin. "Love of God." A child blessed by heaven.

AMADIS — A variation of Amadea.

AMALIA — The Dutch, German, and Spanish form of Amelia.

AMALTHEA — Greek. "Nourishment of the gods." One who provides spiritual uplifting.

AMANDA — Latin. "Worthy of love." Virtuous.

AMARA — Greek. "Everlasting beauty."

AMARANTHA — Greek. "Legendary flower that never fades." Symbol of immortality.

AMARGO — A Portuguese form of Amara.

AMARIS — Hebrew. "What God has promised." Answer to a prayer.

AMARYLLIS — Greek. "Fresh." Also a plant with a lilylike flower.

AMATA — The Italian, Spanish, and Swedish form of Amy.

AMBER — Arabic. "A jewel." A precious child. A stone believed to have curative powers. A dark yellow-orange color.

AMBIKA — Hindu. "Mother." One of the names for the powerful goddess Sakti.

AMBROSINE — Greek. "Immortal." Ambrosia was "the food of the gods." Feminine of Ambrose.

AME — A variation of Amy.

AMELIA — Old German. "Hardworking." Also from the Latin family name meaning "flattering."

AMELINDA — Latin. "Beloved and pretty." A woman who combines beauty and personableness.

AMELINE — A variation of Amelia.

AMETHYST — Greek. "A precious stone." A stone believed by the ancient Greeks to prevent drunkenness.

AMI — A variation of Amy. Also a nickname for Amelia.

AMIE — A variation of Amy.

AMINA — Arabic. "Security." Amina was the mother of the prophet Mohammed.

AMINEH — Arabic. "Faithful." One who can be trusted with the emotions of others.

AMINTA — Latin. "Protectress." In mythology, Amyntha was a shepherdess.

AMISA — A variation of Amissa.

AMISSA — Hebrew. "Truth."

AMITY — Latin. "Friendly." An outgoing personality.

AMORETTE — Latin. "Sweetheart."

AMORITA — Latin. "One who is loved."

AMY — Latin. "Beloved." To know her is to love her.

ANA — A Spanish form of Ann.

ANANDA — Hindu. "Complete happiness."

ANASTASIA — Greek. "Of the Resurrection." Of the greatest of miracles. The feminine of Anastasius.

ANASTASIE — The French form of Anastasia.

ANASTASSIA — The Russian form of Anastasia.

ANATOLA — Greek. "From the East."

ANCELIN — Latin. "Handmaid." A child who is a comfort in one's weariness.

ANDREA — Latin. "Womanly." Epitome of feminine virtues. Feminine form of Andreas or Andrew.

ANDREANA — A variation of Andrea.

ANDRIA — A variation of Andrea.

ANDRIANA — A variation of Andrea.

ANDROMEDA — Greek. Maiden in Greek mythology who was chained to a rock because of her beauty and rescued by Perseus. A constellation.

ANDULA — A Russian nickname for Ann.

ANE — The Hawaiian form of Ann.

ANEMONE — Greek. "Windflower."

ANGEL — A variation of Angela.

ANGELA — Greek. "Messenger from heaven."

ANGELE — The French form of Angela.

ANGELICA — The Italian form of Angela.

ANGELIKA — A Greek form of Angela.

ANGELINA — A variation of Angela.

ANGELINE — A variation of Angela.

ANGELITA — A Spanish nickname for Angela.

ANICA — A Spanish form of Ann.

ANITA — A variation of Ann.

ANN — Hebrew. "One of grace." From the name Hannah.

ANNA — The Italian, German, Slavic, Scandinavian, and Russian form of Ann.

ANNABEL — Hebrew and Latin. "Beautiful and graceful." One who is a lovely sight to behold.

ANNABELLA — A variation of Annabel.

ANNABELLE — A variation of Annabel.

ANNABLA — An Irish variation of Annabel.

ANNE — A variation of Ann.

ANNETTE — A variation of Ann.

ANNICE — A variation of Ann.

ANNORA — A variation of Anora.

ANNUNCIACION — A Spanish variation of Annunciata.

ANNUNCIATA — Latin. "Bearer of news from heaven." The feast of the Annunciation, March 25, commemorates the announcement to the Virgin Mary that she was to be the mother of God.

ANNUNZIATA — An Italian variation of Annunciata.

ANONA — Latin. Annona, goddess of the crops. The warmth of the spring giving life to the fields. Used for girls born under the earth signs of the Zodiac: Capricorn, Taurus, Virgo.

ANORA — English. "Grace and honor." Combination of Ann and Nora.

ANSELMA — Old Norse. "Divine protectress." Feminine form of Anselm.

ANSTICE — A variation of Anastasia.

ANTHEA — Greek. "Lady of the flowers." A woman who surrounds herself with the beauty of life.

ANTHIA — A variation of Anthea.

ANTOINETTE — A French form of Antonia.

ANTONETTE — A variation of Antonia.

ANTONIA — Latin. "Most precious." Priceless jewel of one's life.

ANTONIETTA — The Italian form of Antonette.

ANUSKA — A Czechoslovakian form of Ann.

ANYA — A Russian form of Ann.

APOLLINE — Greek. "Sunshine." One who radiates warmth and strength.

APRIL — Latin. "Open." April was the beginning of spring in the ancient Roman and Greek calendar.

APRILETTE — A variation of April.

AQUENE — American Indian. "Peace." Embodiment of tranquility.

ARA — Latin. "Altar." Or Old Norse for "eagle maid." Ara was the Greek goddess of destruction.

ARABELA — A Spanish form of Arabella.

ARABELLA — Latin. "Beautiful altar." Also from the Old Norse meaning "eagle heroine."

ARABELLE — The French and German form of Arabella.

ARAH — Latin. "Lion cub." Refers to the zodiacal sign Leo, the Lion. Appropriate for a girl born between July 23 and August 22.

ARAMINTA — Hebrew. "Superior." Excellence of mind and body.

ARCITE — Latin. "The Archer." Symbol for the astrological sign Sagittarius, the Archer.

ARDA — A variation of Adelle.

ARDATH — Hebrew. "Flowering field." From the apocryphal Bible.

ARDEEN — A variation of Ardelle.

ARDELIA — A variation of Ardelle.

ARDELIS — A variation of Ardelle.

ARDELLE — Latin. "Ardent enthusiasm."

ARDENE — A variation of Ardelle.

ARDILLA — Spanish. "Squirrel." A lovable warm creature.

ARDINE — A variation of Ardelle.

ARDIS — A variation of Ardelle.

ARDITH — Old German. "Rich gift."

ARDRA — Latin. "Hardworking."

ARELA — A variation of Arella.

ARELLA — Hebrew. "Messenger."

ARETA — Greek. "Virtuous." Of incomparable moral worth.

ARETE — A Greek variation of Areta.

ARETHA — Greek. "Best." Popularized by singer Aretha Franklin.

ARETHI — A variation of Aretha.

ARETINA — A variation of Areta.

ARETTE — The French form of Areta.

ARGEMONE — Greek. "Poppy." Woman with intoxicating aura.

ARGENTA — Latin. "Silver."

ARGYRIA — Greek. "Shining."

ARIADNE — Greek. "Most holy." Goddess of spring and daughter of the Greek sun god. Daughter of the Cretan king Minos who loved and rescued Theseus and was later deserted by him.

ARIANA — A variation of Ariadne.

ARIEL — A variation of Ariella.

ARIELA — A variation of Ariella.

ARIELLA — Hebrew. "Lioness of God." Strong and courageous. A fairy sprite of the air in Shakespeare's *The Tempest*.

ARILDA — Old German. "Maid of the house."

ARISTA — Latin. "Harvest." The fruition of crops planted, tended, and collected.

ARLANA — A variation of Arlene.

ARLEEN — A variation of Arlene.

ARLENA — A variation of Arlene.

ARLENE — Gaelic. "A pledge." A promise of devotion. A feminine form of Arlen.

ARLETA — A variation of Arlene.

ARLINE — A variation of Arlene.

ARLYNE — A variation of Arlene.

ARMIDA — Latin. "Small armed one."

ARMILDA — Old German. "Armed battle-maid." One who is prepared for all adversities.

ARMILLA — Latin. "Bracelet." A charming adornment.

ARMINA — Old German. "Maiden warrior."

ARMONA — Hebrew. "Palace."

ARNA — Hebrew. "Cedar tree." Of sturdy character.

ARNALDA — Old German. "Strong as the eagle." A feminine form of Arnold.

ARNI — A variation of Arnina.

ARNICE — A variation of Arna and Arnina.

ARNINA — Hebrew. "Enlightened." The feminine of Aaron.

ARNIT — A variation of Arna and Arnina.

ARNOLDA — A variation of Arnoldine.

ARNOLDINE — Old German. "Mighty as the eagle."

ARTHA — Hindu. "Prosperity." One of the four goals of man.

ARVA — Latin. "Farming land."

ARVIA — A variation of Arva.

ASA — Japanese. "Born in the morning."

ASABI — African. "Of privileged birth."

ASELA — Latin. "Ash tree."

ASELMA — Old Norse. "Divine providence." One endowed with the protection of the angels.

ASIA — A Russian nickname for Anastassia.

ASISA — Hebrew. "Ripe."

ASPASIA — Greek. "Welcome." In ancient Greece, the intelligent and charming mistress of Pericles.

ASTA — Greek. "Star." One who inspires men to outstanding achievements. Aster, flowering star.

ASTERA — A variation of Asta.

ASTERIA — A variation of Asta.

ASTRA — A variation of Asta.

ASTRED — A variation of Asta.

ASTRID — Old Norse. "Divine strength."

ATA — African. "Twin."

ATALANTA — Greek. "Mighty adversary." A huntress in Greek mythology.

ATALAYA — Spanish. "Guardian."

ATALIA — A variation of Athalia.

ATALIE — A variation of Athalia.

ATARA — Hebrew. "A crown."

ATHALIA — Hebrew. "The exaltation of the Lord." Name of the biblical queen of Judah.

ATHENA — Greek. "Wisdom." Beautiful name of the Grecian goddess of wisdom.

ATHENE — A variation of Athena.

ATIDA — Hebrew. "Future." A child born with promise.

ATIRA — Hebrew. "A prayer."

ATLANTA — A variation of Atalanta.

AUBERTA — Old English. "Noble and brilliant." Feminine of Aubert, a form of Albert.

AUBINE — The French form of Alberta.

AUDEY — A nickname for Audrey.

AUDREY — Old English. "Noble strength."

AUDRIE — A variation of Audrey.

AUDRIS — Old German. "Fortunate."

AUDRY — A variation of Audrey.

AUGUSTA — Latin. "The queenly one." Title given to the wives and daughters of Roman emperors.

AUGUSTE — The Danish, Dutch, French, and German form of Augusta.

AUGUSTINA — A variation of Augusta.

AUGUSTINE — A variation of Augusta.

AURA — Latin. "Gentle wind."

AUREA — A variation of Aurelia.

AURELIA — Latin. "Golden."

AURÉLIE — The French form of Aurelia.

AURORA — Latin. "Daybreak." The dawning of hope.

AURORE — The French form of Aurora.

AUSTINA — A variation of Augusta.

AUSTINE — A variation of Augusta.

AVA — Latin. "Birdlike."

AVASA — Hindu. "Independent."

AVELINE — A variation of Evelyn.

AVENA — Latin. "Vats or "oat fields." An appropriate name for a child born under an earth sign of the Zodiac: Capricorn, Taurus, Virgo.

AVERIL — Old English. "Born in the month of April." Used as a name for an Aries child.

AVERILL — A variation of Averil.

AVERYL — A variation of Averil.

AVICE — Old French. "Quick to anger." A woman to approach with gentleness and sensitivity.

AVIS — Old English. "Refuge in battle." One who provides comforting relief and sustenance from the woes of life. Also a variation of Ava.

AVIVA — Hebrew. "Springtime." Embodiment of refreshment and vigor.

AVIVAH — A variation of Aviva.

AVIVICE — A variation of Aviva.

AVRIT — A variation of Aviva.

AWENDELA — American Indian. "A child born before dawn."

AWENITA — American Indian. "Fawn." Soft, timid, and warm.

AYAME — Japanese. "Iris."

AYLA — Hebrew. "Oak tree." Sturdy and dependable.

AYLET — Hebrew. "Deer" or "gazelle."

AZALEA — Latin. "Dry earth." A flower that can exist with little water.

AZELIA — A variation of Azalea.

AZURA — Old French. "Blue sky." Possessing beguiling blue eyes.

BAB — A nickname for Barbara.

BABARA — The Hawaiian form of Barbara.

BABETTE — A French form of Barbara.

BABITA — A nickname for Barbara.

BABS — A nickname for Barbara.

BAKA — Hindu. "Crane." Symbolizing long life.

BALBINA — Latin. "Little stammerer." One who has difficulty putting thoughts into words.

BAMBI — Italian. "Child." A product of love.

BAPTISTA — Latin. "One who baptizes." Commemorating St. John the Baptist.

BAPTISTE — A French form of Baptista.

BARBARA — Latin. "Stranger."

BARBE — A French form of Barbara.

BARBETTE — A French form of Barbara.

BARBIE — A nickname for Barbara.

BARBO — The Swedish form of Barbara.

BASILIA — Greek. "Queenly." A feminine form of Basil.

BASYA — A variation of Batya.

BATHILDA — Old German. "Commanding battle maiden." A capable leader.

BATHILDE — A French form of Bathilda.

BATHSHEBA — Hebrew. "Daughter of an oath."

BATISTA — An italian form of Baptista.

BATTISTA — An Italian form of Baptista.

BATYA — Hebrew. "Daughter of God." Woman of heavenly virtues.

BEA — A nickname for Beatrice.

BEATA — Latin. "Blessed."

BEATRICE — Latin. "She who makes others happy."

BEATRISA — A Spanish variation of Beatrice.

BEATRIX — Spanish and German form of Beatrice.

BECKIE — A nickname for Rebecca or Beatrice.

BECKY — A nickname for Rebecca or Beatrice.

BEDA — Old English. "Maiden of war."

BEE — A nickname for Beatrice.

BEHIRA — Hebrew. "Brilliant." A woman of outstanding virtue, beauty, and intelligence.

BELANTHA — An occult name used in ceremonies to invoke spirits.

BELIA — A Spanish variation of Isabel.

BELICIA — A variation of Isabel.

BELINDA — Old Spanish. "Beautiful." An attractive name.

BELITA — A variation of Isabel.

BELL — A nickname for Isabelle or Isabella. Also a variation of Belle.

BELLA — A nickname for Isabelle or Isabella. Also a variation of Belle.

BELLANCA — Italian. "Fair-haired."

BELLE — Latin. "Beautiful." Also a nickname for Isabelle or Isabella.

BELLOMA — Latin. "Warlike." Appropriate name for girls born under the astrological signs governed by Mars: Aries and Scorpio.

BENDITE — A French form of Benedicta.

BENEDETTA — The Italian form of Benedicta.

BENEDICTA — Latin. "Blessed." A feminine form of Benedict.

BENEDIKTA — The German form of Benedicta.

BENETTA — A nickname for Benedicta.

BENIGNA — Latin. "Gracious and kind." Personification of the gentlest of virtues.

BENITA — A Spanish form of Benedicta.

BERDINE — Old German. "Glorious." A woman who radiates from within.

BERENGARIA — Old English. "Spear-maiden." Queen of Richard the Lion-Hearted.

BERGET — The Danish form of Bridget.

BERNADENE — A variation of Bernadine.

BERNADETTE — The French form of Bernadine. The Blessed Virgin appeared to St. Bernadette at Lourdes, France (1858).

BERNADINA — The Italian and Spanish form of Bernadine.

BERNADINE — French. "Brave warrior." Feminine of Bernard.

BERNETA — A variation of Bernadine.

BERNETTA — A variation of Bernadine.

BERNETTE — A variation of Bernadine.

BERNIA — Latin. "Battle-maid." A courageous woman.

BERNICE — Greek. "Forerunner of victory." One who brings the message of success.

BERNIE — A nickname for Bernadette, Bernadine, or Bernice.

BERTA — The German, Italian, and Spanish form of Bertha. A nickname for Bertha and names ending in "berta."

BERTHA — Old German. "Brilliant, glorious one." In German mythology, the goddess of fertility.

BERTHE — The French and German form of Bertha.

BERTIE — A nickname for Bertha.

BERTILDE — A variation of Bathilda.

BERTINA — Old German. "Bright or shining."

BERTRADE — Old English. "Brilliant counsel." A source of wise direction.

BERTY — A nickname for Bertha.

BERURA — Hebrew. "Pure." A woman worthy of devotion.

BESS — A nickname for Elizabeth.

BETH — Hebrew. "Home." A woman devoted to her home and family. A nickname for Bethel and Elizabeth.

BETHEL — Hebrew. "House of God." Temple of purity.

BETHESDA — Hebrew. "House of mercy." Source of sympathetic understanding. Name of the pool in Jerusalem believed to have miraculous powers.

BETSY — A nickname for Elizabeth.

BETTINE — A nickname for Elizabeth.

BETULA — Hebrew. "Maiden." One of youthful joy and beauty.

BEULA — A variation of Beulah.

BEULAH — Hebrew. "A married woman."

BEVERLY — Old English. "One who lives near the bearer field."

BEVIN — Irish. "Lady with a sweet song." She who entrances men with rapture of her voice.

BIAN — Vietnamese. "Secretive."

BIANCA — The Italian form of Blanche.

BIBI — Arabic. "Lady." Most gracious of manner.

BIDDIE — A nickname for Bridget.

BIDDY — A nickname for Bridget.

BILL — A variation of Billie.

BILLIE — Old English. "Strong-willed." A lady of determination. Also a nickname for Wilhelmina.

BIRD — English. "Little and birdlike."

BIRDELLA — A variation of Bird.

BIRDIE — A nickname for Bird.

BIRGIT — The Norwegian form of Bridget.

BIRGITTA — The Swedish form of Bridget.

BLANCA — The Spanish form of Blanche.

BLANCH — A variation of Blanche.

BLANCHE — Old French. "Fair and white."

BLANDA — Latin. "Flirtatious."

BLANDINA — A variation of Blanda.

BLANKA — The German form of Blanche.

BLASIA — Latin. "Stammerer." Profundity of thought can be difficult to express verbally.

BLENDA — Old German. "Glorious."

BLESSING — Old English. "Divinely protected." A promise of happiness.

BLISS — Old English. "Joy." A woman of unending delight.

BLITHE — A variation of Blythe.

BLOSSOM — Old English. "Flowerlike." Refreshing and sweet.

BLUM — Hebrew. "Flower."

BLYTHE — Old English. "Joyous." A child blessed with a light-hearted nature.

BO — Chinese. "Priceless."

BOBBIE — A nickname for Roberta.

BOBBY — A nickname for Roberta and Barbara.

BOBINA — A Czechoslovakian nickname for Roberta.

BOHDANA — Russian. "From God."

BONA — Hebrew. "A builder."

BONITA — Spanish. "Pretty."

BONNIBELLE — Latin. "Good and beautiful."

BONNIE — English. "Sweet one." A nickname for Bonita.

BONNY — A variation of Bonnie.

BRENDA — Old English. "Firebrand." A woman who stirs excitement.

BRENNA — Irish. "Raven." A dark-haired beauty.

BRIANA — Irish. "Strong." The feminine form of Brian.

BRIDGET — Irish. "Strong." St. Bridget is a patron saint of Ireland.

BRIDIE — A nickname for Bridget.

BRIGIDA — The Italian and Spanish form of Bridget.

BRIGITTE — The French and German form of Bridget.

BRITA — A nickname for Bridget.

BRONWEN — Welsh. "Of snow-white breast."

BRUCIE — Old French. "Thicket dweller." Feminine of Bruce.

BRUELLA — A variation of Brunella.

BRUNELLA — Old French. "Woman with dark hair."

BRUNETTA — Italian. "Brown-haired one."

BRUNHILDA — Old German. "Battle-maid with an armored breastplate."

BRUNHILDE — A variation of Brunhilda.

BRYANA — A variation of Briana.

BUENA — Spanish. "A good woman." An image of the feminine graces.

BUNNY — A nickname for Bernice and Barbara.

BURURIA — A variation of Berura.

CACILIA — Old German form of Cecilia.

CACILIE — A German form of Cecilia.

CADENA — A variation of Cadence.

CADENCE — Latin. "Melodious."

CADENZA — The Italian form of Cadence.

CAI — Vietnamese. "Female."

CAL — A nickname for Calandra.

CALANDRA — Greek. "Lark."

CALANDRE — A French form of Calandra.

CALANDRIA — The Spanish form of Calandra.

CALANTHA — Greek. "Elegant blossom." One of soothing natural beauty.

CALEDONIA — Latin. "From Scotland." A Celtic lass.

CALIDA — Latin. "Loving, ardent." One whose love is sincere.

CALISTA — Greek. "Most beautiful woman."

CALLA — Greek. "Beautiful."

CALLIDA — A variation of Calida.

CALLIE — A nickname for Calandra.

CALLULA — Latin. "Little one of beauty."

CALLY — A nickname for Calandra.

CALTHA — Latin. "Yellow blossom."

CALVINA — Latin. "Bold." Feminine of Calvin.

CALYPSO — Greek. "Woman who hides her emotions." A sea nymph who detained Odysseus for seven years.

CAM — A nickname for Camille.

CAMEL — A nickname for Camille.

CAMEO — Italian. "A sculptured jewel."

CAMILIA — The Spanish for Camille.

CAMILLA — A variation of Camille.

CAMILLE — Latin. "Young ceremonial attendant." In mythology, the servant of the goddess Diana.

CAMMIE — A nickname for Camille.

CAMMY — A nickname for Camille.

CANACE — Greek. — "Child of the wind." Daughter of the wind god, Aeolus.

CANDACE — Greek. "Sparkling white." Woman of unquestionable virtue.

CANDEE — A nickname for Candace.

CANDI — A nickname for Candida.

CANDICE — A variation of Candace.

CANDIDA — Latin. "Pure white." Heroine of Bernard Shaw's play.

CANDIE — A nickname for Candace.

CANDRA — Latin. "Luminescent." Astrological name for the "moon" that governs Cancer.

CANDY — A nickname for Candace.

CAPRI — Middle English. "The goat." Appropriate name for a girl born under the sign of Capricorn.

CAPRICE — Italian. "Whimsical." Of unpredictable nature.

CARA — Italian. "Dear one." Also Irish for "friend."

CAREL — A variation of Carol.

CARESSE — French. "Beloved one." A woman who captivates all she meets.

CARI — Turkish. "Flows like water." She moves with the perfection that only nature can provide.

CARILLA — Old German. "Strong." Of capable character. Feminine form of Charles.

CARIN — Latin. "Keel."

CARINA — A variation of Carin.

CARINE — A variation of Carin.

CARITA — Latin. "Charity." A lady of kindness.

CARLA — A nickname for Carolina or Charlotte. Also the feminine form of Carl.

CARLEN — A nickname for Caroline.

CARLINE — A nickname for Caroline or Charlotte.

CARLITA — A nickname for Caroline or Charlotte.

CARLOTA — The Spanish form of Charlotte.

CARLOTTA — The Italian form of Charlotte.

CARLY — A nickname for Caroline and Charlotte.

CARMA — Hindu. "Fate." In Hinduism and Buddhism, the force of justice that determines one's destiny in the next life by examining currect actions. Also variation of Carmen.

CARMEL — Hebrew. "Garden." Mt. Carmel is famous in the Bible for the feats of Elijah.

CARMEN — Latin. "A song." Lady with a voice like music. Heroine of Bizet's opera of the same name.

CARMENCITA — A Spanish nickname for Carmen.

CARMIA — A variation of Carmen.

CARMINA — A variation of Carmen.

CARMINE — A variation of Carmen.

CARMITA — A nickname for Carmen.

CARNA — Hebrew. "Horn."

CARNATION — French. "Flesh-colored." Designated as the flower of January.

CARNIELLA — A variation of Carna.

CARNIS — A variation of Carna.

CARNIT — A variation of Carna.

CARO — A nickname for Carol or Caroline.

CAROL — Latin. "Strong and womanly." The feminine of Charles and Carl. Also Old French for "song of joy." A nickname for Caroline.

CAROLA — A nickname for Carolina.

CAROLE — A variation of Carol.

CAROLINA — A variation of Caroline.

CAROLINE — Latin. "Little woman."

CAROLYN — A variation of Caroline.

CARON — French. "Pure."

CARRIE — A nickname for Caroline or Carol.

CARY — A nickname for Caroline.

CARYL — A variation of Carol.

CARYN — A variation of Carin.

CASILDA — Latin. "Of the home." One who enjoys making a good home for her family.

CASS — A nickname for Cassandra.

CASSANDRA — Greek. "Disbelieved." A prophetic princess whose warnings were ignored.

CASSANDRE — The French form of Cassandra.

CASSANDRY — A variation of Cassandra.

CASSIE — A nickname for Cassandra.

CASTA — Latin. "Modest and pure." A demure lady.

CATALINA — A Spanish form of Catherine.

CATARINA — An Italian form of Catherine.

CATERINA — An Italian form of Catherine.

CATHERINA — A variation of Catherine.

CATHERINE — Latin. "Woman of purity." Egyptian princess martyred for her Christianity in the 4th century. An extremely popular name.

CATHIE — A nickname for Catherine or Cathleen.

CATHLEEN — A variation of Catherine.

CATHY — A nickname for Catherine or Cathleen.

CATRIONA — The Scottish form of Catherine.

CEARA — Gaelic. "Spear." Female warrior.

CECANIA — Teutonic. "Free."

CECIL — A variation of Cecilia.

CÉCILE — A French form of Cecilia.

CECILIA — Latin. "Blind." Also the patron saint of music, since St. Cecilia sang while being tortured in the 2nd century.

CECILY — A variation of Cecilia.

CELANDINE — Greek. "The swallow."

CELE — A nickname for Ceilia or Celestine.

CELENA — Greek. One of the daughters of the mythological god Atlas.

CELENE — A variation of Celena or Selena.

CELESTA — A variation of Celeste.

CELESTE — Latin. "Heavenly."

CELESTINA — A variation of Celeste.

CELESTYN — A variation of Celeste.

CELESTYNA — A variation of Celeste.

CELESTYNE — A variation of Celeste.

CELIA — A nickname for Cecilia or Celeste.

CELIE — A nickname for Cecilia or Celeste.

CELINA — A Polish form of Celeste.

CELINKA — A Polish form of Celeste.

CELKA — A Polish form of Celeste.

CELOSIA — Greek. "Burning." A woman who is fiercely loyal.

CERELIA — Latin. "Of the spring." Astrologically appropriate for a girl born under the spring signs of the Zodiac: Aries, Taurus, and Gemini.

CERELLA — A variation of Cerelia.

CERISE — French. "Cherry."

CERYL — A variation of Cheryl.

CHANDI — A variation of Chandra.

CHANDRA — Hindu. "Moon goddess." One of the many Sanskrit names of the goddess Sakti.

CHARIS — Greek. One of the Three Graces of mythology; identified with the virtue of charity.

CHARISSA — A variation of Charity.

CHARITA — A variation of Charity.

CHARITY — Latin. "Benevolent, loving," Puritan virtue name.

CHARLA — A nickname for Caroline.

CHARLEEN — A variation of Caroline or Charlotte.

CHARLENE — A variation of Charlotte or Caroline.

CHARLOTTA — The Swedish form of Charlotte.

CHARLOTTE — French. "Little woman." Feminine of Charles. Charlotte Corday was a heroine of the French Revolution.

CHARMAIN — A variation of Charmaine.

CHARMAINE — Latin. "Singer." A woman who enraptures with her voice. A maid to Cleopatra.

CHARMOIN — A variation of Charmaine.

CHARRY — A nickname for Charity.

CHARYL — A nickname for Charlotte.

CHASTITY — Latin. "Pure." Embodiment of virtuous womanhood. A favorite Puritan name.

CHATTIE — A nickname for Charlotte.

CHAVVA — Hebrew. "Life-giving."

CHAYA — A variation of Chavva.

CHENOA — American Indian. "White dove." The symbol of peace.

CHER — French. "Beloved."

CHERI — A variation of Cher.

CHERIE — A variation of Cher.

CHERRY — A nickname for Cerise and Charity.

CHERYL — A variation of Charlotte.

CHIARRA — The Italian form of Clara.

CHIMENE — Greek. "Hospitable."

CHIQUITA — Spanish. "Little one."

CHIZU — Japanese. "A thousand storks." The stork was an ancient Japanese symbol of longevity.

CHIZUKO — A variation of Chizu.

CHLOE — Greek. "Blooming green bird." Summer name of Grecian deity of agriculture, Demeter. Pastoral name popularized by Elizabethan poets.

CHLORIS — Greek. "The pale." In mythology, the goddess of flowers, who when chased by Apollo turned white.

CHO — Japanese. "Butterfly." Also name for a child born at dawn.

CHRIS — A nickname for Christine.

CHRISELDA — A variation of Griselda.

CHRISTA — A nickname for Christine.

CHRISTABEL — A variation of Christabelle.

CHRISTABELLA — A variation of Christabelle.

CHRISTABELLE — Latin. "Fair and beautiful Christian." First used in England during the 16th century.

CHRISTEL — The Scottish form of Christine.

CHRISTEN — A variation of Christine.

CHRISTIANE — A variation of Christine.

CHRISTINE — Greek. "Christian or anointed one."

CHRYSEIDA — A variation of Cressida.

CHRYSEIS — Latin. "Daughter of the golden one." A beautiful maid given to Agamemnon by the Greeks in the *Iliad*.

CHU HUA — Chinese. "Chrysanthemum." Symbol of the autumn in China. In the West, the flower of the month of November.

CHUN — Chinese. "Spring."

CICILY — A variation of Cecilia.

CILKA — A Slavic nickname for Cecilia.

CINDERELLA — French. "Little one of the ashes." From the fairy tale of the same name.

CINDIE — A nickname for Cinderella, Cynthia, or Lucinda.

CINDY — A nickname for Cinderella, Cynthia, or Lucinda.

CIPRIANA — Greek. "Cyprian."

CISSY — A nickname for Cecilia.

CLAIR — A variation of Claire.

CLAIRE — The French form of Clara.

CLARA — Latin. "Brilliant, illustrious." St. Clara of Assisi founded the first order of nuns in the early 13th century.

CLARABELLE — Latin. "Brilliant and beautiful." Claribel was the name used by Shakespeare in *The Tempest* for the Queen of Tunis.

CLARAMAE — English. Contemporary amalgamation of Clara and Mae.

CLARE — A variation of Claire.

CLARESTA — English. "Most beautiful one."

CLARETA — A Spanish form of Clara.

CLARETTE — A variation of Clara.

CLARICE — A variation of Clarissa.

CLARIE — A nickname for Clara or Clarissa.

CLARIMOND — Latin and German. "Distinguished protectress."

CLARINDA — A variation of Clara.

CLARINE — A variation of Clara.

CLARISSA — Latin. "Making famous." A name popularized in 18th-century England because of the novel *Clarissa Harlowe* by Samuel Richardson.

CLARITA — A Spanish form of Clara.

CLARY — A nickname for Clara.

CLAUDETTE — A French form of Claudia. A popular name in France.

CLAUDIA — Latin. "Lame." Claudius was a famous Latin family name.

CLAUDIE — A nickname for Claudia.

CLAUDINA — An Italian form of Claudia.

CLAUDINE — The French form of Claudia.

CLEATHA — A variation of Cliantha.

CLEATHE — The French form of Cliantha.

CLEM — A nickname for Clementia, Clementina, and Clementine.

CLEMATIS — Greek. "Flowering vine."

CLEMENCE — A French form of Clemency.

CLEMENCY — A variation of Clementia.

CLEMENTIA — Latin. "Mild, calmone."

CLEMENTINA — A variation of Clementia. The first name of the wife of Sir Winston Churchill.

CLEMENTINE — A variation of Clementia. A name popularized by the song "Oh My Darling Clementine" during the Gold Rush days in California.

CLEMMIE — A nickname for Clementia.
Clementine.

CLEMMY — A nickname for Clementia, Clementina, and Clementine.

CLEO — A nickname for Cleopatra.

CLEOPATRA — Greek. "Her father's glory." Queen of Egypt (69-30 B.C.) known for her seductive charms.

CLEVA — Middle English. "Cliff dweller." Feminine form of Clive.

CLIANTHA — Greek. "Flower of glory." Child of a blessed nature.

CLIO — Greek. "The announcer." Name of the muse of history in ancient Greece.

CLODAGH — Irish. Name of a river in Ireland.

CLORINDA — Latin. Fictional name devised by Italian poet Tasso for his heroine in *Jerusalem Delivered.*

CLOTILDA — Old German. "Famous in battle." St. Clotilda was the wife of the 6th-century King of France, Clovis I, who persuaded her husband to embrace Christianity.

CLOVER — Old English. "Clover blossom." A child who is as refreshing as the sight of a field of clover.

CLYMENE — Greek. "Renowned." In mythology, the mother of Atlas and Prometheus.

CLYTE — Greek. "Beautiful." Beloved of Apollo, the sun god in mythology; she was turned into a flower that always turned to the sun.

CLYTIE — A variation of Clyte.

COLETTE — A variation of Collette.

COLLEEN — Gaelic. "Girl, maiden." Used mostly in the United States.

COLLETTE — Latin and French. "Successful in battle." Also a diminutive of Nicolette.

COMFORT — French. "Consoling." An 18th-century Puritan name.

CONCEPCION — A variation of Conception.

CONCEPTION — Latin. "Beginning." Hispanic use honoring the Virgin Mother.

CONCHA — Spanish. "Shell." Beauty of the sea. Also a variation of Conception.

CONCORDIA — Latin. "Harmony." Soul of calmness. Roman goddess governing the peace after war.

CONNIE — A nickname for names beginning with "Con."

CONNY — A nickname for names beginning with "Con."

CONRADINE — Old German. "Bold, wise counselor." Feminine of Conrad.

CONSOLATA — Italian. "Consolation." A name honoring one of the virtues of the Blessed Virgin Mary.

CONSTANCE — Latin. "Fidelity."

CONSTANCIA — The Portuguese form of Constance.

CONSTANCY — A variation of Constance.

CONSTANTA — A variation of Constance.

CONSTANTIA — An Italian and Spanish form of Constance.

CONSTANTINA — A variation of Constance.

CONSTANZA — An Italian and Spanish form of Constance.

CORA — Greek. "Maiden." In mythology, Kore was the child of Demeter, the goddess of agriculture.

CORABELL — A variation of Corabelle.

CORABELLA — A variation of Corabelle.

CORABELLE — Greek and French. "Beautiful maiden."

CORAH — Hindu. "Consistent." A dependable woman.

CORAL — Latin. "Coral from the sea." In ancient Greece, coral was worn as a charm to ward off evil spirits.

CORALIE -- A French form of Coral.

CORALINE — A variation of Coral.

CORDELIA — Welsh. "Jewel of the sea." Daughter of the legendary King Lear, ruler of the sea.

CORDELIE — A French form of Cordelia.

CORELLA — A variation of Cora.

CORETTE — A variation of Cora.

CORINNA — A variation of Cora.

CORINNE — A variation of Cora.

CORISSA — A variation of Cora.

CORLISS — Old English. "Cheerful and generous."

CORNELA — A variation of Cornelia.

CORNELIA — Latin. "Yellow or horn-colored." The feminine of Cornelius.

CORNELIE — A French form of Cornelia.

CORNELLE — A variation of Cornelia.

CORONA — Spanish. "Crowned." A woman of regal presence.

COSETTA — An Italian form of Nicolette.

COSETTE — A variation of Nicolette.

COSIMA — Greek. "Worldly order." Feminine of Cosmos.

CRESCENT — Old French. "One who creates." A child blessed with talent.

CRESCENTIA — A variation of Crescent.

CRESSIDA — Greek. Character in a troubadour's tale used by authors including Boccaccio, Chaucer, and Shakespeare, who gives herself to many men, among them Troilus the Trojan hero.

CRISPIANA — Latin. "Curlyhaired." Feminine of Crispin.

CRISTIN — The Irish form of Christine.

CRISTINA — The Italian and Spanish form of Christine.

CRYSTAL — Latin. "Unquestionably clear." A woman without a deceptive nature.

CYBELE — Greek. Nature goddess from ancient Asia Minor.

CYNARA — Greek. "Thistle." One of a self-protective nature.

CYNTH — A nickname for Cynthia.

CYNTHIA — Greek. "The moon." Another name for the moon goddess Artemis.

CYNTHIE — A nickname for Cynthia.

CYPRIS — Greek. "From the island of Cyprus."

CYRENA — A variation of Cyrene.

CYRENE — Greek. Name of a water nymph who was loved by the god Apollo of mythological legend.

CYRILA — A Spanish form of Cyrilla. Also spelled Cirila.

CYRILLA — Latin. "A lady of dignity."

CYTHEREA — Greek. In mythology, one of the titles for Aphrodite of Venus, from the island of Cythera.

CYTHERIA — A variation of Cytherea.

DACIA — Greek. "From Dacia." An ancient Roman province in Eastern Europe.

DAFFODIL — Greek. "The daffodil flower." The gaily-colored spring blossom. These originally white flowers were turned to yellow when touched by Pluto, according to Greek myth.

DAGNA — Old German. "A splendid day."

DAGNY — A Norwegian form of Dagna.

DAHLIA — Old German. "From the valley."

DAILE — A variation of Dale.

DAISY — Old English. "Eye of the day." A flower whose petals radiate from its dense yellow center as the light beams from the sun.

DALE — Old English. "From the valley."

DALICE — A variation of Dalit.

DALILA — African. "Gentle." Woman of grace and ease.

DALIT — Hebrew. "To draw water."

DAMALIS — Greek. "One who gentles." She can tame even the savage beast.

DAMARA — A variation of Damaris.

DAMARIS — Greek. "Heifer." Of a gentle, trusting nature. Popular name with the Puritans in 17th-century England.

DAMITA — Spanish. "Little noble lady." A child with dignity.

DANELLA — A variation of Daniela.

DANELLE — A variation of Daniela.

DANETTE — A nickname for Daniela.

DANI — A nickname for Daniela.

DANICA — Slavic. "The morning star." A beautiful name for one whose presence brings the promise of a new day.

DANICE — A variation of Denise and a nickname for Daniela.

DANIELA — Hebrew. "God is my judge." Feminine form of Daniel.

DANIELLE — The French form of Daniela.

DANIT — A Hebrew form of Daniela.

DANITA — A Hebrew form of Daniela.

DANYA — A nickname for Bohdana or Daniela.

DAPHNE — Greek. "Laurel tree." A nymph who escaped the advances of Apollo by being turned into a laurel tree, according to Greek mythology.

DARA — Hebrew. "Heart of wisdom."

DARALICE — A variation of Daralis.

DARALIS — Old English. "Beloved."

DARDA — A variation of Dara.

DARIA — Greek. "Regal." One who is born to be queen.

DARICE — A feminine form of Darius.

DARLENE — Old English. "Little beloved one."

DARLINE — A variation of Darlene.

DARYA — A variation of Dara.

DASHA — A nickname for Doroteya.

DASYA — A nickname for Doroteya.

DAVIDA — Hebrew. "The beloved one." Feminine of David.

DAVINA — A variation of Davida.

DAWN — Old English. "The awakening of a new day."

DAYLE — A variation of Dale.

DEANNA — A variation of Diane.

DEB — A nickname for Deborah.

DEBBIE — A nickname for Deborah.

DEBBY — A nickname for Deborah.

DEBORA — A variation of Deborah.

DEBORAH — Hebrew. "Bee." To the ancient Egyptians, the bee symbolized majestic power; while to the Greeks, it meant prophecy. Deborah was a biblical prophetess who assisted the Israelites in their struggle against the Canaanites.

DECIMA — African. "The tenth-born."

DEDE — African. "First-born daughter."

DEE — A nickname for Diane.

DEIANIRA — Greek. Wife of the legendary hero Heracles.

DEIRDRA — A variation of Deidre.

DEIRDRE — Gaelic. "Sorrow." A maid of great beauty in Irish folklore who destroyed herself when her lover was killed.

DELA — A nickname for Adela.

DELCINA — A variation of Dulcie.

DELCINE — A variation of Dulcie.

DELFINE — Greek. "The larkspur flower."

DELIA — Greek. "Visible." A name for the moon goddess who was born on the island of Delos. Also a nickname for Cordelia.

DELICIA — Latin. "Delightful." A woman whose mere presence is refreshing.

DELIGHT — Old French. "Delight or pleasure."

DELILA — A variation of Delilah.

DELILAH — Hebrew. "Brooding." Name of the biblical temptress who betrayed Samson by cutting his hair, the mark of his strength.

DELLA — A nickname for Adelaide and Adelle.

DELMA — Spanish. "Of the sea."

DELORA — Latin. "From the sea-shore." Used for girls born under the astrological water signs Cancer, Scorpio, and Pisces.

DELORES — A variation of Dolores.

DELPHINE — A variation of Delfine.

DELTA — Greek. Fourth letter to the Greek alphabet. Name for a fourth daughter.

DEMETER — Greek goddess of grain, symbol of fertility.

DEMETRIA — A variation of Demeter.

DENA — Old English. "From the valley." Feminine form of Dean.

DENEBOLA — Arabic. Star in the tail of the constellation Leo the Lion.

DENICE — A variation of Denise.

DENISE — French. Derived from the Greek god of wine, Dionysos. A feminine form of Dennis.

DENNIE — A nickname for Denise.

DENNY — A nickname for Denise.

DENYSE — A variation of Denise.

DERORA — Hebrew. "Bird" or "Freedom." Nature name.

DERORICE — A variation of Derora.

DERORIT — A variation of Derora.

DESDEMONA — Greek. "The ill-fated one." Famous character in Shakespeare's *Othello* who is unjustly killed for unfaithfulness.

DESIRÉE — French. "Desired." A much-wished-for child.

DESMONA — A variation of Desdemona.

DEVA — Hindu. "Divine." Name for the moon goddess.

DEVAKI — Hindu. "Black." Goddess who mothered the powerful Krishna.

DEVI — Hindu. "Goddess." Another name for Sakti, the powerful deity of destruction.

DEVONA — Old English. "The defender." The people of Devonshire were noted for their bravery in defending themselves from a Danish invasion.

DEVORA — The Russian form of Deborah.

DEXTRA — Latin. "Skillful." A handy woman. The feminine of Dexter.

DI — A nickname for Diana.

DIAMANTA — French. "Like a diamond." A precious and rare child.

DIAN — A nickname for Diana.

DIANA — Latin. "Divine one." Roman moon goddess associated with fertility.

DIANE — A French form of Diana.

DIANTHA — Greek. "Flower of Zeus."

DIANTHE — A variation of Diantha.

DIANTHIA — A variation of Diantha.

DICKLA — Hebrew. "Palm tree."

DIDO — Greek. "Teacher." Ancient princess reputed to be the founder of Carthage who, according to legend, fell in love with Aeneas and committed suicide when he returned to Italy.

DIELLA — Latin. "Worships God."

DIELLE — A variation of Diella.

DIKLICE — A variation of Djkla.

DIKLIT — A variation of Dikla.

DILYS — Welsh. "Genuine."

DINA — A variation of Dinah. Also a nickname for Adina and Constantine.

DINAH — Hebrew. "Judged."

DIONE — Greek. Mythological daughter of heaven and earth and the mother of Aphrodite.

DIONIS — A variation of Dione.

DISA — Old Norse. "Active spirit." Or Greek for "double."

DITA — A Czechoslovakian name for Edith.

DIXIE — French. "Ten" or "tenth." Also Dixieland was a name for the Southern states. Dixie has been used as a name for a girl born in the South.

DOANNA — American. Contemporary combination of Dorothy and Anna.

DOCILA — Latin. "Teachable."

DOCILLA — A variation of Docila.

DODIE — Hebrew. "Beloved."

DOLL — A nickname for Dorothy.

DOLLY — A nickname for Dorothy.

DOLORA — A variation of Dolores.

DOLORES — Spanish. "Sorrows." Name commemorating the Lady of Sorrows.

DOLORITA — A nickname for Dolores.

DOLORITAS — A Spanish diminutive form of Dolores.

DOMELA — Latin. "Mistress of the home."

DOMINA — Latin. "Lady." A woman of culture and refinement.

DOMINI — A variation of Domina and Dominica.

DONALDA — Gaelic. "World-mighty." A woman capable of conquering the world.

DONATA — Latin. "Gift." A present from God.

DONELLA — Latin. "Little mistress." Or Celtic, "dark-haired, elflike girl."

DONI — A nickname for Donalda.

DONIA — A nickname for Donalda.

DONICA — Latin. "A gift."

DONNA — Latin. "Lady." Mistress of the home. A lady of refinement and charm.

DONNI — A nickname for Donalda.

DORA — Greek. "A gift." Also a nickname for Dorothy.

DORALIA — A variation of Dora.

DORALIN — A variation of Dora.

DORALYNNE — A variation of Dora.

DORCAS — Greek. "A gazelle." Literally "with large dark eyes." Also the name of groups of women in the Bible who made clothes for the poor. A popular name with the Puritans.

DORCEA — A variation of Dorcas.

DORCIA — A variation of Dorcas.

DORÉ — French. "Golden one." A blond-haired beauty.

DOREA — A variation of Doré.

DOREEN — Irish. "The sullen one." A child of a reflective nature. Also a nickname for Dora.

DORELIA — A variation of Dora.

DORETTE — A variation of Dora.

DORI — A nickname for names beginning with "Dor."

DORIA — Greek. "A Dorian." The Dorians were a race of people from ancient Greece known for their sturdy simplicity. Also a variation of Doris.

DORICE — A variation of Doria or Doris.

DORINDA — Greek and Spanish. "Beautiful gift." Name was invented in 18th-century England, when such combinations as Belinda and Clarinda became popular.

DORIS — Greek. "From the sea." In mythology, the daughter of Oceanus, and goddess of the sea nymphs.

DORISA — The Hawaiian form of Doris.

DORITA — A nickname for Doris or Dorothy.

DORLISA — A German form of Dorothy.

DOROLICE — A French form of Dorothy.

DOROTEA — The Italian and Spanish form of Dorothy.

DOROTEYA — The Russian form of Dorothy.

DOROTHEA — The German form of Dorothy.

DOROTHÉE — The French form of Dorothy.

DOROTHY — Greek. "Gift of God."

DORTHEA — A variation of Dorothy.

DRINI — A nickname for Alexandra.

DRISA — A variation of Drisana.

DRISANA — Hindu. "Daughter of the sun." Astrologically appropriate for a girl born under the sign of Leo.

DRU — A nickname for Druella and Drusilla.

DRUCIE — A nickname for Drusilla.

DRUELLA — Old German. "Fairy-like vision." A child with pixielike mirth.

DRUSIE — A nickname for Drusilla.

DRUSILLA — Latin. "Child of Drusus, the strong."

DUA — Latin. "Of two natures."

DUANA — Gaelic. "Song." One of poetic essence.

DUENA — Spanish. "Chaperone." One who tenderly guards the things she loves.

DULCE — A variation of Dulcie.

DULCEA — A variation of Dulcie.

DULCIA — A variation of Dulcie.

DULCIANA — A variation of Dulcie.

DULCIBELLE — Latin and French. "Sweet and beautiful."

DULCIE — Latin. "Sweet."

DULCINE — A variation of Dulcie.

DULCINEA — A variation of Dulcie. The country maid who was idolized by Don Quixote.

DULCY — A variation of Dulcie.

DUNA — A variation of Duana.

DUSCHA — Russian. "Soul." Everyday term of endearment.

DWANA — A variation of Duana.

DYAN — A nickname for Diana.

DYANE — A variation of Diana.

DYMPHNA — Gaelic. "Suitable one." Famous Irish virgin saint.

EARLENE — Old English. "Noble woman."

EARLEY — A nickname for Earlene.

EARLIE — A nickname for Earlene.

EARLINE — A variation of Earlene.

EARTHA — Old English. "Child of the earth." A daughter of natural simplicity and strength.

EBA — A variation of Eva.

EBBA — Old English. "Flowing back of the tide." A romantic name. Also a variation of Eve.

EBERTA — Old German. "Overwhelmingly brilliant." Feminine of Egbert.

EBONY — Greek. Type of wood. Symbol of black beauty.

ECHO — Greek. "Repeated sound." In mythology, a nymph whose unrequited love for Narcissus caused her to pine away until only her voice remained.

EDA — Old English. "Prosperity." A child bestowed with an abundance of blessings. Also a variation of Edda.

EDANA — Gaelic. "Fiery one." Possibly one who possesses the stereotypic Irish temper.

EDDA — Old Norse. "Poetry."

EDE — Greek. "Generation." The fulfilled promise of continuation of the race. Also the Russian form of Edda and nickname for Edith.

EDELINE — A variation of Adeline.

EDI — A nickname for Edith.

EDIE — A nickname for Edith.

EDINA — Scottish. "From the city of Edinburgh." Also a variation of Eda.

EDITA — The Italian and Slavic form of Edith.

EDITH — Old English. "Rich gift."

EDITHA — A variation of Edith.

EDITHE — A variation of Edith.

EDIVA — A variation of Edith.

EDLA — A variation of Edlyn.

EDLYN — Old English. "Noble woman." Lady of fine breeding.

EDMÉE — The French form of Edmonda.

EDMONDA — Old English. "Happy protectress." One who cares for her family with pleasure. Feminine of Edmond.

EDMUNDA — A variation of Edmonda.

EDNA — Hebrew. "Rejuvenation." One whose very presence provides a breath of fresh air. Edna St. Vincent Millay was a famous American poet.

EDOLIE — Old German. "Noble."

EDRA — A variation of Edrea.

EDREA — Old English. "Prosperous." Feminine of Edric.

EDRIS — A variation of Edrea.

EDWARDINE — Old English. "Prosperous guardian." Feminine of Edward.

EDWINA — Old English. "Valuable friend." A woman who can withstand the test of true friendship. Feminine of Edwin.

EDYTH — A variation of Edith.

EFFIE — A nickname for Euphemia.

EFRONA — Hebrew. "A bird." Feminine of Efron.

EFUA — African. Name of a child "born on a Friday."

EGBERTA — Old English. "Shining sword." A most capable warrior. Feminine of Egbert.

EGBERTINA — A variation of Egberta.

EGBERTINE — A variation of Egberta.

EGERIA — Latin. "Counselor." According to legend, a nymph who advised the lawgiver Numa Pompilius, King of Rome.

EGLANTINE — Old French. "Sweet briar rose." A beautiful nature name.

EILEEN — Gaelic. "Light." Irish form of Helen.

EIMILE — The Irish form of Emily.

EIR — Old Norse. "Peace." Norse goddess of healing.

EIRENA — A variation of Irene.

EIRENE — A variation of Eir.

EITHNE — A variation of Aithe.

EKATERINA — The Russian form of Catherine.

EKU — African. Name for a child "born on Wednesday."

ELA — A nickname for names beginning with "El."

ELAINE — Greek. "Light." Elaine was the maid of the lilies who pined and died of her love for Launcelot in the legend of King Arthur. A variation of Helen.

ELANE — A variation of Elaine.

ELATA — Latin. "The exalted one." One who has been elevated to the heights of adoration for her beauty and charm.

ELAYNE — A variation of Elaine.

ELBERTA — Old English. "Nobly brilliant." Feminine of Elbert.

ELBERTINE — A variation of Elberta.

ELDORA — Spanish. "The gilded one." Believed to be a contraction of the name Eldorado given to a Colombian tribal chief who covered himself with gold dust in a religious ritual. In literature, Eldorado is used to signify a land of opportunity.

ELDORIS — A variation of Eldora.

ELDRIDA — Old English. "Wise counselor." Feminine of Eldred and Eldrid.

ELEANOR — A variation of Eleanore.

ELEANORE — Greek. "Light." A form of Helen. Eleanore Roosevelt was a renowned American stateswoman.

ELECTRA — Greek. "Bright and shining." Daughter of the Greek hero Agamemnon in Greek history.

ELENA — The Italian and Spanish form of Helen.

ELENI — A Greek form of Helen.

ELEONORA — A variation of Eleanore.

ELEONORE — A variation of Eleanore.

ELEORA — A variation of Eliora.

ELFRIDA — A variation of Alfreda.

ELFRIEDA — A variation of Elfrida.

ELGA — Gothic. "Holy." A model of saintliness.

ELIANORA — The Hawaiian of Eleanore.

ELIDI — Greek. "Gift of the sun." Astrological name for a child born under the sign of Leo, which is ruled by the sun.

ELINOR — A variation of Eleanore.

ELIORA — Hebrew. "The Lord is my light." One who uses the Word of God as a guide for life.

ELISA — A Spanish form of Elizabeth.

ELISABET — The Swedish form of Elizabeth.

ELISABETH — The French, Dutch, and German form of Elizabeth.

ELISABETTA — The Italian form of Elizabeth.

ELISE — A French form of Elizabeth.

ELISSA — A nickname for Elizabeth.

ELITA — Old French and Latin. "The chosen one.'

ELIZABET — The Greek form of Elizabeth.

ELIZABETH — Hebrew. "Oath of God." St. Elizabeth was the mother of St. John the Baptist, and a cousin of the Blessed Virgin. A popular name in all European languages, it has numerous variations.

ELLA — Old English. "Beautiful fairy maiden." Elves were considered supernatural beings who influenced the lives of men. Also a nickname for Eleanore.

ELLADINE — A variation of Eleanore.

ELLAMA — Hindu. Mother goddess who protects southern India.

ELLAMAE — A variation of Ellamay.

ELLAMAY — Contemporary combination of Ella and May.

ELLEN — A variation of Helen.

ELLETTE — A nickname for Ella.

ELLI — An Estonian form of Helen.

ELICE — Hebrew. "Jehovah is God." A feminine of Elias.

ELLIE — A nickname for Eleanore and Ella.

ELLY — A nickname for Eleanore and Ella.

ELMA — Greek. "Amiable." Feminine of Elmo.

ELMINA — Old English. "Noble and famous."

ELMIRA — A variation of Elmina.

ELNA — A variation of Helen.

ELNORA — A variation of Eleanore.

ELODIE — Greek. "Marshy." White blossom of the water-thyme.

ELOINE — Latin. "Worthy to be chosen." Feminine of Eloy.

ELOISA — A variation of Louise.

ELOISE — A variation of Louise.

ELORA — A nickname for Eleanore.

ELSA — Old German. "Noble one." Also a Dutch and German nickname for Elizabeth.

ELSBETH — A Scottish form of Elizabeth.

ELSE — A Danish form of Elsa.

ELSIE — A nickname for Elsa.

ELSPETH — A Scottish form of Elizabeth.

ELUNED — Welsh. "Uncertain."

ELVA — Old English. "Elfin." Also a variation of Alfreda.

ELVERA — A variation of Elvira.

ELVERDA — Latin. "Virginal." Occult name suitable for a child born under the sign of Virgo.

ELVINA — Old English. "Befriended by the elves." A child placed under the protection of the little people.

ELVIRA — Latin. "The fair one."

ELVITA — Latin. "Life." A child capable of living a full existence.

ELWIRA — The Polish form of Elvira.

ELYN — A variation of Helen.

ELYSE — A variation of Elsa and Elsie.

ELYSIA — Latin. "Sweetly blissful." Elysium was the final resting place of heroes and virtuous souls in Greek legend.

ELZA — Hebrew. "God is my joy." Also the Russian form of Elsa.

EM — A nickname for names beginning with "Em."

EMA — A Spanish form of Emma.

EMALIA — A variation of Emelia.

EMBER — Old English. "Smoldering remains of a fire." A woman who emanates warmth.

EMELDA — A variation of Emily.

EMELIA — Latin. "Flatterer." A woman of complimentary speech.

EMELINA — A variation of Emily or Emma.

EMELINE — A variation of Emily or Emma.

EMELYNE — A variation of Emma.

EMERA — A variation of Emily.

EMERALD — Old French. "The green gem." Birthstone of May.

EMILIA — The Dutch, Italian, Portuguese, and Spanish form of Emily.

EMILIE — The French and German form of Emily.

EMILY — Latin. "Industrious."

EMINA — Latin. "Lady of prominence."

EMLYNNE — A variation of Emily.

EMMA — Old German. "Universal."

EMMALINE — A variation of Emma.

EMMIE — A nickname for names beginning with "Em."

EMMYLOU — Modern combination of Emmy and Lou.

EMOGENE — A variation of Imogene.

ENA — Gaelic. "Little ardent one." Or from the Greek, meaning "praise."

ENGELBERTA — Old German. "Bright angel." Little messenger from God.

ENGRACIA — A Spanish form of Grace.

ENID — Celtic and Latin. "Spirit." In Tennyson's *Idylls of the King*, the story of the fair maiden Enid is told.

ENNEA — Greek. "Nine." The ninth child.

ENRICA — Italian. "Mistress of the estate."

ENRICHETTA — An Italian form of Henrietta.

ENRIQUETA — A Spanish form of Henrietta.

EOLANDE — A variation of Yolanda.

ERANTHE — Greek. "Spring flower."

ERASMA — Greek. "Amiable."

ERDA — A variation of Eartha.

ERENA — A variation of Irene.

ERICA — Old Norse. "Ever-powerful." Feminine of Eric.

ERIKA — A variation of Erica.

ERIN — Gaelic. "Peace." Also used as a name for Southern Ireland itself.

ERINA — A variation of Erin.

ERLENE — A variation of Earlene.

ERLINA — A variation of Earlene.

ERLINE — A variation of Earlene.

ERMA — Old German. "Army maiden." Or Latin, meaning "noble one."

ERMINA — A variation of Erma.

ERMINIA — A variation of Erma.

ERMINIE — A variation of Erma.

ERMYNTRUDE — Old German. "Universal strength."

ERNA — Old English. "Eagle."

ERNALINE — A variation of Erna.

ERNESTA — A variation of Ernestine.

ERNESTINE — Old English. "Earnest one."

ERTHA — A variation of Eartha.

ERWINA — Old English. "Friend from the sea." Feminine of Erwin.

ESMA — A nickname for Esmeralda.

ESMERALDA — Spanish. "The emerald." Precious child with bright green eyes.

ESSIE — A nickname for Estelle or Esther.

ESTA — Italian. "From the East." An exotic woman.

ESTELLA — A variation of Estelle.

ESTELLE — Latin. "A star."

ESTHER — Hebrew. "A star." The biblical Jewish Queen of Persia who uncovered a plot to exterminate her people in the 5th century B.C.

ESTRA — Old English. "Goddess of spring."

ESTRELLA — The Spanish form of Estelle.

ESTRELLITA — A nickname for Estrella.

ETHEL — Old English. "Noble one."

ETHELDA — A variation of Ethel.

ETHELIN — A variation of Ethel.

ETHELINDA — Old German. "Honorable serpent." In the ancient world, the serpent symbolized sagacity and immortality.

ETHELJEAN — A modern combination of Ethel and Jean.

ETHNE — A variation of Aithne.

ETTA — Old German. "Little." Name by itself or as an ending on various names to form diminutives.

ETTY — A variation of Etta.

EUCLEA — Greek. "Glory." A child destined for greatness.

EUDICE — A Hebrew form of Judith.

EUDOCIA — Greek. "Esteemed." A woman beyond reproach.

EUDORA — Greek. "Generous."

EUDORE — The French form of Eudora.

EUDOSIA — A variation of Eudocia.

EUDOXIA — A variation of Eudocia.

EUFEMIA — The Italian and Spanish form of Euphemia.

EUGENIA — Greek. "Well-born."

EUGENIE — The French form of Eugenia.

EULALIA — Greek. "Well-spoken." St. Eulalia is the patron saint of Barcelona.

EUNICE — Greek. "Happy in victory."

EUPHEME — A variation of Euphemia.

EUPHEMIA — Greek. "Of auspicious fame." St. Euphemia was a 4th-century virgin-martyr.

EUPHÉMIE — The French form of Euphemia.

EURYDICE — Greek. In Greek mythology, the wife of Orpheus, whom Hades permitted to take from the Underworld, on the condition that he not look at her until he reached earth; a promise he was not able to keep and so he lost her forever.

EUSTACIA — Latin. "Fruitful." Feminine of Eustace.

EVA — The Slavic, Scandinavian, German, Italian, Russian, Spanish, and Portuguese form of Eve.

EVADINE — Greek. A name used frequently in Greek poetry and mythology in ancient times

EVAGELIA — The Greek form of Angela.

EVALEEN — The Irish form of Eve.

EVALINA — A variation of Eve.

EVANGELINE — Greek. "Bearer of good tidings." Longfellow revived the name in his popular poem *Evangeline* in 1849.

EVANIA — Greek. "Tranquil." One who will be untroubled by life's adversities.

EVANTHE — Greek. "A flower." A child like a flourishing blossom.

EVE — Hebrew. "Life." "And Adam called his wife's name Eve, because she was the mother of the living" (Genesis iii:20).

EVELEEN — An Irish form of Eve.

EVELINA — A Russian and Spanish form of Eve.

EVELYN — A variation of Eve and Helen.

EYDE — A nickname for Edith.

EYDIE — A nickname for Edith.

EZRAELA — A variation of Ezrela.

EZRAELLA — A variation of Ezrela.

EZRELA — Hebrew. "God is my strength." A name reaffirming one's belief in God.

FABIA — Latin. "Bean grower." A maid who tills the land.

FABRIENNE — Latin. "Mechanical."

FAE — A variation of Fay.

FAITH — Middle English. "Fidelity." A virtue name, popular after the Reformation.

FAN — A nickname for Frances.

FANCHON — French. "Free."

FANECHKA — A Russian form of Frances.

FANIA — A Slavic form of Frances.

FANNIE — A nickname for Frances.

FANNY — A nickname for Frances.

FANYA — A Slavic form of Frances.

FARCIA — A nickname for Fredericka.

FAUNA — A variation of Fawn.

FAUSTA — A variation of Faustine.

FAUSTINA — An Italian form of Faustine.

FAUSTINE — Latin. "The fortunate one." The feminine of Faust.

FAVOR — Old French. "Gracious concern for another."

FAWN — Old French. "Young deer."

FAWNIA — A variation of Fawn.

FAY — Old French. "A fairy." A child blessed with the good fortune of the little people. A nickname for Faith.

FAYANNE — Current compound of Fay and Anne.

FAYE — A variation of Fay.

FAYINA — A Russian form of Frances.

FAYME — Old French. "Held in high esteem." Her praises will be proclaimed far and near.

FAYOLA — African. "Good luck."

FAYRE — Old English. "Beautiful."

FEALTY — Old French. "Allegiance."

FEDERICA — The Spanish and Italian form of Frederica.

FEDORA — A Slavic form of Theodora.

FELDA — Old German. "From the field." This name can be used for girls born under the earth signs of the Zodiac: Capricorn, Taurus, and Virgo.

FELICE — Latin. "The happy one."

FELICIA — The Italian and Polish form of Felice.

FELICIDAD — The Spanish form of Felice.

FELICIE — A French form of Felice.

FELICITY — A variation of Felice.

FELIPA — A Spanish form of Phillipa.

FELISE — A French form of Felice.

FELITA — A variation of Felice.

FENELLA — Gaelic. "White-shouldered."

FEODORA — A Slavic form of Theodora.

FEODOSIA — A Slavic form of Theodosia.

FERDINANDA — A variation of Fernanda.

FERN — Old English. "Fern." Lush and soft and refreshing.

FERNANDA — Gothic. "Life adventurer."

FERNANDE — A variation of Fernanda.

FERNANDINA — A variation of Fernanda.

FIDELIA — A variation of Fidelity.

FIDELITY — Latin. "Faithfulness." A Puritan virtue name. *Fidelio* was the title of Beethoven's only opera.

FIFI — The French nickname of Josephine.

FIFINE — The French form of Josephine.

FILIDE — The Italian form of Phyllis.

FILIPA — An Italian form of Phillipa.

FILMA — Old English. "A mist."

FIONA — Gaelic. "Fair lady."

FIORA — The Italian form of Flora.

FIORENZA — The Italian form of Florence.

FLANNA — Gaelic. "Red-haired." A lass with flaming red locks.

FLAVIA — Latin. "Blonde."

FLEDA — A variation of Fleta.

FLETA — Old English. "Swift, fleet."

FLEUR — French. "Flower."

FLEURETTE — A nickname for Fleur.

FLO — A nickname for Florence.

FLOR — A Spanish form of Flora.

FLORA — Latin. "Flowering." Florida was discovered on Easter Sunday, known as *Pascua florida*, by Ponce de Leon.

FLORE — The French form of Flora.

FLORELLA — A form of Flora.

FLORENCE — Latin. "Blooming." Florence, Italy, is a city where the arts flourished during the Renaissance.

FLORENCIA — The Spanish form of Florence.

FLORIA — A variation of Flora.

FLORIDA — A Spanish form of Flora.

FLORIE — A nickname for Flora and Florence.

FLORINDA — A variation of Florence.

FLORINE — A variation of Florence.

FLORIS — A variation of Flora and Florence.

FLORRIE — A nickname for Flora and Florence.

FLORRY — A nickname for Flora and Florence.

FLOSSIE — A nickname for Florence.

FONDA — Spanish. "Profound." Or from the Middle English meaning "affectionate."

FORTUNA — The Italian and Spanish form of Fortune.

FORTUNE — Latin. "The fortunate one." Fortuna was the Roman goddess of good luck.

FRAN — A nickname for Frances.

FRANCES — Latin. "Free," or from "France." Feminine of Francis.

FRANCESCA — The Italian form of Frances.

FRANCI — A nickname for Frances.

FRANCIE — A nickname for Frances.

FRANCINE — A variation of Frances.

FRANCISCA — The Spanish form of Frances.

FRANCISKA — A Slavic form of Frances.

FRANÇOISE — A French form of Frances.

FRANCYNE — A variation of Frances.

FRANKIE — A nickname for Frances.

FRANNIE — A nickname for Frances.

FRANNY — A nickname for Frances.

FREDA — A variation of Frieda.

FREDDIE — A nickname for Frederica.

FREDDY — A nickname for Frederica.

FREDELLA — A contemporary combination of Fred and Ella.

FRÉDÉRICA — Old German. "Peaceful ruler." A feminine form of Frederick.

FREDERICKA — A variation of Frederica.

FRÉDÉRIQUE — The French form of Frederica.

FREYA — Old Norse. "Noble lady." The Scandinavian Venus after whom Friday is named.

FRIDA — A variation of Frieda.

FRIEDA — Old German. "Woman of peace."

FRIEDERIKE — The German form of Frederica.

FRITZI — Old German. "Peaceful ruler." A feminine form of Fritz.

FRITZIE — A variation of Fritzi.

FRODINA — A variation of Frodine.

FRODINE — Old German. "Learned friend."

FRONDE — Latin. "A leafy branch." One who is richly attired."

FRONIA — Latin. "Forehead." A woman of intelligence.

FULVIA — Latin. "Golden-haired."

FUYU — Japanese. A girl born in the "winter."

GABIE — A nickname for Gabrielle.

GABRIELA — The Spanish form of Gabrielle.

GABRIELLA — A variation of Gabrielle.

GABRIELLE — Hebrew. Feminine of Gabriel, "man who takes his strength from God."

GABY — A nickname for Gabrielle.

GAEA — Greek. "The earth." Gaia was the Greek deity of the earth, and the mother of Uranus. Astrologically appropriate for a girl born under the earth signs and also Aquarius, which is ruled by Uranus.

GAFNA — Hebrew. "Wine."

GAIA — A variation of Gaea.

GAIL — Old English. "Gaiety." Also a nickname for Abigail.

GALA — Old Norse. "Singer."

GALATEA — Greek. "Milky-white." In mythology, the name given by Pygmalion, the sculptor, to an ivory statue that was brought to life by Aphrodite.

GALE — A variation of Gail and Gala.

GALI — Hebrew. "Fountain."

GALICE — A variation of Gali.

GALIENA — Old German. "The dignified one."

GALINA — The Russian form of Helen.

GALIT — A variation of Gali.

GANA — Hebrew. "Garden."

GANESE — Hindu. Deity of good fortune and wisdom.

GANICE — A variation of Ganit.

GANIT — A variation of Gana.

GARDA — A variation of Gerda.

GARDENIA — Latin. "White flower with the delicious scent."

GARLAND — Old French. "A wreath of flowers."

GARNET — Middle English. "The dark gem." The birthstone for the month of January.

GARNETTE — A variation of Garnet.

GARUDA — Hindu. Name of the half-giant, half-eagle sun-bird upon whom the god Vishnu rides.

GAURI — Hindu. "Yellow." Another name for the goddess Sakti.

GAVRA — A Slavic form of Gabrielle.

GAVRILA — A Slavic form of Gabrielle.

GAY — Old French. "Lively."

GAYLE — A variation of Gail.

GAZELLA — Latin. "Gazelle." A woman of graceful movement.

GEELA — Hebrew. "Joy."

GELASIA — Greek. "Predisposed to laughter." A child with a bubbling nature.

GELTRUDA — The Italian form of Gertrude.

GELYA — A Russian nickname for Angelina.

GEMINA — Latin. Name signifying a child born under the sign of Gemini, the third constellation of the Zodiac.

GEMMA — Italian. "A rare jewel."

GENE — A nickname for Eugenia.

GENEVA — Old French. "Juniper tree."

GENEVIÈVE — Old German and French. "White waves." St. Geneviève is the patron saint of Paris. She is credited with saving the city from the Huns in the 15th century.

GENEVRA — An Italian form of Geneviève.

GENIE — A nickname for Eugenia.

GENOVERA — An Italian form of Geneviève.

GEORGENE — A variation of Georgia.

GEORGETTE — The French form of Georgia.

GEORGIA — Latin. "Farmer." The feminine form of George.

GEORGIANA — A variation of Georgia.

GEORGIE — A nickname for Georgia.

GEORGIENNE — A French form of Georgia.

GEORGINA — A Dutch and German form of Georgia.

GEORGINE — A French form of Georgia.

GEORGY — A nickname for Georgia.

GERALDA — A variation of Geraldine.

GERALDINA — A variation of Geraldine.

GERALDINE — Old German and French. "Mighty with the spear." Feminine for Gerald.

GERANIUM — Greek. "Crane." Now known because of the red-flowering plant for which this name is used.

GERDA — Old Norse. "An enclosed, protected area." The word "garden" is derived from the same root.

GERHARDINE — The German form of Geraldine.

GERMAINE — French. "A German. From the Celtic for "shoulder."

GERMANA — A variation of Germaine.

GERRIE — A nickname for Geraldine.

GERRY — A nickname for Geraldine.

GERT — A nickname for Gertrude.

GERTRUD — The German form of Gertrude.

GERTRUDE — Old German. "Spear-maiden." The name of one of the Valkyries, the young women who carried the souls of heroes to the heaven of Norse mythology, Valhalla.

GERTRUDIS — The Spanish form of Gertrude.

GERTY — A nickname for Gertrude.

GIANCINTA — The Italian form of Hyacinth.

GIANINA — An Italian form of Jane.

GILADA — Hebrew. "Eternal joy."

GILANA — A variation of Geela.

GILBERTA — Old German. "Brilliant pledge."

GILBERTE — A variation of Gilberta.

GILBERTINA — A variation of Gilberta.

GILBERTINE — A variation of Gilberta.

GILDA — Old English. "Covered with gold." Or from the Celtic, meaning "servant of God."

GILL — A nickname for Gilberta and Gillian.

GILLIAN — Latin. "Young down-haired child."

GILLIE — A nickname for Gilberta and Gillian.

GILLY — A nickname for Gilberta and Gillian.

GINA — Japanese. "Silvery." In ancient folklore, metals were believed to be capable of combating evil spirits.

GINEVRA — The Italian form of Guinevere.

GINGER — Latin. "Ginger flower or spice." A nickname for Virginia.

GIORGIA — An Italian form of Georgia.

GIORSA — The Scottish form of Grace.

GIOVANNA — The Italian form of Jane.

GIPSY — A variation of Gypsy.

GIRALDA — An Italian form of Geraldine.

GISA — Hebrew. "Hewn stone."

GISELA — The Italian and Spanish form of Giselle.

GISELE — The French form of Giselle.

GISELLE — Old German. "Pledge."

GITA — Hebrew. "Good."

GITANA — Spanish. "Gypsy."

GITEL — A variation of Gytha.

GIZA — Old German. "Gift."

GIZELA — A Slavic form of Giselle.

GIZI — A nickname for Giselle.

GLAD — Old English. "Merry." Also nickname for Gladys.

GLADI — A nickname for Gladys.

GLADYS — Latin. "Lame," or "small sword."

GLEDA — Old English. "Make happy." Also a variation of Gladys.

GLEN — A nickname for Glenna.

GLENDA — A variation of Glenna.

GLENNA — Gaelic. "One who dwells in the valley." An example of a name denoting a place of residence.

GLENNIS — A variation of Glenna.

GLORI — A nickname for Gloria.

GLORIA — Latin. "Glorious."

GLORIANA — A variation of Gloria.

GLORIANE — A variation of Gloria.

GLYNIS — A varitaion of Glenna.

GODIVA — Old English. "Gift of God." The legend of Lady Godiva of Coventry was made famous by Tennyson.

GOLDA — Hebrew. "Golden locks."

GOLDARINA — A variation of Golda.

GOLDIE — A nickname for Golda.

GOLDINA — A variation of Golda.

GRACE — Latin. "Graceful." A 17th-century Puritan name.

GRACIA — The Spanish form of Grace.

GRACIE — A nickname for Grace.

GRANIA — Gaelic. "Love." Name of a popular folk hero.

GRATA — A variation of Grace.

GRATIA — A variation of Grace.

GRATIANA — A variation of Grace.

GRAZIA — An Italian form of Grace.

GREDEL — A German form of Margaret.

GREER — A variation of Gregoria.

GREGORIA — Latin. "The watchful one." Feminine of Gregory.

GRETA — A nickname for Margaret.

GRETAL — A German form of Margaret.

GRETCHEL — A German form of Margaret.

GRETCHEN — A German form of Margaret.

GRETE — A Norwegian form of Grace.

GRETEL — A German form of Margaret.

GRISELDA — Old German. "Gray-haired battle heroine."

GRISELDIS — A variation of Griselda.

GRISHILDA — A German form of Griselda.

GRISHILDE — A German form of Griselda.

GRISSEL — A variation of Griselda.

GRIZEL — The Scottish form of Griselda.

GRIZELDA — A variation of Griselda.

GUADALUPE — A Spanish name taken from St. Mary of Guadalupe.

GUDA — Old English. "Good."

GUENDOLEN — A variation of Gwendolyn.

GUENNA — A nickname for Guinevere and Gwendolyn.

GUGLIELMA — The Italian form of Wilhelmina.

GUILLA — A nickname for Wilhelmina.

GUILLELMINA — The Spanish form of Wilhelmina.

GUILLELMINE — A French form of Wilhelmina.

GUINEVERE — Old Welsh. "Fair spirit." Sir Launcelot failed in his search for the Holy Grail because of his love for Guinevere, the Queen of King Arthur in the legends of the Knights of the Round Table.

GUNDA — A nickname for Gunhilda.

GUNHILDA — Old Norse. "Warrior."

GURICE — A variation of Gurit.

GURIT — Hebrew. "Young of the lion." Astrologically appropriate

for girls born under the sign of
Leo, the Lion.

GUSTAVA — Old German.
"Noble." The feminine of Gustavus.

GUSTEL — A German variation of
Augusta.

GWEN — A nickname for Gwendolyn and Guinevere.

GWENDOLEN — A variation of
Gwendolyn.

GWENDOLIN — A variation of
Gwendolyn.

GWENDOLYN — Old Welsh.
"White circle." An ancient Celtic
goddess, possibly corresponding
to the Roman moon goddess
Diana. Gwendolyn was the wife of
Merlin, the magician in Welsh
folklore.

GWENORA — A variation of
Guinevere.

GWENORE — A variation of
Guinevere.

GWYNETH — Old Welsh. "Fair
one."

GWYNNE — A variation of
Gwyneth.

GYPSY — Old English. "A
wanderer." A woman with an
adventurous spirit.

GYTHA — Old English. "A gift."
Or from Old Norse for "belligerent."

HADRIA — A variation of Adria.

HAGAR — Hebrew. "Forsaken."
In the Bible, Hagar, an Egyptian
concubine of Abraham, was
forced by his wife Sarah to flee
into the desert with her son
Ishmael.

HAIDEE — Greek. "Honored."
Greek maiden who was the heroine of Bryon's *Don Juan.*

HALCYONE — Greek. "Kingfisher
from the sea." In mythology, a
maiden, overcome by grief for her
drowned husband, threw herself
into the sea and was transformed
into a kingfisher.

HALDANA — Old Norse. "Half
Danish." Feminine of Haldan.

HALETTE — A nickname for
Haralda and Henrietta.

HALFRIDA — Old German.
"Peaceful home."

HALI — A nickname for Halimeda.

HALIMEDA — Greek. "Thinking
of the sea." A daughter who contemplates faraway places.

HALLY — A nickname for Halimeda, Haralda, or Henrietta.

HALONA — American Indian.
"Fortunate."

HAMUDA — Hebrew. "Precious."

HANA — Japanese. "Flower." Also
a German form of Hannah.

HANAE — A Japanese variation of
Hana.

HANAKO — A Japanese variation
of Hana

HANE — A German form of
Hannah.

HANELE — A German form of
Hannah.

HANIA — Hebrew. "Place of rest."

HANIYA — A variation of Hania.

HANNAH — Hebrew. "One
favored by God." Biblical name;
mother of the prophet Samuel.

HANNIE — A nickname for
Hannah.

HANNY — A nickname for
Hannah.

HAPPY — Contemporary. Meaning self-explanatory.

HARA — Hindu. One of the names
of the god of destruction, Shiva.
Feminine of Hari.

HARALDA — Old Norse. "Mighty
warrior." Feminine of Harold.

HARELDA — A variation of
Haralda.

HARMONIA — A variation of
Harmony.

HARMONIE — A variation of
Harmony.

HARMONY — Latin. "Complete
peace."

HARRIET — Old French. "Mistress of the home." Feminine of
Henry.

HARRIETTA — A variation of Harriet.

HARRIETTE — A variation of Harriet.

HARRIOT — A variation of Harriet.

HASINA — Hebrew. "Strong."

HATTIE — A nickname for Harriet or Henrietta.

HAZEL — Old English. "Commander." In ancient Europe, the hazel branch was a symbol of authority.

HEATHER — Middle English. "Flowering heather." Popular presenty in the United States.

HEBE — Greek. "Bloom of youth." In mythology, the goddess of youth was the daughter of Zeus and also the wife of Heracles.

HECATE — Greek. Goddess of the sky, earth, and underworld. Patroness of witches.

HEDA — A variation of Hedwig.

HEDDA — A variation of Hedwig.

HEDDI — A nickname for Hedwig.

HEDDY — A nickname for Hedwig.

HEDVIGE — A French form of Hedwig.

HEDWIG — Old German. "Strife."

HEDWIGA — A variation of Hedwig.

HEDY — Greek. "Pleasant." Also a nickname for Hedwig.

HELEN — Greek. "Light." The abduction of Helen of Troy by Paris was the cause of the Trojan War.

HELENA — A German form of Helen. St. Helena was the mother of Constantine.

HÉLENÈ — A French and German form of Helen.

HELENKA — The Polish form of Helen.

HELGA — Old German. "Pious." Also a variation of Olga.

HELICE — Greek. "Spiral." Nymph in mythology.

HELLI — A Finnish form of Helen.

HELMA — Old German. "Protection."

HÉLOÏSE — A French form of Louise. Famous French abbess and lover of Abelard.

HELSA — A Danish nickname for Elizabeth.

HENDRIKA — A Dutch form of Henrietta.

HENKA — A Polish form of Henrietta.

HENRIETA — A Polish form of Henrietta.

HENRIETTA — French. "Mistress of the household." A feminine form of Henry.

HENRIETTE — The French and German form of Henrietta.

HENRIKA — The Swedish form of Henrietta.

HEPHZIBAH — Hebrew. "My delight is in her." A biblical reference to Israel, the Promised Land.

HEPHZIBETH — A variation of Hephzibah.

HEPSIBA — A variation of Hephzibah.

HERA — Greek. "Queen." Heavenly goddess and wife of Zeus in Greek mythology.

HERMANDINE — A variation of Hermione.

HERMIA — A variation of Erma and Hermione.

HERMINA — A variation of Erma and Hermione.

HERMINE — A variation of Erma and Hermione.

HERMIONE — Greek. "Earthly." Daughter of Helen of Troy.

HERMOSA — Spanish. "Beautiful."

HERTA — A variation of Eartha.

HERTHA — A variation of Eartha.

HESPER — Greek. "Evening star." Hespira was the Greek name for Italy.

HESTER — Greek. "Star." A Dutch form of Esther.

HESTIA — A variation of Hester.

HETTY — A nickname for Hester.

HIBERNIA — Latin. Ancient for Ireland.

HIBISCUS — Latin. The flower name.

HILARIA — Latin. "Cheerful." Feminine of Hilary.

HILDA — Old German. "Maiden of war." In Norse mythology, the name for one of the Valkyries.

HILDE — A variation of Hilda.

HILDEGARDE — Old German. "Battle fortress."

HILDEMAR — Old German. "Celebrated battle."

HILDRETH — Old German. "Battle counselor."

HILLELA — Hebrew. "Praise."

HILMA — A variation of Helma.

HINDA — Hebrew. "Deer."

HIPPOLYTA — Greek. In Greek legend, the name of the leader of the Amazons, a group of women warriors.

HOA — Vietnamese. "Blossom."

HOLDA — Old German. "Beloved."

HOLDE — A variation of Holda.

HOLLE — A variation of Holda.

HOLLY — Old English. "Holly tree." Traditional Christmastide decoration.

HONEY — Old English. "Sweet one." Frequently used as a general term of endearment. Also a nickname for Honoria.

HONORIA — Latin. "Lady of honor."

HOPE — Old English. "Encouragement." Favorite Puritan virtue name.

HORACIA — A variation of Horatia.

HORATIA — Latin. "One who is responsible for watching the time."

HORTENSE — Latin. "Gardener."

HORTENSIA — The German form of Hortense.

HOSHI — Japanese. "A star."

HOSHIE — A variation of Hoshi.

HUBERTA — Old German. "Brilliant."

HUETTE — A variation of Huberta.

HUGETTE — A variation of Huberta.

HUGHETTE — A variation of Huberta.

HULDA — Hebrew. "Weasel." Name of a biblical prophetess. Also a variation of Holda.

HULDIE — A nickname for Hulda or Holda.

HULDY — A nickname for Hulda and Holda.

HUYANA — American Indian. "Rain falling." Name usually given to a child who was born during a rainstorm.

HYACINTH — Greek. "Hyacinth flower." A sweet-smelling flower.

HYACINTHA — A variation of Hyacinth.

HYACINTHE — A variation of Hyacinth.

HYACINTHIA — A variation of Hyacinth.

HYACINTHIE — A German form of Hyacinth.

HYPATIA — Greek. "Surpassing A beautiful Greek philosopher of 5th-century Alexandria.

IANTHA — Greek. "Violet-colored flower."

IANTHINA — A variation of Iantha.

IB — A nickname for Isabel.

IDA — Old German. "Hard-working." Or Old English for "prosperous."

IDALIA — A variation of Ida.

IDALINA — A variation of Ida.

IDALINE — A variation of Ida.

IDELLE — A variation of Ida.

IDETTE — A variation of Ida.

IDOLA — Greek. "A vision."

IDONA — A variation of Iduna.

IDONIA — A variation of Iduna.

IDUNA — Old German. "Industrious," or from the Old Norse for "lover." Name of the Norse goddess who fed the golden apples of immortality to the gods.

IERNE — Latin. "Ireland."

IGNACIA — A variation of Ignatia.

IGNATIA — Latin. "Fiery or ardent." A feminine form of Ignatius.

ILA — Old English. "From the island." Also from the Old English meaning "battle."

ILANA — Hebrew. "Tree."

ILANIT — A variation of Ilana.

ILEANA — Greek. "From the city of Ilion" or Troy. Also a variation of Helen.

ILIA — Latin. In Roman mythology, the mother of Romulus and Remus, the founders of Rome.

ILKA — A contraction of Milka.

ILONA — Hungarian. "Beauty." Also a Slavic form of Helen.

ILONKA — A Slavic form of Helen.

IMOGEN — A variation of Imogene.

IMOGENE — Latin. "Image." Shakespeare's heroine in *Cymbeline*.

IMPERIA — Latin. "Imperial mistress."

INA — Latin. Name suffix to the feminine equivalents of masculine names.

INDRA — Hindu. God of power whose position was usurped by Vishnu and Siva.

INES — A Spanish form of Agnes.

INESITA — A nickname of Ines.

INESSA — A Russian form of Agnes.

INEZ — A Spanish form of Agnes.

INGA — A variation of Ingrid.

INGABERG — A variation of Ingrid.

INGER — A variation of Ingrid.

INGRID — Old Norse. "A hero's daughter." Ing was the hero god of Norse mythology.

INGUNNA — A variation of Ingrid.

INIGA — A Spanish form of Ignatia.

IOLA — Greek. "Violet-colored." Heracles captured the princess Iola according to mythology.

IOLANTHE — A variation of Iola.

IOLE — A variation of Iola.

IONA — A variation of Ione.

IONE — Greek. "Violet-colored stone."

IPHIGENIA — Greek. In mythology, Iphigenia was offered as a sacrifice by Agamemnon to placate the gods, but, in later versions of the legend, she was rescued by Artemis.

IRA — A Russian nickname for Irina.

IRENA — A variation of Irene.

IRENE — Greek. "Peace." Appropriately, Irene was the Greek goddess of peace.

IRETA — Latin. "The enraged one."

IRETTA — A variation of Ireta.

IRETTE — A variation of Irete.

IRINA — The Russian form of Irene.

IRIS — Greek. "The rainbow." Iris was the goddess of the rainbow and messenger of the gods in Greek mythology.

IRISA — The Russian form of Iris.

IRMA — Latin. "Noble woman."

IRMINA — A variation of Irma. Also a nickname for Hermione.

IRVETTE — Old English. "Friend from the sea."

ISA — Old German. "Strongwilled." Also a nickname for Isabel.

ISABEAU — The French form of Isabel.

ISABEL — The Spanish form of Elizabeth.

ISABELITA — A nickname for Isabel.

ISABELLA — An English and Italian variation of Elizabeth.

ISABELLE — An English and German variation of Isabel.

ISADORA — Egyptian. "Gift of Isis." Isadora was the goddess of the moon. The feminine of Isador.

ISADORE — A variation of Isadora.

ISEABAL — The Scottish form of Isabel.

ISHI — Japanese. "Stone."

ISIDORA — A variation of Isadora.

ISIS — Egyptian. "Supreme goddess." Egyptian moon goddess of maternity and fertility.

ISLEEN — A variation of Aislim.

ISOLDA — A variation of Isolde.

ISOLDE — Old Welsh. "Fair lady." A princess in the Arthurian legends.

ISSIE — A nickname for Isabel.

ISSY — A nickname for Isabel.

ISTA — American Indian. "Snow."

ITA — Gaelic. "Thirst." A woman who craves knowledge.

IVA — Old French. "Yew tree." Also a Russian form of Jane.

IVANE — A Russian form of Jane.

IVANNA — A Russian form of Jane.

IVRIA — Hebrew. From the Hebrew word used for the Jewish people in the Bible.

IVRIAH — A variation of Ivria.

IVY — Old English. "The ivy vine." The ivy vine was sacred in mythology.

IZA — A Polish nickname for Luisa.

IZABEL — A Portuguese form of Isabel.

JACINTA — A Spanish form of Hyacinth.

JACINTHA — A variation of Hyacinth.

JACKELYN — A variation of Jacqueline.

JACKIE — A nickname for Jacqueline.

JACKY — A nickname for Jacqueline.

JACOBA — Hebrew. "The supplanter."

JACOBINA — A variation of Jacoba.

JACOBINE — A variation of Jacoba.

JACQUELINE — Old French. "The supplanter."

JACQUELYN — A variation of Jacqueline.

JACQUETTE — A nickname for Jacqueline.

JADE — Spanish. "The jade gem."

JAEN — Hebrew. "Ostrich."

JAFFA — Hebrew. "Beautiful."

JAFIT — A variation of Jaffa.

JAKOBA — A variation of Jacoba.

JAMILA — Arabic. "Beautiful."

JAN — A variation of Jane.

JANA — A Slavic nickname for Janina.

JANE — Hebrew. "God is gracious." The feminine of John.

JANECZKA — A Polish form of Jane.

JANELLA — A variation of Jane.

JANET — A variation of Jane.

JANETTA — A variation of Jane.

JANETTE — A variation of Jane.

JANEY — A nickname for Jane.

JANIA — A Slavic form of Jane.

JANICE — A variation of Jane.

JANIE — A nickname of Jane.

JANINA — A Slavic form of Jane.

JANKA — A Polish form of Jane.

JANTHIUM — A form of Ianthe.

JANYTE — A Slavic form of Jane.

JAQUENETTA — A variation of Jacqueline.

JAQUENETTE — A variation of Jacqueline.

JARDENA — Hebrew. "Descender." Feminine of Jordan.

JARITA — Hindu. A legendary bird who was given a human soul because she risked her life to save her offspring.

JARVIA — Old German. "Spearkeen." Swift-minded.

JASISA — A Polish form of Jane.

JASMINE — Persian. "The jasmine flower."

JAYNE — A variation of Jane.

JEAN — A French form of Jane.

JEANETTE — A French variation of Jean.

JEANEY — A nickname for Jane.

JEANI — A nickname for Jane.

JEANIE — A nickname for Jane.

JEANNE — A variation of Jane.

JEANNETTE — A variation of Jane.

JELENA — A Russian form of Helen.

JEMIE — A nickname for Jemima.

JEMIMA — Hebrew. "A dove." A symbol of peace.

JEMINA — Hebrew. "Right-handed."

JEMMIE — A nickname for Jemima.

JENICA — The Rumanian form of Jane.

JENNIE — A nickname for Jane and Jennifer.

JENNIFER — A form of Guinevere.

JENNY — A nickname for Jane and Jennifer.

JENSINE — The Danish variation of Jane.

JERI — A nickname for Geralda and Geraldine.

JERRI — A nickname for Geralda and Geraldine.

JERRY — A nickname for Geralda and Geraldine.

JERUSHA — Hebrew. "Married."

JESS — A nickname for Jessica.

JESSALYN — A variation of Jessica.

JESSAMINE — A variation of Jessica.

JESSICA — Hebrew. "Rich lady." A woman of wealth and position.

JESSIE — A nickname for Jessica.

JESSY — A nickname for Jessica.

JESUSA — Spanish. An abbreviated form of Maria de Jesus, honoring the Virgin Mary.

JEWEL — Latin. "Gem."

JILL — A nickname for Gillian and Julia.

JINX — Latin. "A charm."

JO — A nickname for Josephine.

JOAKIMA — Hebrew. "The Lord will judge."

JOAN — A variation of Jane. Joan of Arc is a famous French saint.

JOANA — A Portuguese form of Joan.

JOANKA — A Polish form of Joan.

JOANNA — A variation of Joan.

JOBINA — Hebrew. "The persecuted." The feminine of Job.

JOBIE — A nickname for Jobina.

JOBY — A nickname for Jobina.

JOBYNA — A variation of Jobina.

JOCELIN — Latin. "Merry." Also from the Old English for "just."

JOCELINE — A variation of Jocelin.

JOCELYN — A variation of Jocelin.

JOCOSA — Latin. "Gleeful." A child with a cheerful nature.

JODY — A variation of Judith.

JOELA — Hebrew. "The Lord is willing."

JOELLA — A variation of Joela.

JOELLE — A variation of Joela.

JOELLEN — A contemporary combination of Jo and Ellen.

JOETTE — A nickname for Josephine.

JOHANNA — The German form of Jane.

JOICE — A variation of Joy.

JOLA — The nickname for Jolan.

JOLAN — The Hungarian form of Yolande.

JOLANKA — A nickname for Jolan.

JOLANTA — A Slavic variation of Yolande.

JOLETTE — A variation of Julia.

JOLINE — A variation of Josephine.

JONATI — A variation of Jonina.

JONINA — Hebrew. "Dove." A symbol of tranquility.

JONIT — A variation of Jonina.

JORA — Hebrew. "Autumn rain."

JORDANA — A variation of Jardena.

JOSCELIN — A variation of Jocelin.

JOSCELYN — A variation of Jocelin.

JOSEFA — A Spanish form of Josephine.

JOSEFINA — A Spanish form of Josephine.

JOSEPHA — A variation of Josephine.

JOSEPHINE — Hebrew. "He shall add." Feminine of Joseph.

JOVITA — Latin. "Joyful."

JOY — A variation of Jovita.

JOYCE — A popular variation of Joy.

JOYITA — A nickname for Joyuela.

JOYOUS — A variation of Joy.

JOYUELA — Spanish. "A small jewel."

JUANA — A nickname for Juanita.

JUANITA — A Spanish form of Jane.

JUDITH — Hebrew. "Praised."

JUDITHA — A variation of Judith.

JUDY — A nickname for Judith.

JULIA — Latin. "Youthful." The feminine form of Julius.

JULIANA — A variation of Julia.

JULIANE — A variation of Julia.

JULI — A nickname for Julia.

JULIE — A nickname for Julia.

JULIENNE — A French form of Julia.

JULIET — A French form of Julia. The romantic heroine of the tragedy *Romeo and Juliet* has popularized this name.

JULIETA — A Spanish form of Julia.

JULIETTA — A variation of Julia.

JULIETTE — A variation of Julia.

JULITA — A nickname for Julietta.

JUNE — Latin. "Youthful." From the name of the Roman family Janius, from which comes the name of the month June.

JUNELLA — A contemporary combination of June and Ella.

JUNO — Latin. In Roman mythology, Juno was the wife of Jupiter, queen of the heavens and protectress of women.

JUSTINA — A variation of Justine.

JUSTINE — Latin. "Just." The feminine of Justin.

KAKALINA — A Hawaiian form of Katherine.

KALANIT — Hebrew. A flower common in Israel.

KALI — Hindu. "Energy." Another name for Sakti, the goddess who embodies both virtue and devastation.

KALIKA — Greek. "Rosebud."

KALILA — Arabic. "Loved one." A general term of endearment.

KALINDA — Hindu. "The Sun."

KALINDI — A variation of Kalinda.

KALLI — A nickname for Calandra or Kalika.

KALLIE — A nickname for Calandra or Kalika.

KAMARIA — African. "Moonlike." Appropriate name for a Cancer child.

KAMEKO — Japanese. "Child of the tortoise." The tortoise was a symbol of longevity.

KAMILLA — A Slavic form of Camilia.

KARA — A variation of Cara.

KAREN — The Danish form of Katherine.

KARENA — A Norwegian form of Katherine.

KARI — A variation of Carol.

KARIDA — Arabic. "Virginal." An appropriate name for a Virgo child.

KARIN — A Norwegian form of Karen.

KARKA — Hindu. "Crab." Appropriate for a child born under the sign of Cancer.

KARLA — A German form of Caroline.

KARLOTTE — The German form of Charlotte.

KARMA — Hindu. "Action." Each individual's state of being, which is determined by his actions in this and past lives.

KARMEL — A variation of Carmel.

KAROLINA — A variation of Caroline.

KAROLY — A Hungarian form of Carol.

KASMIRA — Slavic. "One who brings peace."

KASSIA — A Polish form of Katherine.

KATA — A Slavic form of Katherine.

KATALIN — A Hungarian form of Katherine.

KATE — A nickname for Katherine.

KATERINA — A Slavic form of Katherine.

KATHA — A German form of Katherine.

KATHERINE — Greek. "Pure." A name found in almost all Western languages.

KATHIE — A nickname for Katherine.

KATHLEEN — A variation of Katherine.

KATHY — A nickname for Katherine.

KATINA — A Greek form of Katherine.

KATINKA — A Slavic form of Katherine.

KATUSCHA — A Russian form of Katherine.

KATYA — A Russian form of Katherine.

KAY — A nickname for Katherine.

KAYE — A variation of Kay.

KAZU — Japanese. "First." Possibly the first-born child.

KAZUKO — A variation of Kazu.

KEELY — Gaelic. "Beautiful one."

KEI — Japan. "Adoration." A child to worship.

KEIKO — A variation of Kei.

KELDA — Old Norse. "A spring." A child refreshing as a clear mountain stream.

KEMA — Hebrew. "Eastward."

KENDRA — Old English. "The knowledgeable."

KENNIS — Gaelic. "Beautiful." Feminine form of Kenneth.

KESHET — Hebrew. "Rainbow."

KETTI — A nickname for Katherine.

KIKILIA — The Hawaiian form of Cecilia.

KIKU — Japanese. "Chrysanthemum." In the West, the flower of November.

KIKUKO — A variation of Kiku.

KINETA — Greek. "Energetic."

KIRSTEN — A Scandinavian form of Christine.

KIRSTIE — A Scottish nickname for Christine.

KIRSTINA — A Scandinavian form of Christine.

KISMET — Turkish. "Fate."

KIT — A nickname for Katherine.

KITTIE — A nickname for Katherine.

KLARA — The German form of Clara.

KLARIKA — A Slavic form of Clarissa.

KLARRISA — A Russian form of Clarissa.

KLEMENTINE — A German form of Clementine.

KOKO — Japanese. "Stork." In ancient Japan, the symbol of longevity.

KONA — Hindu. Another name for Saturn, who is the black god in mythology.

KONSTANZE — The German form of Constance.

KORA — Greek. "Maiden."

KORDULA — The German form of Cordelia.

KOREN — A variation of Kora.

KORIE — A variation of Kora.

KOSTYA — The Russian nickname for Constance.

KOSTYUSHA — The Russian nickname of Constance.

KRISTEL — A German form of Christine.

KRISTEN — A Scandinavian form of Christine.

KRISTIN — A Scandinavian form of Christine.

KRYSTA — A Polish form of Christine.

KRYSTYNA — A Polish form of Christine.

KUMA — African. "Younger."

KUMUDA — Hindu. "Lotus." Honored in Eastern religions as the resting place of the gods.

KYNA — Gaelic. "Wise." The feminine of Conan.

KYNAH — A variation of Kyna.

KYNTHIA — The Greek form of Cynthia.

KYOKO — Japanese. "Mirror."

LALA — Slavic. "Tulip." The harbinger of spring.

LALAGE — Greek. "Free-speaking."

LALITA — Hindu. "Winsome." One of the names for the goddess Sakti.

LANA — A nickname for Alanna. Also a variation of Helen.

LANETTE — A nickname for Alanna.

LANNA — A nickname for Alanna.

LARA — Latin. "Famous." Daughter of Almo, the river god, who was punished for her garrulity. Name was popularized in the last decade by film of Boris Pasternak's novel, *Doctor Zhivago*.

LARAINE — Latin. "Seagull." One who has a life of freedom and graceful flight. Also a variation of Lorraine.

LARENTA — Latin. The foster mother of Romulus and Remus.

LARINA — A variation of Laraine.

LARINE — A variation of Laraine.

LARISSA — Greek. "Cheerful."

LARK — Middle English. The name of a bird known for its song.

LASCA — Latin. "Weary."

LASSIE — Middle English. "Little girl."

LATONIA — Latin. In Roman mythology, Latona was the mother of the sun god Apollo and the moon goddess Diana.

LAURA — Latin. "Laurel." The symbol of victory. The feminine of Lawrence.

LAURÉ — The French form of Laura.

LAUREEN — A variation of Laura.

LAUREL — From the same root as Laura.

LAUREN — A variation of Laura.

LAURENA — A variation of Laura.

LAURETTA — A variation of Laura.

LAURETTE — A variation of Laura.

LAURICE — A variation of Laura.

LAVEDA — Latin. "The innocent one." A girl of virtue.

LAVERNA — Latin. "Spring." The Roman goddess of gain.

LAVERNE — A variation of Laverna.

LAVINA — A variation of Lavinia.

LAVINIA — From the same root as Laveda. The name of Aeneas's wife.

LAVINIE — The French form of Lavinia.

LEA — A variation of Leah.

LEAH — Hebrew. "Weary." In the Bible, the wife of Jacob.

LEALA — Old French. "Loyal."

LEALIE — A variation of Leala.

LEANA — A variation of Liana.

LEANOR — The Spanish form of Eleanore.

LEATRICE — Contemporary compound of Leah and Beatrice.

LEDA — A nickname for Letita. Name made famous by Yeats' poem "Leda and the Swan."

LEDAH — Hebrew. "Birth." A reawakening of hope.

LEE — A variation of Leah.

LEENA — An Estonian form of Hélène.

LEETICE — The French form of Letitia.

LEILA — Persian. "Dark-haired."

LELA — A variation of Leila. A Spanish nickname for Alita.

LELAH — A variation of Leila.

LELIA — A variation of Leila.

LEMUELA — Hebrew. "Dedicated to God." The feminine form of Lemuel.

LENA — Latin. "Alluring." A temptress. Also a nickname for names ending in "lena," "lina," and "line."

LENETA — A variation of Lenis.

LENIS — Latin. "Gentle."

LENITA — A variation of Lenis.

LENKA — A Slavic form of Helen.

LENORA — A Russian form of Eleonora.

LENORE — A variation of Eleanore and Helen.

LEODA — Old German. "Woman of the people." A female patriot.

LEOINE — A variation of Leola.

LEOLA — Latin. "Lionlike." The feminine of Leo.

LEOMA — Old English. "Shining."

LEONA — The French form of Leola.

LEONARDA — Old French. "Brave as a lion."

LEONARDE — An Italian form of Leonarda.

LEONELLE — A variation of Leola.

LEONIE — A French form of Leola.

LEONORA — A variation of Eleanore.

LEONORE — A variation of Eleanore.

LEOPOLDA — Old German. "Fearless." Feminine form of Leopold.

LEOPOLDINE — A variation of Leopolda.

LEORA — A nickname for Eleanore.

LEOTA — A variation of Leoda.

LEOTIE — American Indian. "Prairie flower."

LEOTINE — From the same root as Leola.

LEOTYNE — A variation of Leotine.

LESYA — A Russian nickname for Alexandra.

LETA — A nickname for Letha and Letitia.

LETHA — Greek. "Oblivion." A mythological river whose waters caused forgetfulness.

LETICIA — A Spanish form of Letitia.

LETITIA — Latin. "Gladness."

LETIZIA — The Italian form of Letitia.

LETTIE — A nickname for Letitia or Leatrice.

LETTY — A nickname for Letitia or Leatrice.

LEVANA — Latin. "The rising sun." Levana was the Roman goddess of childbirth. Appropriate for a child born under the sign of Leo.

LEVINA — Latin. "Flash." A woman with a quick, winning smile.

LEWANNA — Hebrew. "The moon." One who beams with inner radiance. A name for a Cancer child.

LEXA — A Czechoslovakian nickname for Alexandra.

LEXIE — A nickname for Alexandra.

LEYA — Spanish. "Loyalty to the law."

LIA — An Italian form of Leah.

LIAN — Chinese. "The flowing willow."

LIANA — French. "Binding."

LIANE — A variation of Liana.
LIBBY — A nickname for Elizabeth.
LIEN — Chinese. "Lotus." The flower symbolizes past, present, and future.
LIESA — A German nickname for Elizabeth.
LIL — A nickname for Lilith or Lillian.
LILA — A variation of Leila and a nickname for Lillian.
LILAC — Persian. "Bluish-purplish flower." A beautifully-scented spring flower.
LILAS — The Scottish form of Lillian.
LILI — A German form of Lillian. Also a nickname for Lillian.
LILIA — A variation of Lillian.
LILIANA — A variation of Lillian.
LILIANE — A variation of Lillian.
LILITH — Arabic. "Of the night." According to Eastern mythology, Lilith was the first wife of Adam who challenged his authority and was replaced by God with Eve.
LILLIAN — Latin. "The lily flower." In ancient Egypt, the lily was revered as the symbol of resurrection and is the flower of Easter, the Christian feast celebrating Jesus Christ's return from the grave. The lily also represents purity.
LILLIE — A nickname for Lillian or Lilith.
LILLIS — A variation of Lillian or Lilith.
LILLY — A nickname for Lillian or Lilith.
LILY — A variation and nickname for Lillian or Lilith.
LILYBELL — Latin. "Fair lily."
LINA — A nickname for names ending in "lene," "lina," and "line." Also used as an independent name.
LINDA — Spanish. "Pretty one." A popular name for little beauties.
LINDY — A variation of Linda.

LINET — A variation of Linette.
LINETTE — Celtic. "Graceful."
LINNEA — Old Norse. "Lime tree."
LINNETTE — A variation of Linette.
LIS — The French form of Lillian.
LISA — A nickname for Elizabeth. Also used as an independent name.
LISABET — A variation of Elizabeth.
LISABETTA — A variation of Elizabeth.
LISABETTE — A variation of Elizabeth.
LISETA — A Spanish form of Elizabeth.
LISETTE — A French form of Louise and of Elizabeth.
LISSA — A nickname for Melissa and Millicent.
LITA — A nickname for names ending in "lita."
LIUKA — A Greek form of Lillian.
LIUSADH — A Scottish variation of Louise.
LIVANA — A variation of Levana.
LIVIA — A nickname for Olivia.
LIVIE — A nickname for Olivia.
LIZA — A nickname for Elizabeth. Also used as an independent name.
LIZABETH — A variation of Elizabeth.
LIZZIE — A nickname for Elizabeth.
LODEMA — Old English. "Guide."
LOIS — A variation of Louise.
LOLA — A nickname for Dolores.
LOLETA — A nickname for Dolores.
LOLITA — A nickname for Dolores.
LONA — Middle English. "Solitary."
LORA — A variation of Laura and Eleanore.
LORAINE — A variation of Lorraine.
LORELEI — German. "Lurer to the rock." In folklore, a siren of the

Rhine whose singing charmed sailors to their doom.

LORENA — A variation of Laura.

LORENE — A variation of Laura.

LORENZA — The Italian and Spanish form of Laura.

LORETTA — A variation of Laura.

LORETTE — A nickname for Laura.

LORI — A nickname for Laura.

LORINDA — A variation of Laura.

LORITA — A nickname for Laura.

LORNA — A variation of Laura.

LORRAINE — German. "Famous in battle."

LOTTA — A nickname for Charlotte.

LOTTIE — A nickname for Charlotte.

LOTTY — A nickname for Charlotte.

LOTUS — Greek. "The lotus flower." In ancient Egypt, the lily of the Nile.

LOU — A nickname for Laura.

LOUELLA — A contemporary combination of Lou and Ella. Also a variation of Luella.

LOUISA — A variation of Louise.

LOUISE — Old German. "Famous in battle."

LOVE — Old English. "Cherished affection."

LOYCE — A variation of Louise.

LUANA — German and Hebrew. "Graceful warrior." A woman who maintains her elegance even in battle.

LUCIA — Latin. "Light." A lady who brings a glow to even the darkest lives.

LUCIANA — An Italian form of Lucia.

LUCIE — A French and German. form of Lucia. Also a nickname for Louise or Lucia.

LUCIENNE — A French form of Lucia.

LUCILLA — A variation of Lucia.

LUCILLE — A French form of Lucia.

LUCINA — A variation of Lucia.

LUCINDA — A variation of Lucia.

LUCITA — A Spanish form of Lucia.

LUCRÈCE — A French form of Lucretia.

LUCRETIA — Latin. "Bringer of light." Also from the Latin word for "reward."

LUCY — A nickname for Lucia and Louise.

LUDMILLA — Old Slavic. "Beloved by the people." Revered by all who know her.

LUDOVIKA — A German form of Ludmilla.

LUELLA — Old English. "Elf." Also from the Latin "atonement," or a contemporary compound of Lou and Ella.

LUISA — An Italian and Spanish form of Louise.

LUISE — A German form of Louise.

LULITA — A nickname for Louise.

LULU — A nickname for Louise.

LUNA — Latin. "Shining." The Roman goddess of the moon. The moon governs Cancer children.

LUNETTA — An Italian form of Luna.

LUPE — A Spanish nickname for Guadalupe.

LURLING — A variation of Lorelei.

LUSA — A Finnish nickname for Elizabeth.

LUVENA — Old English and Latin. "Little beloved one."

LUZ — A Spanish form of Lucia.

LYDIA — Greek. "A woman from Lydia." A part of Asia Minor known for its culture.

LYDIE — A variation of Lydia.

LYNDA — A variation of Linda.

LYNETTE — A variation of Linette.

LYRA — Latin. A constellation name.

LYRIS — Greek. "Player of the lyre." The music of the gods.

LYSANDRA — Greek. "Emancipation." Lysander was a Greek hero believed to raise men's souls to the height of beauty.

MAB — Gaelic. "Joy." In mythology, Mab was the queen of the fairies, the subject Shelley's famous long poem *Queen Mab*.

MABEL — Latin. "Lovable."

MABELLE — A French form of Mabel.

MADA — A nickname for Madeline.

MADALENA — A Spanish form of Madeline.

MADALYN — A variation of Madeline.

MADDALENA — The Italian form of Madeline.

MADDIE — A nickname for Madeline.

MADELAINE — A French form of Madeline.

MADELEINE — A variation of Madeline.

MADELENA — A variation of Madeline.

MADELINA — A variation of Madeline.

MADELINE — Greek. "Tower." A woman of strength.

MADELLE — A nickname for Madeline.

MADELON — A French form of Madeline.

MADGE — A nickname for Margaret.

MADLEN — A variation of Madeline.

MADLIN — A variation of Madeline.

MADORA — A variation of Media.

MADRE — Spanish, "Mother."

MADY — A German form of Madeline.

MAE — A variation of May.

MAG — A nickname for Magdalen or Magnolia.

MAGDA — A German nickname for Magdalen.

MAGDALA — A variation of Magdalen.

MAGDALEN — Greek. "Tower." Magdala was the birthplace of St. Mary Magdalen. From the same root as Madeline.

MAGDALENA — A Spanish form of Magdalen.

MAGDALENE — A German form of Magdalen.

MAGGIE — A nickname for Margaret.

MAGNILDA — Old German. "Strong battle-maiden." A child destined for leadership.

MAGNOLIA — Latin. "Magnolia plant." A delicately-scented blossom. Name taken from the 17th-century French botanist, Pierre Magnol.

MAHALA — A Hebrew. "Affection." A loving child.

MAHALIA — A variation of Mahala.

MAHOGANY — Name for a beauty of reddish-brown complexion.

MAIA — A variation of May. Name of the goddess of spring.

MAIBLE — The Irish form of Mabel.

MAIDA — Old English. "A maiden."

MAIDIE — A nickname for Maida.

MAIR — A Welsh form of Mary.

MAIRE — An Irish form of Mary.

MAIRGHREAD — The Irish form of Madeline.

MAISIE — A Scottish nickname for Margaret.

MAITILDE — The Irish form of Mathilda.

MAJESTA — Latin. "Magnificent." Majesta was another name for the goddess Maia.

MALA — A nickname for Madeline.

MALENA — A variation of Madeline and Magdalen.

MALIA — The Hawaiian form of Mary.

MALINA — A variation of Madeline, Magdalen, and Malinda.

MALINDA — Greek. "Gentle one." A pretty name.

MALVA — Greek. "Soft."

MAME — A nickname for Mary.

MAMIE — A nickname for Mary.

MANDA — A nickname for Amanda.

MANDY — A nickname for Amanda.

MANETTE — A variation of Manon.

MANON — A French form of Mary.

MANU — African. "Second." A birth-order name.

MANUELA — Spanish. "God is with us." Feminine of Emmanuel.

MANYA — A Russian form of Mary.

MARA — Hebrew. "Bitter."

MARALINE — A variation of Mara.

MARCELLA — Latin. "Warlike." A fierce opponent. The feminine of Mark.

MARCELLE — A French form of Marcella.

MARCELLINA — A variation of Marcella.

MARCELLINE — A variation of Marcella.

MARCIA — Latin. "Bellicose." From the same root as Marcella.

MARCY — A variation of Marcia.

MARELDA — Old German. "Well-known battle-maid."

MARGALO — A variation of Margaret.

MARGARET — Greek. "A pearl." A rare beauty of milk-white complexion.

MARGARETA — A variation of Margaret.

MARGARETE — A Danish form of Margaret.

MARGARETHA — A Dutch form of Margaret.

MARGARETHE — A German form of Margaret.

MARGARETTA — A variation of Margaret.

MARGARID — The Armenian form of Margaret.

MARGARITA — A Spanish form of Margaret.

MARGE — A nickname for Margaret.

MARGERY — A nickname for Margaret.

MARGIE — A nickname for Margaret.

MARGIT — A Slavic form of Margaret.

MARGOLO — A variation of Margaret.

MARGOT — A form of Margaret.

MARGUERITE — A French form of Margaret.

MARIA — The Spanish and Italian form of Mary.

MARIAM — A form of Mary.

MARIAN — Hebrew. "Graceful-bitter." A combination of Mary and Ann. Maid Marian was the love of the legendary Robin Hood.

MARIANNE — A form of Marian.

MARIBEL — Hebrew. "Beautiful but bitter."

MARICE — A form of Mary.

MARIE — The French form of Mary.

MARIEL — A German form of Mary.

MARIETTA — A nickname for Mary.

MARIGOLD — English. "The marigold flower." A golden-haired child.

MARIJA — A Slavic form of Mary.

MARILDA — A variation of Marelda.

MARILLA — A variation of Marelda.

MARILYN — A variation of Mary.

MARINA — Latin. "Maid of the sea."

MARION — A French form of Mary.

MARIQUILLA — A Spanish form of Mary.

MARIS — Latin. "Of the sea."

MARISKA — A Hungarian form of Mary.

MARITA — A Spanish form of Mary.

MARITSA — A Slavic form of Mary.

MARJA — A Finnish form of Mary.

MARJORIE — A Scottish form of Mary.

MARKETA — A Czechoslovakian form of Margaret.

MARLA — A German form of Mary.

MARLEEN — A variation of Madeline.

MARLENA — A variation of Madeline.

MARLENE — A German form of Madeline.

MARMARA — Greek. "Radiant." A lady with magnetic charm.

MARNIA — A variation of Marina.

MARQUITA — A Spanish form of Marcia.

MARSHA — A variation of Marcia.

MARTA — The Italian, Scandinavian, Slavic, and Spanish form of Martha.

MARTELLE — A nickname for Martha.

MARTHA — Aramaic. "Mistress." A biblical name.

MARTINA — Latin. "Warlike." Feminine of Martin.

MARTINE — A variation of Martina.

MARTITA — A Spanish nickname for Marta.

MARVEL — Old French. "A wondrous happening."

MARVELA — A variation of Marvel.

MARY — Hebrew. "Bitter." The mother of Jesus, who is revered as the Blessed Virgin. A very popular name throughout the world.

MARYA — A Polish form of Mary.

MARYANN — A contemporary combination of Mary and Ann.

MARYANNE — A variation of Maryann.

MARYJANE — A contemporary combination of Mary and Jane.

MARYLOU — A contemporary combination of Mary and Louise.

MARYSA — A French form of Mary.

MASHA — A Russian form of Mary.

MATELDA — The Italian form of Mathilda.

MATHEA — A variation of Mattea.

MATHIA — A variation of Mattea.

MATHILDA — Old German. "Powerful in battle." The name of William the Conqueror's queen.

MATHILDE — A variation of Mathilda.

MATILDA — A variation of Mathilda.

MATILDE — The Spanish form of Mathilda.

MATRIKA — Hindu. "Mother." Another of the many names of the goddess Sakti.

MATTEA — Hebrew. "Gift of God." A feminine form of Matthew.

MATTIE — A nickname for Mathilda.

MATTY — A nickname for Mathilda.

MAUD — A variation of Mathilda.

MAUDE — A variation of Mathilda.

MAURA — Latin. "Dark." Also an Irish form of Mary.

MAURE — A variation of Maura, also an Irish form of Mary.

MAURELLA — Latin and Old German. "Dark and elflike."

MAUREEN — Gaelic. "Little Mary." Or "dark-complected,"; from the same root as Maura.

MAURINE — A variation of Maureen.

MAURITA — A nickname for Maura.

MAURIZIA — The Italian form of Maureen.

MAUVE — Latin. "Violet-colored." Child with violet eyes.

MAVIS — French. "The song thrush." A woman with graceful movements and voice.

MAVRA — A Russian form of Maura.

MAXIE — A nickname for Maxine.

MAXINE — Latin. "Greatest."

MAY — Old English. "Kinswoman." Or from the Middle English for "maiden." Also a variation of Maia, the Roman goddess of growth; or a nickname for Mary.

MAYA — Hindu. "Divine creative force found in all things."

MAYBELLE — Middle English and French. "Beautiful maiden."

MAYE — A variation of May.

MAYME — A variation of Mame.

MAZAL — Hebrew. "Luck." A child blessed with good fortune.

MEARA — Gaelic. "Mirth." A lass with a bubbling personality.

MEAVE — A variation of Mab.

MEDEA — Ruling. "Greek." Also from the Latin for "middle child." Legendary sorceress who assisted Jason with winning the Golden Fleece.

MEDORA — A variation of Medea.

MEDIA — A variation of Medea.

MEG — A Scottish nickname for Margaret.

MEGAN — Greek. "The strong one." Also an Irish form of Margaret.

MEHETABEL — Hebrew. "Advantaged by God."

MEHITABEL — A variation of Mehetabel.

MEL — A nickname for Melanie.

MELA — A Polish nickname for Melanie.

MELANIA — A Polish form of Melanie.

MELANIE — Greek. "Dark" or "clad in dark clothes." Melanie was the Greek earth goddess who mourned during the winter for her daughter, Persephone, goddess of spring.

MELANTHA — Greek. "Dark flower."

MELANY — A variation of Melanie.

MELBA — A variation of Malva.

MELINA — Latin. "Canary yellow."

MELINDA — A variation of Malinda."

MELISANDE — A French form of Millicent.

MELISE — A variation of Melissa.

MELISENDA — A Spanish form of Millicent.

MELISSA —Greek. "A honey bee." A sweet child.

MELOSA — A Spanish form of Melissa.

MELVA — A variation of Malvina.

MELVINA — A variation of Malvina.

MENORAH — Hebrew. "Candelabrum." Lighting the menorah is a significant part of the services for Hanukkah, the Jewish celebration commemorating the Dedication of the Temple.

MENSAH — African. "Third." A birth-order name.

MERCEDES — A Spanish form of Marcy.

MERCIA — Old English. "From Merce." An antiquated name for a part of England. Also a variation of Mercy.

MERCY — French and Latin. "Compassionate." A Puritan virtue name.

MERDYCE — A variation of Mertice.

MERIS — A variation of Maris.

MERNA — A variation of Myrna.

MERRY — Middle English. "Joyful." A cheerful child.

MERTA — A variation of Myrtle.

MERTICE — Old English. "Well-known and pleasant." A woman whose graciousness is recognized.

MESHA — Hindu. "Ram." Appropriate for a child born under the astrological sign of the Ram, Aries.

MESSINA — Latin. "Middle child."

META — Latin. "Ambitious." Also a nickname for Almeta and Margaret.

METIS — Greek. "Ability." The first wife of Zeus in mythology.

METTABEL — A variation of Mehetabel.

MIA — A nickname for Marie and Michaela.

MICAELA — A variation of Michaela.

MICHAELA — Hebrew. "Who is like God." A feminine form of Michael.

MICHAELINA — A variation of Michaela.

MICHAELINE — A variation of Michaela.

MICHAELLA — The Italian form of Michaela.

MICHEL — A French form of Michaela.

MICHELLE — A French form of Michaela.

MIGNON — French. "Dainty darling." Heroine of Goethe's *Wilhelm Meister.*

MIGNONETTE — A nickname for Mignon.

MIGUELA — A Spanish form of Michaela.

MIKAELA — A variation of Michaela.

MILDRED — Old English. "Gentle counselor." One to whom her friends can always turn.

MILENA — A Slavic form of Melanie.

MILKA — A Slavic form of Emily.

MILLICENT — Old German. "Ambitious."

MILLIE — A nickname for Millicent.

MILLY — A nickname for Millicent.

MIMI — A nickname for Miriam.

MIMOSA — Latin. Tropical tree with small blossoms.

MINA — A variation of Minna. Also a nickname for Wilhelmina.

MINDY — A nickname for Minna.

MINERVA — Greek. "Wisdom." Or from the Latin for "reflective." The most significant goddess of Roman mythology.

MINETTA — A form of Minna.

MINETTE — A form of Minna.

MINNA — Old German. "Love." An embodiment of tender affection. Also a nickname for Hermina and Wilhelmina.

MINNIE — A variation of Minna.

MINNY — A variation of Minna.

MINTA — Greek. "Mint." Refreshing as a cool stream.

MINTHA — A variation of Minta.

MIQUELA — A Spanish form of Michaela.

MIRA — Latin. "A lady of wonder."

MIRABEL — A variation of Mirabelle.

MIRABELLA — A variation of Mirabelle.

MIRABELLE — Latin and French. "Of spectacular beauty."

MIRANDA — Latin. "To be admired." Shakespeare's heroine in *The Tempest.*

MIRELLE — A variation of Mira.

MIRIAM — A variation of Mary.

MIRILLA — A variation of Mira.

MIRNA — A variation of Mira.

MITZI — A nickname for Miriam.

MODESTA — The Italian form of Modesty.

MODESTIA — The Spanish form of Modesty.

MODESTY — Latin. "Humility." Popularized by the Puritans of the 17th century.

MOINA — Gaelic. "Gentle."

MOIRA — An Irish form of Mary.

MOIRE — An Irish form of Mary.

MOLLIE — A nickname for Mary.

MOLLY — A nickname for Mary.

MONA — Gaelic. "Noble." Also from the Greek for "solitary." The Mona Lisa is the most famous of Leonardo da Vinci's paintings.

MONCA — The Irish form of Monica.

MONICA — Latin. "Adviser." A 14th-century saint who was the mother of St. Augustine.

MORAG — Gaelic. "Great."

MOREEN — A variation of Maureen.

MORENA — A Spanish variation of Maureen.

MORGANA — Old Welsh. "Of the sea."

MORIA — A variation of Maureen.

MORNA — A variation of Myrna.

MORWENNA — Old Welsh. "Sea wave."

MOSELLE — Hebrew. "Taken from the water." Astrologically appropriate for a child born under the water signs Pisces, Cancer, or Scorpio.

MOYNA — A variation of Myrna.

MOZELLE — A variation of Moselle.

MUIRE — A Scottish form of Mary.

MURIEL — Arabic. "Myrrh." An aromatic gum that was considered extremely valuable and presented as one of the gifts of the Wise Men to the baby Jesus.

MUSETTA — Old French. "A song."

MUSIDORA — Greek. "Gift of the Muses." The Muses were the goddesses who ruled the arts and sciences.

MYFANWY — Welsh. "Rare one."

MYRILLA — A variation of Mira.

MYRTA — A variation of Myrtle.

MYRTICE — A variation of Myrtle.

MYRTLE — Greek. "The myrtle." A type of evergreen that symbolized victory in ancient Greece.

NADA — Slavic. "Hope."

NADIA — A Slavic form of Nada.

NADINE — A French form of Nada.

NADYA — A Slavic form of Nada.

NAN — A nickname for Ann, Hannah, or Nancy.

NANA — A nickname for Ann, Hannah, or Nancy.

NANCY — A popular variation of Ann or Hannah.

NANELIA — A variation of Nan.

NANELLA — A variation of Nan.

NANNA — A variation of Nan.

NANNETTA — A variation of Nan.

NANNETTE — A variation of Nan.

NANNIE — A variation of Nan.

NANNY — A variation of Nan.

NAOMA — A variation of Naomi.

NAOMI — Hebrew. "Pleasant." An Old Testament name popularized by the Puritans.

NANON — A variation of Ann.

NAPEA — Latin. "Of the valleys."

NARA — Old English. "Near."

NARCISSA — Greek. "Beauty."

NARDA — Latin. "Fragrantly anointed." She brings a scent of loveliness.

NAT — A nickname for Natalie.

NATA — Hundu. "Rope dancer." A woman who moves with the grace of a ballerina.

NATALA — A variation of Natalie.

NATALIA — The Spanish and Italian form of Natalie.

NATALIE — Latin. "Christmas child." A name often given to a child born at Christmastide.

NATALINE — A variation of Natalie.

NATASCHA — A Russian form of Natalie.

NATASHA — A Russian form of Natalie.

NATHALIA — A variation of Natalie.

NATHANIA — Hebrew. "Given by God." The feminine of Nathan.

NATHENE — A variation of Nathania.

NATICA — A Russian nickname for Natscha.

NATIVIDAD — Spanish. "Christmas." Another name for a Christmas child.

NATTIE — A nickname for Natalie.

NATTY — A nickname for Natalie.

NEALA — Gaelic. "Chieftain." A feminine form of Neal.

NEBULA — Latin. "Cloud."

NEDA — Slavic. "Born on Saturday." From the nursery rhyme: ". . . the child that is born on the Sabbath Day is blithe, and bonny and good and gay."

NEDDA — A variation of Neda.

NEELY — A variation of Neala.

NELDA — Old English. "At the elder tree." Also a variation of Nell.

NELIA — A nickname for Cordelia.

NELINA — A variation of Nell.

NELITA — A variation of Nell.

NELL — A nickname for Cornelia, Eleanore, or Helen.

NELLA — A variation of Nell.

NELLIANA — A variation of Nell.

NELLIE — A variation of Nell.

NELLIS — A variation of Nell.

NELLY — A variation of Nell.

NELMA — A variation of Nell.

NENEMOOSHA — American Indian. "Sweetheart."

NEOLA — Greek. "Youthful." An ageless woman.

NEOMA — Greek. "New moon." Name given to a child born at the time of a new moon.

NERICE — A variation of Nerine.

NERINE — Greek. "A nereid, one from the sea." The sailors in mythology were assisted by the Nereids, the daughters of the sea god.

NERISSA — A variation of Nerine.

NESSA — A nickname for Agnes.

NETIS — American Indian. "Trusted friend."

NETTA — A nickname for various names ending in "net," "nette," or "netta."

NETTIE — A variation of Netta.

NETTY — A variation of Netta.

NEVA — Spanish. "Snowy."

NEVADA — Spanish. "White as snow."

NEYSA — A Slavic nickname for Agnes.

NICK — A nickname for Nicole.

NICKI — A nickname for Nicole.

NICKIE — A nickname for Nicole.

NICKY — A nickname for Nicole.

NIKKI — A nickname for Nicole.

NICOLA — A variation of Nicole.

NICOLE — Greek. "Victory of the people." A feminine form of Nicholas.

NICOLETTE — A variation of Nicole.

NICOLINA — A variation of Nicole.

NICOLINE — A variation of Nicole.

NIÑA — Spanish. "Girl."

NINETTA — A variation of Nina.

NINETTE — A variation of Nina.

NINITA — A nickname for Nina.

NINON — A variation of Ann.

NITA — A nickname for names ending in "nita."

NIXIE — Old German. "A water spirit."

NOAMI — A variation of Naomi.

NOEL — French. "Christmas."

NOELLA — A variation of Noel.

NOKOMIS — American Indian. "Grandmother."

NOLA — Latin. "A small bell." Also Gaelic for "noble."

NOLANA — A variation of Nola.

NOLETA — Latin. "Unwilling."

NOLITA — A variation of Noleta.

NONA — Latin. "The ninth." A birth-order name.

NONIE — A nickname for Nona.

NORA — A nickname for Eleanore or Honoria.

NORAH — A variation of Nora.

NORBERTA — Old German. "Outstanding heroine."

NORDICA — German. "From the North."

NORINA — A nickname for Honoria.

NORINE — A nickname for Honoria.

NORMA — Latin. "Rule."

NORNA — Old Norse. A viking goddess of fate.

NOVA — Latin. "Young."

NOVELLA — A form of Natalie.

NOVIA — A variation of Nova.

NUALA — Gaelic. "Fair-shouldered."

NUMIDIA — Latin. "A wanderer." A woman who seeks adventure.

NUNCIATA — A variation of Annunciata.

NYDIA — Latin. "Refuge."

NYSSA — Greek. "Beginning."

NYX — Greek. "Night."

OBELIA — Greek. "A pillar." Strength is the core of her being.

OCTAVIA — Latin. "Eighth child." The feminine of Octavius.

OCTAVIE — A French form of Octavia.

ODELET — A variation of Odelette.

ODELETTE — French. "Little song."

ODELIA — Old Anglo-French. "Wealthy." Rich in spirit.

ODELINDA — A variation of Odelia.

ODELLA — A variation of Odelia.

ODESSA — Greek. "A long journey." Taken from the name of the epic poem relating the travels of Odysseus.

ODILE — A variation of Odelia.

OFELIA — The Spanish form of Ophelia.

OFILIA — A variation of Ophelia.

OLA — Old Norse. "Relic." A woman with the mark of her ancestors.

OLATHE — American Indian. "Beautiful."

OLENKA — A Slavic form of Olga.

OLETHEA — A variation of Alethea.

OLGA — Old Norse. "Holy." St. Olga was a Russian saint in the 10th century.

OLIA — A Slavic form of Olga.

OLIMPIA — The Italian form of Olympia.

OLINDA — Latin. "Beautifully scented."

OLIVE — Latin. "The olive." The olive branch serves as a symbol of peace. A feminine form of Oliver.

OLIVETTE — A variation of Olive.

OLIVIA — A variation of Olive.

OLYMPIA — Greek. "Heavenly." Olympus was the mythological home of the gods.

OLYMPIC — A German form of Olympia.

OMA — Arabic. "Commander."

ONA — Latin. "Unity."

ONAWA — American Indian. "Wide-awake one." An alert child.

ONELLI — A Hungarian variation of Helen.

ONIDA — American Indian. "The expected one."

OONA — The Irish variation of Ona.

OONAGH — An Irish form of Ona.

OPAL — Hindu. "Precious stone." The opal was believed to have magical powers.

OPALINA — A variation of Opal.

OPALINE — A variation of Opal.

OPHELIA — Greek. "Serpent." In ancient times, the serpent signified immortality. A famous dramatic character in *Hamlet*.

OPHÉLIE — A French form of Ophelia.

ORA — Latin. "Seacoast," "gold," or "pray."

ORABEL — A variation of Ora.

ORABELLE — A variation of Ora.

ORAH — Hebrew. "Light." Also a variation of Ora.

ORALIA — A variation of Aurelia.

ORALIE — A variation of Aurelia.

ORDELLA — Old German. "Elf-like spear."

OREA — Greek. "From the mountain." A girl with simple beauty.

ORELA — Latin. "An announcer from heaven."

ORLANDA — The Italian form of Rolanda.

ORLANTHA — Old German. "From the land."

ORLENE — A variation of Ordelia.

ORNA — Gaelic. "Olive-colored." Also Hebrew for "cedar tree."

ORPAH — Hebrew. "A fawn."

ORSA — A nickname for Ursula.

ORTENSIA — The Italian form of Hortense.

ORTRUD — Old German. "Maid of the serpent." In most ancient cultures, the serpent represented wisdom.

ORTRUDE — A variation of Ortrud.

ORVA — Old English. "Brave friend." Or from the Old French for "of the value of gold." The feminine of Orin.

OTTAVIA — The Italian form of Octavia.

OTTILIA — Old German. "Girl of the fatherland."

OTTILIE — A variation of Ottilia.

OZORA — Hebrew. "Strength of God."

PALLAS — Greek. "Wisdom." Another name for the goddess Athena.

PALMA — Latin. "A palm." A palm was the symbol of triumph at the time of Christ.

PALOMA — Spanish. "Dove." A symbol of peace in many cultures.

PALOMETA — A variation of Paloma.

PAM — A nickname for Pamela.

PAMELA — Greek. "All honey." The name is traced to Sir Philip Sidney's *Arcadia* (1590).

PAMELINA — A variation of Pamela.

PANDORA — Greek. "All-gifted." In mythology, Pandora was believed to be the first woman, who brought with her to earth a box containing all the evils of the gods. When she opened the box, they all escaped, leaving only hope.

PANPHILA — Greek. "All-loving." Lover of mankind.

PANSY — Old French. "A thought." The little flower with a pretty face.

PANTHEA — Greek. "Of all the gods." The Pantheon was a temple built to honor the deities of ancient Rome.

PAOLA — The Italian form of Paula.

PAOLINA — A variation of Paula.

PARNELLA — Old French. "Little rock." A feminine form of Parnell.

PARTHENIA — Greek. "Maiden."

PAT — A nickname for Patricia.

PATIENCE — French. "Enduring." A 17th-century virtue name.

PATRICE — A French form of Patricia.

PATRICIA — Latin. "Well-born." The feminine of Patrick.

PATRIZIA — The Italian form of Patricia.

PATSY — A nickname for Patricia.

PATTY — A nickname for Patricia.

PAULA — Latin. "Small." The feminine of Paul.

PAULE — A French form of Paula.

PAULETTE — A French form of Paula.

PAULINA — A Spanish form of Paula.

PAULINE — A French form of Paula.

PAULITA — A nickname for Paula.

PAVLA — A Slavic form of Paula.
PAZ — Hebrew. "Golden."
PAZA — A variation of Paz.
PAZIA — A variation of Paz.
PAZICE — A variation of Paz.
PAZIT — A variation of Paz.
PEACE — Latin. "Tranquility." A Puritan virtue name.
PEARL — Latin. "Pear." A name derived from its shape.
PEARLA — A variation of Pearl.
PEARLE — A variation of Pearl.
PEARLINE — A variation of Pearl.
PEG — A nickname for Margaret.
PEGGY — A nickname for Margaret.
PELAGIA — Greek. "From the sea."
PEN — A nickname for Penelope.
PENELOPA — A Slavic form of Penelope.
PENELOPE — Greek. "The weaver." The name of Odysseus' wife, who during his absence deflected all rivals for her affections by promising them an answer when she finished a piece of weaving, which she unraveled at the end of each day.
PENINA — Hebrew. "Coral" or "Pearl."
PENINIT — A variation of Penina.
PENNY — A nickname for Penelope and Penina.
PENTHEA — Greek. "Fifth" or "mourner." Can be considered a birth-order name.
PEONY — Latin. "From the god of healing." A flower believed in ancient times to have medicinal powers; named for Paeon, the Greek god of healing.
PEPITA — A Spanish nickname for Josephine.
PERDITA — Latin. "The lost." The name of the king's daughter in Shakespeare's The Winter's Tale.
PERFECTA — Spanish. "Perfect."
PERLA — A Slavic form of Pearl.
PERNELLA — A variation of Parnella.

PERPETUA — Latin. "Eternal."
PERRINE — A French form of Petra.
PERSEPHONE — Greek. The goddess of the underworld.
PERSIS — Greek. "Woman from Persia."
PETRA — Latin. "Rock." The feminine of Peter.
PETRINA — A variation of Petra.
PETRONELLA — A variation of Petra.
PETRONIA — A variation of Petra.
PETRONILLE — A German form of Petra.
PETULA — Latin. "Seeker." A woman who searches for knowledge.
PETUNIA — American Indian. "Plant with the reddish-purple flowers."
PHAEDRA — A variation of Phedra.
PHEBE — A variation of Phoebe.
PHEDRA — Greek. "Bright." The daughter of Minos and wife of Theseus who is the heroine of Racine's Phèdre (1677).
PHIL — A nickname for names beginning with "Phil."
PHILANA — Greek. "Lover of humanity."
PHILANTHIA — Greek. "Flower lover."
PHILBERTA — Old English. "Extraordinarily bright."
PHILENE — A variation of Philana.
PHILINA — A variation of Philana.
PHILIPPA — Greek. "Lover of horses." The horse was the ancient symbol of divinity.
PHILLIDA — Greek. "The loving."
PHILLINA — A variation of Phillida.
PHILLIPPINE — A German form of Philippa.
PHILLIS — A variation of Phyllis.
PHILOMEL — A variation of Philomela.

PHILOMELA — Greek. "Lover of the moon." A mythological maiden who was transformed into a nightingale.

PHILOMENA — A variation of Philana or Philomela.

PHOEBE — Greek. "The shining."

PHOENIX — Greek. "Reincarnated." A legendary bird in ancient Egypt that after living 500 years was consumed by fire and rose anew from the ashes.

PHYLLIS — Greek. "A green bough." A mythological maiden who was changed into a fruitless almond tree upon the disappearance of her lover. The tree is said to have blossomed upon his return.

PIERRETTE — A French form of Petra.

PILAR — Spanish. "Pillar." A name referring to the Virgin Mary.

PILISI — A Hawaiian form of Phyllis.

PIPER — Old English. "A pipe player."

PIPPA — An Italian nickname for Phillippa.

PIXIE — Of unknown origin. "A cheerful mischievous sprite."

PLÁCIDA — Latin. "Serene, peaceful."

PLÁCIDIA — A variation of Plácida.

PLATONA — Greek. "Broadshouldered." The feminine of Plato.

PLECIA — A Polish nickname for Penelope.

POLLY — A nickname for Mary or Paula.

POLLYANNA — A combination of Polly and Anna.

POMONA — Latin. "Fruitful." The Roman goddess of the fruit.

PORTIA — Latin. "An offering." Also from the title of the Roman clan, the Porcii, whose ancestors were "pig farmers." Portia is the heroine of Shakespeare's *The Merchant of Venice*.

PRANE — A Slavic form of Frances.

PRIMA — Latin. "The first." A birth-order name.

PRIMALIA — A variation of Prima.

PRIMAVERA — Latin. "Spring."

PRIMROSE — Latin. "First rose."

PRIS — A nickname for Priscilla.

PRISCILLA — Latin. "The ancient." St. Priscilla assisted St. Paul, the Apostle to the Gentiles.

PRISSIE — A nickname for Priscilla.

PROSPERA — Latin. "Favorable."

PRU — A nickname for Prudence.

PRUDENCE — Latin. "Cautious and discreet." A name popularized by the Puritans.

PRUE — A nickname for Prudence.

PRUNELLA — Old French and Latin. "Prune-colored."

PSYCHE — Greek. "The soul." A maiden in mythology who loved Cupid but was kept from him until her suffering made her worthy of true love.

PYRENA — Greek. "Fiery."

PYTHIA — Greek. "Prophet." Name of the diviners of the Delphic Oracle of Apollo.

QUEENA — Old English. "A queen."

QUEENIE — A nickname for Queena.

QUENBY — Scandinavian. "Womanly."

QUERIDA — Spanish. "Beloved."

QUINTINA — Latin. "The fifth." A birth-order name.

RACHEL — Hebrew. "Ewe." In the

Bible, Rachel was the wife of Jacob and the mother of Benjamin and Joseph.

RACHELE — The Italian form of Rachel.

RACHELLE — The French form of Rachel.

RADELLA — Old English. "Elfin adviser."

RADINKA — Slavic. "Active."

RADMILLA — Slavic. " Handmaid of the people."

RAE — A nickname for Rachel.

RAFAELA — The Spanish feminine form of Raphael.

RAHEL — The German form of Rachel.

RAINA — Old German. "Mighty." Also a variation of Regina.

RAISSA — Old French. "Thinker."

RAKEL — The Swedish form of Rachel.

RAMONA — Spanish. "Mighty, wise protectress." The feminine of Ramon.

RANA — A variation of Rani, the goddess of the sea in Norse mythology.

RANEE — A variation of Rani.

RANI — Hindu. "A queen."

RANIA — A variation of Rani.

RANICE — A variation of Rani.

RANIT — A variation of Ranita.

RANITA — Hebrew. "Song." Woman with a melodious voice.

RAPHELA — Hebrew. "Divinely healed." The feminine of Raphael.

RAQUEL — The Spanish form for Rachel.

RASIA — A variation of Rose.

RATRI — Hindu. "Night." Another name for the goddess Sakti.

RAY — A nickname for Rachel.

REA — A variation of Rhea.

REBA — A nickname for Rebecca.

REBECA — The Spanish form of Rebecca.

REBECCA — Hebrew. "Knotted cord." The wife of Isaac in the Old Testament.

REBEKAH — A variation of Rebecca.

REBEKKAH — A German form of Rebecca.

REGAN — A variation of Regina.

REGGIE — A nickname for Regina.

REGINA — Latin. "A queen." Commemorates the Blessed Virgin as Regina Caeli, the Queen of heaven.

REINA — The Spanish form of Regina.

REINE — The French form of Regina.

RENA — A nickname for Irene.

RENATA — Latin. "Reborn."

RENATE — The German form of Renata.

RENE — A nickname for Irene and Renata.

RENÉE — The French form of Renata.

RENITA — Latin. "Self-possessed."

RESEDA — Latin. "Curative." Name of the mignonette flower.

REVA — Latin. "Reviving."

REXANA — Latin. "With queenly grace."

RHEA — Greek. "A stream." The Greek goddess who gave birth to Zeus.

RHETA — Greek. "An orator."

RHODA — A variation of Rose.

RHODANTHE — Greek. "Flower of the rose bush."

RHODIA — A variation of Rose.

RIA — Spanish. "Mouth of a river."

RICADONNA — English and Latin. "Ruling lady."

RICARDA — Old English. "Powerful ruler." The feminine of Richard.

RICKIE — A nickname for Ricardoa and Ricardonna.

RINA — A nickname for Regina.

RISA — Laughter. "Latin."

RITA — A nickname for Margaret. Also used as an independent name.

RIVA — French. "Shore."

ROANNA — A variation of Roseann.

ROBERTA — Old English. "Shining fame." The feminine form of Robert.

ROBINA — A variation of Roberta.

ROBINE — A French form of Roberta.

ROBINETTE — A variation of Roberta.

ROBINIA — A variation of Roberta.

ROCH — A nickname for Rochelle.

ROCHELLA — A variation of Rochelle.

ROCHELLE — French. "From the little rock."

ROCHETTE — A variation of Rochelle.

RODDY — A nickname for Roderica.

RODERICA — Old German. "Famous princess." A feminine form of Roderick.

ROHANA — Hindu. "Sandalwood." Beautifully-scented incense.

ROIS — The Irish form of Rose.

ROLANDA — Old German. "From a well-known place." The feminine of Roland.

ROLANDE — The French form of Rolanda.

ROMELDA — A variation of Romilda.

ROMILDA — Old German. "Glorious battle maiden."

ROMOLA — Latin. "The Roman." The title of George Eliot's novel.

RONALDA — Old Norse. "Mighty warrior."

ROSA — The Italian, Spanish, Dutch, and Swedish form of Rose.

ROSABEL — A variation of Rosabella.

ROSABELLA — Latin. "Beautiful rose "

ROSABELLE — A variation of Rosabella.

ROSALBA — Latin. "White rose."

ROSALEEN — An Irish form of Rose.

ROSALIA — A variation of Rose.

ROSALIE — A variation of Rose.

ROSALIND — A variation of Rosalinda.

ROSALINDA — Spanish. "Fair rose."

ROSAMOND — Old German. "Famed protection."

ROSAMONDE — The French form of Rosamond.

ROSAMUND — A variation of Rosamond.

ROSAMUNDA — The Italian form of Rosamond.

ROSANNA — A variation of Rose and Anne.

ROSANNE — A combination of Rose and Anne.

ROSE — Greek. "A rose." The flower of Gemini.

ROSELLA — A variation of Rose.

ROSEMARIE — A variation of Rosemary.

ROSEMARY — A combination of Rose and Mary.

ROSETTE — The French form of Rose.

ROSIE — A nickname for Rose and all names beginning with "Ros."

ROSINA — A variation of Rose.

ROSITA — A Spanish form of Rose.

ROWENA — Old English. "Well-known friend." The heroine's name in Sir Walter Scott's *Ivanhoe* (1819).

ROXANA — A variation of Roxanne.

ROXANE — The French form of Roxanne.

ROXANNE — Persian. "Dawn." The love of Cyrano de Bergerac in Rostand's classic story.

ROXIE — A nickname for Roxanne.

ROXINE — A variation of Roxanne.

ROYALE — Old French. "Regal." One who moves with queenly grace.

ROZALIE — A variation of Rosalie.

ROZALIN — A variation of Rosalinda.

ROZALLA — A variation of Rose.

ROZE — A Slavic form of Rose.

ROZELE — A variation of Rose.

ROZINA — A variation of Rose.

RUBETTA — A nickname for Ruby.

RUBIA — The Spanish form of Ruby.

RUBINA — A variation of Ruby.

RUBY — Old French. "The ruby gem."

RUDELLE — Old German. "Famous one."

RUE — Greek. Plant name. Once used in Christian baptismal services.

RUELLA — A combination of Ruth and Ella.

RUFINA — Latin. "Red-haired." A feminine form of Rufus.

RULA — Latin. "Ruler."

RUPERTA — The German form of Roberta.

RUTH — Hebrew. "A friend of beauty." The story of Ruth is told in the Old Testament.

RUTHANN — A combination of Ruth and Ann.

RUTHIE — A nickname for Ruth.

RUTHMARY — A combination of Ruth and Mary.

SABA — Greek. "Woman of Sheba."

SABINA — Latin. "From the Sabine." The Sabine were a tribe in ancient Italy.

SABINE — A variation of Sabina.

SABRA — Hebrew. "Thorny cactus." Name for native-born Israelis.

SABRINA — Latin. "From the border."

SACHI — Japanese. "Joy." A happy child.

SADIE — A nickname for Sarah.

SADIRA — Arabic. "Ostrich returning from water."

SAKTI — Hindu. "Energy." A major deity who embodies both innocence and cruelty.

SALINA — Latin. "Salty."

SALIVIA — Latin. "Sage." The herb.

SALLIE — A nickname for Sarah.

SALLY — A nickname for Sarah.

SALOMA — A variation of Salome.

SALOME — Hebrew. "Peaceful."

SALOMI — A variation of Salome.

SALVINA — A variation of Salivia.

SAM — A nickname for Samantha.

SAMANTHA — Aramaic. "A listener." An excellent quality for a friend.

SAMARA — Hebrew. "Ruled by God."

SAMUELA — Hebrew. "Asked by God." Feminine of Samuel.

SAMUELLE — A variation of Samuela.

SANCHA — A Spanish form of Sancia.

SANCHIA — A Spanish form of Sancia.

SANCIA — Latin. "Holy."

SANDI — A nickname for Alexandra.

SANDRA — A nickname for Alexandra. Very often used as an independent name.

SAPPHIRA — Hebrew. "Beautiful." Or the name of the jewel derived from the Greek.

SAPPHIRE — A variation of Sapphira.

SARA — The French, German, Italian, and Spanish form of Sarah.

SARAH — Hebrew. "Princess." In the Bible, the wife of Abraham and the mother of Issac.

SARENE — A variation of Sarah.

SARINE — A variation of Sarah.

SARITA — A Spanish form of Sarah.

SASHA — Russian. Nickname for Alexandra.

SAVANNA — Spanish. "An open grassland."

SAVINA — A variation of Sabina.

SAXONA — Old English. "A Saxon."

SCARLETT — English. "Bright red color." The famous heroine of *Gone With the Wind*, Scarlett O'Hara.

SEBASTIANA — Greek. "Majestic." The feminine of Sebastian.

SEBASTIANE — A variation of Sebastiana.

SECUNDA — Latin. "The second." A birth-order name.

SELA — Hebrew. "A rock."

SELDA — A nickname for Griselda.

SELENA — Greek. "The moon." Astrologically appropriate name for a Cancer child.

SELENE — A variation of Selena. The mythological deity of the moon.

SELETA — A variation of Sela.

SELIA — A nickname for Selena.

SELIMA — Arabic. "Peace."

SELINA — A variation of Selena.

SELINDA — A variation of Selena.

SELMA — Gaelic. "Fair."

SEMELE — Latin. "Once." Grecian earth goddess.

SENA — A nickname for Selena.

SENALDA — Spanish. "Signal."

SEPTIMA — Latin. "Seventh." September was the seventh month of the Roman calendar.

SERAFINA — A variation of Seraphina.

SERAFINE — A variation of Seraphina.

SERAPHINA — Hebrew. "Ardent one." Seraph was an angel of the highest acclaim according to the Bible.

SERENA — Latin. "Tranquil."

SERILDA — Old German. "Armed maiden of war."

SHAINA — Hebrew. "Beautiful."

SHAKO — American Indian. "Mint." Refreshing.

SHANE — A variation of Shaina.

SHANI — African. "Marvelous."

SHARAI — Hebrew. "Princess."

SHARLEEN — A variation of Charlene.

SHARON — The English derivation of Sharai.

SHARRY — A nickname for Sharon.

SHEBA — A variation of Saba.

SHEELA — A variation of Sheila.

SHEELAH — A variation of Sheila.

SHEENA — An Irish form of Jane.

SHEILA — The Irish form of Cecilia.

SHEREE — A nickname for Charlotte.

SHERILL — A nickname for Charlotte.

SHERRY — A nickname for Charlotte or Sharon.

SHERYL — A variation of Sherill.

SHIRA — Hebrew. "Spring."

SHIRI — A nickname for Shirley.

SHIRIL — A nickname for Shirley.

SHIRLEE — A variation of Shirley.

SHIRLEEN — A variation of Shirley.

SHIRLEY — Old English. "From the bright meadow." A residence name.

SHIRLINE — A variation of Shirley.

SHOSHANA — Hebrew. "Rose."

SIB — A nickname for Sibyl.

SIBEAL — The Irish form of Sibyl.

SIBEL — A variation of Sibyl.

SIBIL — A variation of Sibyl.

SIBLEY — A variation of Sibyl.

SIBYL — Greek. "Prophetic." In Roman mythology, the Sibyls were prophetesses.

SIBYLLA — The Dutch form of Sibyl.

SIBYLLE — The French and German form of Sibyl.

SIDONIA — Hebrew. "Binding."

SIDONIE — A variation of Sidonia.

SIDRA — Latin. "Like a star."

SIGFREDA — Old German. "Victory on peace."

SIGNA — Latin. "A sign."

SIGRID — Old Norse. "Beautiful victory."

SILVA — A variation of Sylvia.

SILVIA — The Italian and Spanish form of Sylvia.

SILVIE — The nickname for Sylvia.

SIMONA —Hebrew. "Heard." The feminine form of Simon.

SIMONE — A beautiful French form of Simona.

SIMONETTE — A nickname for Simona.

SIRENA — Greek. "A siren." In mythology, the Sirens were sea nymphs who enticed sailors away from their course to their death.

SIUSAN — The Scottish form of Susan.

SOFIA — The Italian and Spanish form of Sophie.

SOFIE — The French and Dutch form of Sophie.

SOLITA — Latin. "Solitary."

SOLVIG — Old German. "Maiden successful in battle."

SONIA — A Slavic and Scandinavian form of Sophie.

SONJA — A Slavic and Scandinavian form of Sophie or Sophronia.

SOPHIA — A variation of Sophie.

SOPHIE — Greek. "Wisdom."

SOPHRONIA — Greek. "Foresighted."

SOPHY — A variation of Sophie.

SORCHA — The Irish form of Sarah.

SOSANNA — The Irish form of Susan.

SPICA — The name of the brightest star in the constellation of Virgo.

SPRING — Old English. "The season of growth."

STACIA — A nickname for Anastasia.

STACIE — A nickname for Anastasia.

STACY — A nickname for Anastasia.

STEFFIE — A nickname for Stephanie.

STELLA — A nickname for Estelle.

STELLE — A nickname for Estelle.

STEPHA — A nickname for Stephanie.

STEPHANA — A variation of Stephanie.

STEPHANIA — A variation of Stephanie.

STEPHANIE — Greek. "Crowned." The feminine of Stephen.

STESHA — A Russian nickname for Stephanie.

STEVANA — A variation of Stephanie.

STEVENA — A variation of Stephanie.

STINA — A nickname for Christine.

STORM — Old English. "Impetuous by nature."

SUE — A nickname for Susan.

SUKEY — A nickname for Susan.

SUKI — A nickname for Susan.

SUNNY — English. "Cheerful."

SUSAN — Hebrew. "The lily." A model of purity.

SUSANA — The Spanish form of Susan.

SUSANNA — The Italian form of Susan.

SUSANNAH — A variation of Susan.

SUSANNE — The French and German form of Susan.

SUSIE — A nickname for Susan.

SUSY — A nickname for Susan.

SUZANNA — A variation of Susan.

SUZANNE — A French form of Susan.

SUZETTE — A French form of Susan.

SUZIE — A nickname for Susan.

SWANHILDA — Old Norse. "Swan maiden." Name derived from the Valkyries, who transformed themselves into swans.

SYBIL — A variation of Sibyl.

SYLVA — A variation of Sylvia.

SYLVAVNA — A variation of Sylvia.

SYLVIA — Latin. "From the forest."

SYNA — Greek. "Two together."

TABITHA — Aramaic. "The gazelle." An animal that served as an ancient symbol of beauty. An intriguing name.

TACITA — Latin. "Silent."

TALETHA — A variation of Talitha.

TALITHA — Aramic. "Young woman."

TALLIE —A nickname for Tallula.

TALLULA — American Indian. "Leaping water."

TALLULAH — A variation of Tallula.

TALLY — A nickname for Tallula.

TAMARA — Hebrew. "Palm tree." An Oriental symbol of beauty.

TAMMIE — A nickname for Tamara or Thomasina.

TAMMY — Hebrew. "Perfection." Also a nickname for Tamara or Thomasina.

TANGERINE — French. "From Tangiers." An exotic woman.

TANSY — Latin. "Persistent." A woman of perseverance.

TANYA — A nickname for Tatiana.

TAO — Chinese. "Peach." A Buddhist symbol of immortality.

TARA — Gaelic. "Tower." Tara Halls was the home of the ancient Irish kings.

TATIANA — Russian. "Fairy queen."

TAVIE — A nickname for Octavia.

TAVY — A nickname for Octavia.

TEDDIE — A nickname for Theodora.

TEDDY — A nickname for Theodora.

TEMINA — Hebrew. "Honest." A trustworthy girl.

TEMPEST —Old French. "Stormy."

TEMPLA — Latin. "A temple."

TEODORA — The Italian and Spanish form of Theodora.

TERENTIA — Greek. "Guardian." The feminine form of Terence.

TERESA — The Italian and Spanish form of Theresa.

TERESE — A variation of Theresa.

TERESINA — The Italian nickname for Theresa.

TERESITA — A Spanish nickname for Theresa.

TEREZA — The Portuguese form of Theresa.

TERRI — A nickname for Terentia or Theresa.

TERRIE — A nickname for Terentia or Theresa.

TERRY — A nickname for Terentia or Theresa.

TERTIA — Latin. "The third." A birth-order name.

TERZA — A variation of Tertia and Theresa.

TESS — A nickname for Tessa and Theresa.

THADA — A nickname for Thadea.

THADEA — Greek. "Courageous." Also from the Hebrew for "praise." The feminine of Thaddeus.

THADINE — A variation of Thaddea.

THAIS — Greek. "The bond." The mistress of Alexander the Great.

THALASSA — Greek. "From the sea."

THALIA — Greek. "Blooming." According to mythology, one of the Three Graces and the muse of comedy.

THANCYI — African. "Child of happiness."

THEA — Greek. "Heavenly." According to legend, one of the Titans, a generation of deities whose positions were usurped by Zeus and his followers.

THEANO — Greek. "Divine name."

THECLA — Greek. "Of divine fame."

THEDA — A nickname for Theodora.

THEKLA — A variation of Theodora.

THELMA — Greek. "Nursling."

THEODORA — Greek. "Gift from God." The feminine of Theodore.

THEODOSIA — Greek. "God-given." The feminine form of Theodosius.

THEOLA — Greek. "The divine."

THEONE — Greek. "God's name."

THEOPHANIA — Greek. "Manifestation of God."

THEOPHILA — Greek. "Loved by God." A popular name among the 17th-century Puritans.

THEORA — Greek. "Thinker."

THERA — Greek. "Untamed."

THERESA — Greek. "Reaper."

THERESE — The German and and French form of Theresa.

THETIS — Greek. "Determined." The mother of Achilles who, when he was an infant, plunged him into the river Styx to make him invulnerable, but forgot to bathe the heel by which she held him.

THIRZA — Hebrew. "Pleasant."

THISBE — A mythological maiden whose lover, fearing that she had been slain by a lion, kills himself. Her tale is parodied in Shakespeare's *Midsummer Night's Dream.*

THOMASA — A variation of Thomasina.

THOMASINA — Hebrew. "The twin." A feminine form of Thomas.

THOMASINE — A variation of Thomasina.

THORA — Old Norse. "Thunder." The feminine of Thor.

THORABERTA — Old Norse. "Thunderbright." A feminine form of Thorbert.

THORDIA — A variation of Thora.

THORDIS — A variation of Thora.

TIBBIE — A nickname for Tiberia.

TIBBY — A nickname for Tiberia.

TIBELDA — Old German. "Fearless." A woman of courage.

TIBERIA — Latin. "From the Tiber River." A residence name.

TILDA — A nickname for Mathilda.

TILLIE — A nickname for Mathilda.

TIMOTHEA — Greek. "Honoring God." The feminine form of Timothy.

TINA — A nickname for names ending in "tina." Also used as an independent name.

TIRZA — Hebrew. "Desirable." A woman of magnetism.

TISH — A nickname for Letitia and Patricia.

TITA — Latin. "A title of respect."

TITANIA — Greek. "Grant." The Titans were giant gods who ruled the earth before Zeus and his followers.

TIVONA — Hebrew. "Nature lover."

TOBY — Hebrew. "God is good." The feminine of Tobias.

TOINETTE — A variation of Antoinette.

TOKI — Japanese. "Time."

TOMMIE — A nickname for Thomasina.

TOMMY — A nickname for Thomasina.

TONIA — A nickname for Antonia.

TONYA — A Russian nickname for Antonia.

TOPAZ — Latin. "The dark yellow gem." The birthstone for November.

TOURMALINE — Sinhalese. "The Canelian gem."

TRACY — Latin. "Courageous." Or from the Gaelic for "one who does battle." Also can be a nickname for Theresa.

TRAVIATA — Italian. "One who goes astray." From the name of the well-known Verdi opera *La Traviata*.

TRELLA — A nickname for Estrella.

TRESA — A German form of Theresa.

TRESCHA — A German form of Theresa.

TRICIA — A nickname for Patricia.

TRILBY — Italian. "One who sings musical trills." The beautiful singer in George du Maurier's novel of the same name (1894).

TRINA — A nickname for Catherine.

TRINETTE — A nickname for Catherine.

TRISTA — Latin. "Melancholy." The feminine of Tristan.

TRIX — A nickname for Beatrice.

TRIXIE — A nickname for Beatrice.

TRUDA — A nickname for Gertrude.

TRUDE — A nickname for Gertrude.

TRUDEL — A Dutch form of Gertrude, a nickname.

TRUDY — A nickname for Gertrude.

TRYPHENA — Latin. "Dainty." A fragile child.

TUESDAY — Old English. "Born on Tuesday."

TULLIA — Gaelic. "Serene." A peaceful soul.

TZIGANE — Hungarian. "Gypsy."

UDA — Old German. "Wealthy."

UDELE — A variation of Uda.

UDELLE — A variation of Uda.

ULA — A nickname for Cordula.

ULIMA — Arabic. "Wise."

ULRICA — Old German. "Ruler of all." The feminine of Ulric.

ULRIKA — A variation of Ulrica.

ULTIMA — Latin. "Aloof."

ULVA — Gothic. "Wolf." Symbolizing courage in ancient times.

UMA — Hindu. "Mother." One of the names of the goddess Sakti.

UMEKO — Japanese. "Plum-blossom child." The flower symbolizing patience.

UNA — Latin. "One."

UNDINE — Latin. "Of the wave." A water nymph in mythology who married a mortal.

UNITY — Middle English. "Oneness." A Puritan virtue name.

URANIA — Greek. "Heavenly." The Greek muse of astronomy. An appropriate name for a girl born under the sign of Aquarius, which is ruled by Uranus.

URSA — Greek. "She-bear." In mythology, nymph placed in the sky as a constellation.

URSEL — The German form of Ursula.

URSIE — A nickname for Ursula.

URSOLA — The Spanish form of Ursula.

URSULA — A variation of Ursa.

URSULE — The French form of Ursa.

URSULINE — A variation of Ursula.

VAL — A nickname for names beginning with "Val."

VALA — Gothic. "Chosen."

VALBORGA — Old German. "Protecting ruler."

VALDA — Old Norse. "Spirited warrior."

VALEDA — Latin. "Vigorous." An active child.

VALENCIA — Latin. A variation of Valentia.

VALENKA — The Russian form of Helen.

VALENTIA — Latin. "Strong and healthy."

VALENTINA — A variation of Valentia.

VALERIA — The Italian form of Valerie.

VALERIE — Old French. "Strong."

VALERY — A variation of Valerie.

VALESKA — Old Slavic. "Glorious ruler."

VALLONIA — Latin. "Of the valley." Roman goddess of valleys.

VALMA — A variation of Wilma.

VALONIA — A variation of Vallonia.

VAN — A nickname for names beginning with "Van."

VANDA — A Slavic form of Wanda.

VANESSA — Latin. "Butterfly."

VANGIE — A nickname for Evangeline.

VANGY — A nickname for Evangeline.

VANIA — A variation of Jane.

VANNA — A nickname for Vanessa.

VANNY — A nickname for Vanessa.

VANORA — A variation of Guinevere.

VANYA — A Russian form of Jane.

VARA — A Slavic nickname for Barbara.

VARINA — A Slavic form of Barbara.

VARVARA — A Russian form of Barbara.

VASHTI — Persian. "Beautiful." A woman who enraptures.

VEDA — Hindu. "Sacred knowledge."

VEDETTE — Old French. "Watchtower."

VEDIS — A variation of Veda.

VEGA — Arabic. "Falling like a star."

VELDA — A variation of Valda.

VELEDA — Old German. "Divine wisdom."

VELIKA — Old Slavic. "Great."

VELMA — A variation of Wilhelmina.

VELVET — Middle English. "Velvety." Soft as the plush fabric.

VENETIA — Gaelic. "Blessed."

VENITA — A nickname for Venus.

VENTURA — Spanish. "Good fortune."

VENUS — Latin. "Beauty." The Roman name for Aphrodite, the goddess of beauty.

VERA — Latin. "True." Also possibly from the Russian for "faith."

VERABENA — Latin. "Sacred branches."

VERADIS — A variation of Vera.

VERDA — A variation of Verna.

VERENDA — Old German. "Protector."

VERENE — A variation of Vera.

VERINE — A variation of Vera.

VERITY — English. "Truth."

VERNA — Latin. "Springlike."

VERNE — A variation of Verna.

VERNIS — A variation of Verna.

VERNITA — A nickname for Verna.

VERONICA — A variation of Bernice. St. Veronica came from the crowd and wiped the face of Jesus on his way to Calvary.

VERONIKA — A variation of Bernice.

VERONIKE — The German form of Veronica.

VERONIQUE — A French form of Veronica.

VESPERA — Latin. "Evening star." A beautiful name.

VESTA — Latin. "She who stays behind." The Roman goddess of the household and tender of the fires of the Vestal Virgins.

VEVAY — A nickname for Vivian.

VEVILA — Gaelic. "A woman with a melodious voice."

VIC — A nickname for Victoria.

VICKI — A nickname for Victoria.

VICKIE — A nickname for Victoria.

VICKY — A nickname for Victoria.

VICTOIRE — The French form of Victoria.

VICTORIA — Latin. "Victory." Queen Victoria ruled England for more than half a century.

VICTORINE — A variation of Victoria.

VIDA — Hebrew. "Beloved." A feminine form of David.

VIDETTE — A variation of Vida.

VIDONIA — Portuguese. "A branch of the vine."

VIGILIA — Latin. "Alert."

VIGNETTE — French. "Little vine."

VILETTE — French. "From the country home."

VILHELMINA — The Swedish form of Wilhelmina.

VILMA — A Slavic form of Wilma.

VIÑA — Spanish. "From the vineyard."

VINCENTIA — Latin. "Conquering." The feminine of Vincent.

VINCENZA — An Italian form of Vincentia.

VINCIE — A nickname for Vincentia.

VINE — An English form of Vina.

VINITA — A nickname for Vincentia or Vina.

VINNIE — A nickmane for Vincentia.

VINNY — A nickname for Vincentia.

VIOLA — The Italian form of Violet.

VIOLANTE — The Spanish and Italian form of Violet.

VIOLET — Old French. "The little purple flower." A symbol of purity.

VIOLETTA — The Italian form of Violet.

VIOLETTE — The French form of Violet.

VIRGIE — A nickname for Virginia.

VIRGINIA — Latin. "Maidenly pure."

VIRGINIE — The French and Dutch form of Virginia.

VIRIDIS — Latin. "Youthful and blooming."

VIRINA — A variation of Verna.

VIRNA — A variation of Verna.

VITA — Latin. "Life."

VITIA — A variation of Vita.

VITORIA — The Spanish form of Victoria.

VITTORIA — The Italian form of Victoria.

VIV — A nickname for Vivian.

VIVIAN — Latin. "Vivacious." In the legends of King Arthur, Merlin was imprisoned because of the enchantment of Vivian.

VIVIANA — The Italian form of Vivian.

VIVIE — A nickname for Vivian.

VIVIEN — A variation of Vivian.

VIVIENNE — A French form of Vivian.

VOLANTE — Italian. "Flying."

VOLETA — Old French. "Veiled."

VOLETTA — A variation of Voleta.

VONNIE — A nickname for Veronica.

VONNY — A nickname for Veronica.

VRINDA — Hindu. A woman of great virtue and divine strength in mythology.

WAHKUNA — American Indian. "Beautiful."

WAKENDA — American Indian. "Worshipped."

WALDA — Old German. "Ruler."

WANDA — Old German. "Wanderer."

WANDIE — A nickname for Wanda.

WANDIS — A variation of Wanda.

WANETTA — Old English. "Pale." A fair beauty.

WAPEKA — American Indian. "Skillful."

WARDA — Old German. "Guardian." A feminine form of Ward.

WELCOME — Old English. "Graciously receptive." A Puritan name.

WELDA — A variation of Walda.

WELSA — Old English. "From the west meadow." A residence name.

WENDA — A variation of Wanda.

WENDALINE — A variation of Wanda.

WENDELIN — A variation of Wanda.

WENDY — A nickname for Wanda.

WENONA — American Indian. "First-born daughter."

WILDA — Old English. "Untamed."

WILEEN — A nickname for Wilhelmina.

WILHELMINA — Old German. "Resolute power."

WILHELMINE — The German and Dutch form of Wilhelmina.

WILLA — A variation of Wilhelmina.

WILLABELLE — Old German and Latin. "Beautiful and determined."

WILLAMINA — A variation of Wilhelmina.

WILLETTE — A variation of Wilhelmina.

WILLOW — Middle English. "Freedom." A tree with beautiful sweeping branches.

WILMA — A variation of Wilhelmina.

WILMET — A variation of Wilhelmina.

WILONA — Old English. "Desired."

WILONE — A variation of Wilona.

WINEMA — American Indian. "Female chief."

WINIFRED — Old German. "Peaceful friend."

WINNIE — A nickname for Winifred.

WINNY — A nickname for Winifred.

WINOLA — Old German. "Gracious friend."

WINONA — A variation of Wenona.

WYNNE — Celtic. "Fair."

XANTHE — Greek. "Yellow."

XAVIERA — Arabic. "Brilliant." The feminine of Xavier.

XENA — A variation of Xenia.

XENE — A variation of Xenia.

XENIA — Greek. "Hospitable."

XYLIA — Greek. "Of wood."

XYLONA — Greek. "From the forest."

XYLVINA — A variation of Xylia.

YAMA — Japanese. "Mountain."

YASU — Japanese. "Peaceful."

YASUKO — A variation of Yasu.

YEDDA — Old English. "Singer."

YEKATERINA — A Russian form of Katherine.

YETTA — A variation of Yedda.

YEVETTE — A variation of Yvonne.

YNES — A Spanish form of Agnes.

YNEZ — A Spanish form of Agnes.

YOLANDA — The Italian form of Iolanthe.

YOLANDE — The French form of Iolanthe.

YOLANTHE — A variation of Iolanthe.

YOSHI — Japanese. "Good."

YOSHIKO — A variation of Yoshi.

YSABEL — A Spanish form of Isabel.

YVETTE — A variation of Yvonne.

YVONNE — Old French. "Archer." An appropriate name for a child born under the sign of Sagittarius.

ZABRINA — A variation of Sabrina.

ZADA — Arabic. "Lucky one."

ZANDRA — A variation of Sandra.

ZANETA — A Russian form of Jane.

ZARA — Hebrew. "Dawn." Also a variation of Sarah.

ZARAH — A variation of Sarah.

ZARIA — A variation of Sarah.

ZEA — Latin. "Kind of grain." Appropriate for a child born under the earth astrological signs.

ZELDA — A nickname for Griselda.

ZELE — A variation of Zelia.

ZELIA — Greek. "Zeal."

ZELMA — A nickname for Anselma.

ZENA — A variation of Xenia and Zenobia.

ZENAIDA — A variation of Zenobia.

ZENDA — Persian. "Womanly." Also a variation of Zenobia.

ZENIA — A variation of Xenia and Zenobia.

ZENINA — A variation of Zenobia.

ZENNA — A variation of Zenobia.

ZENOBIA — Greek. "Given life by Zeus."

ZÉNOBIE — The French form of Zenobia.

ZERA — Hebrew. "Seeds." The source of all good things.

ZERELDA — A variation of Serilda.

ZERLINA — A variation of Zerlinda.

ZERLINDA —Hebrew and Spanish. "Dawn-beautiful."

ZETA — Greek. "The letter Z."

ZEVA — Greek. "Sword."

ZIGANA — Hungarian. "Gypsy."

ZILA — Hebrew. "Shadow."

ZILLA — A variation of Zila.

ZILVIA — A variation of Silvia.

ZINIA — Latin. The flower.

ZINNIA — A variation of Zinia.

ZIPPORA — Hebrew. "Sparrow."

ZITA — A Spanish nickname for Rosita.

ZOE — Greek. "Life."

ZOFIA — A Slavic form of Sophia.

ZONA — Latin. "A girth."

ZONNE — A contemporary combination of Zoe and Anne.

ZORA — Slavic. "Aurora" or "dawn."

ZORANA — A variation of Zora.

ZORINA — A variation of Zora.

ZORINE — A variation of Zora.

ZSA ZSA — A Hungarian nickname for Susan.

ZULA — A Czechoslovakian nickname for Susan.

(7)
Boys' Names

AARON — Hebrew. "Enlightened." The brother of Moses and the first high priest of the Jews.

ABAD — The Spanish form of Abbott.

ABBÉ — The French form of Abbott.

ABBOID — The Irish form of Abbott.

ABBOT — A variation of Abbott.

ABBOTSON — Old English. "The son of Abbott."

ABBOTT — Hebrew. "Father." The head of a monastery.

ABDEL — Arabic. "Son of." Usually used with another name.

ABDUL — A variation of Abdel.

ABE — A nickname for Abraham.

ABEL — Hebrew. "Breath, evanescence."

ABELARD — Old German. "Nobly resolute." Famous medieval scholar and lover of Héloïse.

ABIE — A nickname for Abraham.

ABIJAH — Hebrew. "The Lord is my father."

ABISHA — A variation of Abijah.

ABNER — Hebrew. "Father of light."

ABOTT — A variation of Abbott.

ABRAHAM — Hebrew. "Father of the multitude."

ABRAHAMO — The Italian form of Abraham.

ABRAHAN — The Spanish form of Abraham.

ABRAM — Hebrew. "Exalted father."

ABRAMO — The Italian form of Abram.

ABRAN — A Spanish variation of Abraham and Abram.

ABSALOM — Hebrew. "Father of peace."

ACE — Latin. "Unity."

ACEY — A nickname for Ace.

ACHILLES — The Greek hero whose story is portrayed in Homer's *Illiad*.

ACK — A nickname for Ackerley.

ACKERLEY — Old English. "From the oak-tree meadow." A residence name.

AD — A nickname for Adam.

ADABERT — A German form of Albert.

ADAIR — Gaelic. "From the oak-tree ford." A residence name.

ADAL — Old German. "Noble."

ADALARD — Old German. "Noble and brave."

ADALRIC — A variation of Adelric.

ADAM — Hebrew. "Man of red earth." According to the Bible, God created the first man, Adam, from the soil.

ADAMO — An Italian form of Adam.

ADAMS — A variation of Adam.

ADÁN — The Spanish form of Adam.

ADAO — The Portuguese form of Adam.

ADAR — Hebrew. "Fire." An appropriate name for a child born under the fire signs of the Zodiac.

ADDIS — A variation of "Son of Adam."

ADDISON — Old English. "Son of Adam."

ADEL — German. "Noble."

ADELBERT — A German form of Albert.

ADELRIC — Old German. "Noble commander."

ADIN — Hebrew. "Delicate."

ADIR — Hebrew. "Majestic." A princely child.

ADLAI — Hebrew. "A witness of God."

ADLAR — Old German. "Eagle."

ADLER — A variation of Adlar.

ADLEY — Hebrew. "Just." A man of fairness.

ADNEY — Old English. "Dweller on the noble one's island."

ADOLF — The German form of Adolph.

ADOLFO — The Spanish and Italian form of Adolph.

ADOLPH — Old German. "Noble wolf." In ancient times, the wolf was revered for its cunning.

ADOLPHE — The French form of Adolph.

ADOLPHUS — The Swedish form of Adolph.

ADON — Hebrew. "Lord."

ADONIS — The Greek variation of Adon. A beautiful young man loved by Aphrodite in classic Greek mythology.

ADRIAN — Latin. "Man from Adria," a town in Italy.

ADRIANO — The Italian form of Adrian.

ADRIEL — Hebrew. "Of God's congregation."

ADRIEN — The French form of Adrian.

ADULLAH — Arabic. "Servant of God."

AENEAS — Greek. "Worthy of praise." The Trojan hero, revered as the founder of the culture of ancient Rome, whose story is told by Virgil in the *Aeneid.*

AEOLUS — Greek. "A wind." The mythological god of the winds.

AFFONSO — The Portuguese form of Alphonso.

AGNI — Hindu. The god of fire.

AGOSTO — The Italian form of August.

AGUISTIN — The Irish form of August.

AGUSTIN — A Spanish form of August.

AHARON — A variation of Aaron.

AHEARN — Gaelic. "Lord of the horses."

AHERIN — A variation of Ahearn.

AHERN — A variation of Ahearn.

AHERNE — A variation of Ahearn.

AHMAD — Arabic. "The most praised."

AHMED — A variation of Admad.

AHREN — Old German. "Eagle."

AICKIN — A variation of Aikin

AIDAN — Gaelic. "Fiery."

AIKAN — A variation of Aikin.

AIKIN — Old English. "Oaken." Of sturdy stock.

AILBERT — The Scottish form of Albert.

AILEAN — The Scottish form of Alan.

AILFRID — The Irish form of Alfred.

AILIN — The Irish form of Alan.

AINDREAS — The Scottish and Irish form of Andrew.

AINSLEY — Old English. "From the meadow of the revered one." A residence name.

AINSLIE — A variation of Ainsley.

AINSWORTH — Old English. "From the estate of the revered one."

AIRELL — A variation of Earl.

AJAX — Greek. "Eagle." A Greek hero of the Trojan War whose story is told in Homer's *Iliad*.

AKIM — A Russian nickname for Jehoiakim.

AKSEL — A Danish form of Absalom.

AL — A nickname for names beginning with "Al."

ALA — Arabic. "Glorious."

ALAIN — The French form of Alan.

ALAIR — A variation of Hilary.

ALAN — Gaelic. "Handsome." A comely lad.

ALANO — The Italian and Spanish form of Alan.

ALANSON — Old English. "Son of Alan."

ALARD — The French form of Allard.

ALARIC — Old German. "Ruler of all."

ALARICO — The Spanish form of Alan.

ALASTAIR — A variation of Alexander.

ALASTER — The Irish form of Alexander.

ALBA — The Spanish form of Alben.

ALBAN — An Irish form of Albin.

ALBEN — A variation of Albin.

ALBERN — Old English. "Noble warrior."

ALBERT — Old English. "Noble and bright."

ALBERTO — The Italian and Spanish form of Albert.

ALBIE — A nickname for Albert.

ALBIN — Latin. "Fair."

ALBION — A variation of Albin. The ancient name for the British Isles.

ALBRECHT — A German form of Albert.

ALCINOUS — Greek. "Strong-willed."

ALCOTT — Old English. "From the old cottage." A name derived from a place of residence.

ALDEN — Old English. "Old wise protector."

ALDER — Old English. "At the alder tree."

ALDIN — A variation of Alden.

ALDIS — Old English. "From the old house."

ALDO — Italian. "Rich."

ALDOUS — A variation of Aldis.

ALFRED — Old English. "Ancient counselor."

ALDRIC — A variation of Aldrich.

ALDRICH — Old English. "Wise ruler."

ALDRIDGE — A variation of Aldrich.

ALDUS — A variation of Aldis.

ALDWIN — Old English. "Old friend."

ALEC — A nickname for Alexander.

ALEJANDRO — The Spanish form of Alexander.

ALEJO — A nickname for Alejandro.

ALEK — A nickname for Aleksandr.

ALEKSANDR — A Russian form of Alexander.

ALERON — Latin. "Eagle."

ALESSANDRO — The Italian form of Alexander.

ALEX — A nickname for Alexander.

ALEXANDER — Greek. "Helper of mankind." The Macedonian conqueror, Alexander the Great, made this name famous.

ALEXANDRE — The French and Portuguese form of Alexander.

ALEXIO — A Portuguese form of Alexander.

ALF — A nickname for Alfonso, Alford, or Alfred.

ALFIE — A nickname for Alfonso, Alford, or Alfred.

ALFONS — The German form of Alphonso.

ALFONSO — The Italian and Spanish form of Alphonso.

ALFORD — Old English. "From the old ford." A residence name.

ALFRED — Old English. "Elfin counselor." In ancient times, elves were thought to be beings who advised men and influenced their lives.

ALFREDO — The Italian and Spanish form of Alfred.

ALGAR — A variation of Alger.

ALGER — Old German. "Noble spearman."

ALGERNON — Old French. "Bearded."

ALGIE — A nickname for Alger or Algernon.

ALGY — A nickname for Alger or Algernon.

ALI — Arabic. "The greatest."

ALISTER — A variation of Alastair.

ALLAN — A variation of Alan.

ALLARD — Old English. "Nobly determined."

ALLEN — A variation of Alan.

ALLISTER — An Irish form of Alexander.

ALMO — Old English. "Noble and famous."

ALMUND — Old English. "Protector of the temple."

ALOIN — A French form of Alvin.

ALONSO — The Spanish form of Alphonso.

ALONZO — The Spanish form of Alphonso.

ALOYSIUS — Latin. "Famous in war." A man known for his courage.

ALPHEUS — Hebrew. "Substituted."

ALPHONSE — The French form of Alphonso.

ALPHONSO — Old German. "Noble and eager."

ALPHONSUS — The Irish form of Alphonso.

ALPIN — A variation of Albin.

ALRIC — A variation of Aldrich.

ALRICK — A variation of Aldrich.

ALROY — Latin. "Royal."

ALSANDAIR — An Irish form of Alexander.

ALSON — Old English. "Son of all."

ALSTON — Old English. "From the estate of the noble one."

ALTON — Old English. "From the town."

ALUIN — A French form of Alvin.

ALUINO — A Spanish form of Alvin.

ALVA — Latin. "Blond."

ALVAH — Hebrew. "Exalted."

ALVAN — A variation of Alvin.

ALVAR — Latin. "Fair."

ALVER — A variation of Alvar.

ALVIN — Old German. "Beloved by all."

ALVIS — Old Norse. "All wise."

ALVORD — A variation of Alford.

AMADEO — Spanish. "One who loves God."

AMADIS — A variation of Amadeo.

AMADO — A variation of Amadeo.

AMANDO — A variation of Amadeo.

AMASA — Hebrew. "Burdened."

AMBROGIO — An Italian form of Ambrose.

AMBROISE — The French form of Ambrose.

AMBROS — The Irish form of Ambrose.

AMBROSE — Greek. "Immortal."

AMBROSI — An Italian form of Ambrose.

AMBROSIO — The Spanish form of Ambrose.

AMBROSIUS — The German, Swedish, and Dutch form of Ambrose.

AMERIGO — The Italian form of Emery. Amerigo Vespucci was a navigator of the 15th and early 16th century whose signature on maps of the New World gave rise to the name of America.

AMERY — A variation of Emery.

AMIAS — A variation of Amyas.

AMIEL — Hebrew. "Of the Lord's people."

AMIN — Hindu. "Faithful."

AMMON — Egyptian. "The hidden."

AMON — Hebrew. "Related to the sun." An appropriate name for Leos.

AMORY — A variation of Emery.

AMOS — Hebrew. "A burden."

AMSDEN — Old English. "From the Ambrose's valley."

AMYAS — Latin. "One who shall love God."

ANASTASIUS — Latin. "One who shall rise again."

ANATOL — A Slavic form of Anatole.

ANATOLE — Greek. "Man from the East."

ANATOLIO — The Spanish form of Anatole.

ANDERS — The Scandinavian form of Anatole.

ANDERSON — Old English. "The son of Andrew."

ANDIE — A nickname for Andrew.

ANDONIS — A greek form of Andrew.

ANDRE — A French form of Andrew.

ANDREA — An Italian form of Andrew.

ANDREAS — The German, Dutch, and Swedish form of Andrew.

ANDREJ — A Slavic form of Andrew.

ANDRES — The Spanish form of Andrew.

ANDREW — Greek. "Manly." One of the Twelve Apostles of Christ and the patron saint of Scotland.

ANDREY — The Russian form of Andrew.

ANDY — A nickname for Andrew.

ANEURIN — Welsh. "Honorable."

ANGELO — Italian. "Messenger."

ANGIE — A nickname for Angelo.

ANGUS — Gaelic. "Very strong."

ANNAN — Gaelic. "From the stream."

ANNTOIN — The Irish form of Anthony.

ANSCOM — Old English. "From the valley of a noble."

ANSE — A nickname for Anselm.

ANSEL — A variation of Anselm.

ANSELM — Old German. "Divine protection."

ANSELME — The French form of Anselm.

ANSELMI — The Italian form of Anselm.

ANSELMO — The Spanish and Portuguese form of Anselm.

ANSLEY — Old English. "From the pastureland of the noble." A residence name.

ANSON — Old English. "Son of a noble."

ANSTICE — A variation of Anastasius.

ANSTISS — A variation of Anastasius.

ANTOINE — The French form of Anthony.

ANTON — A German, Slavic, and Scandinavian form of Anthony.

ANTONI — A Polish form of Anthony.

ANTONIN — A Slavic form of Anthony.

ANTONIUS — A German and Scandinavian form of Anthony.

ANWELL — Welsh. "Dear."

ANWYL — A variation of Anwell.

ANYON — Welsh. "Anvil." The surface upon which heated metal is shaped.

APOLLO — Greek. "Manly beauty." The Greek god of prophecy, healing, light, and the leader of the muses.

ARALDO — The Italian form of Harold.

ARATT — The Irish form of Harold.

ARBER — Old French. "Herb healer."

ARCH — A nickname for Archard, Arher, or Archibald.

ARCHAIMBAUD — A French form of Archibald.

ARCHAMBAULT — A French form of Archibald.

ARCHARD — German. "Powerful."

ARCHER — Old English. "Bowman." Sagittarius is the sign of the archer.

ARCHERD — A variation of Archard.

ARCHIBALD — French and German. "Sacred and bold."

ARCHIBALDO — The Spanish form of Archibald.

ARDEL — Old English. "From the valley of the hares."

ARDELL — A variation of Ardel.

ARDEN — Latin. "Ardent, fiery."

ARDIN — A variation of Arden.

ARDLEY — Old English. "From the meadow of the well-known."

AREL — Hebrew. "Lion of God." A name appropriate for a child born under the zodical sign of Leo, the Lion.

AREN — A variation of Aleron.

AREND — A Dutch form of Aleron.

ARGUS — Greek. "Vigilant."

ARGYLE — Gaelic. "From the land of the Irish."

ARI — A nickname for Arel.

ARIC — Old English. "Ruler."

ARICK — A variation of Arick.

ARIE — A nickname for Arel.

ARIES — Latin. "A ram." A perfect name for a child born under the first sign of the Zodiac.

ARKWRIGHT — Old English. "Builder of chests." A name that once denoted the occupation of its owner.

ARLEDGE — A variation of Ardel.

ARLEN — Gaelic. "A pledge."

ARLEY — A variation of Harley.

ARLIE — A variation of Arley.

ARLIN — A variation of Arlen.

ARLO — A variation of Harlow.

ARMAN — A Russian form of Armand.

ARMAND — Old German. "Army man." The patron saint of the Netherlands. Also the French form of Herman.

ARMANDO — The Spanish form of Armand and Herman.

ARMIN — A variation of Armand.

ARMSTRONG — Old English. "Strong arm."

ARNALDO — The Spanish form of Arnold.

ARNALL — Old German. "Good-natured eagle."

ARNATT — Old French and German. "Little eagle."

ARNAUD — A French form of Arnold.

ARNE — A Norwegian form of Arney.

ARNELL — A variation of Arnall.

ARNETT — A variation of Arnatt.

ARNEY — Old German. "Eagle."

ARNIE — A variation of Arney and a nickname for Arnold.

ARNO — Old German. "Eagle-wolf."

ARNOLD — Old German. "Strong as an eagle."

ARNOLDO — The Italian form of Arnold.

ARNOT — A variation of Arnatt.

ARNOTT — A variation of Arnatt.

ARNOU — A French form of Arno.

ARNOUX — A French form of Arno.

ARON — A Slavic form of Aaron.

ARPAD — A Hungarian form of Arvad. A Magyay hero of the late 19th century.

ARRIO — Spanish. "Warlike."

ART — A nickname for Arthur.

ARTAIR — The Scottish form of Arthur.

ARTE — A nickname for Arthur. Also used as an independent name.

ARTEMAS — Greek. "Gift of Artemis."

ARTEMIS — A variation of Artemas. Artemis was the Greek goddess of the moon.

ARTHUR — Welsh. "Bear-man." A man of courage. The name was popular in England because of the legendary King Arthur of the Round Table.

ARTUR — An Irish form of Arthur.

ARTURO — The Spanish and Italian form of Arthur.

ARTUS — The French form of Arthur.

ARUNDEL — Old English. "Dweller at the eagle dell." A name that once denoted a place of residence.

ARVAD — Hebrew. "Wanderer."

ARVAL — Welsh. "Wept-over." Also from the Latin for "cultivated land."

ARVEL — A variation of Arval.

ARVIN — Old German. "Friend of the people."

ASA — Hebrew. "Physician."

ASCOT — Old English. "Dweller at the east cottage."

ASCOTT — A variation of Ascot.

ASHBURN — Old English. "Ash-tree brook."

ASHBY — Old English. "From the ash-tree farm."

ASHER — Hebrew. "Happy blessed."

ASHFROD — Old English. "One who lives at the ash-tree ford."

ASHLEY — Old English. "One who lives at the ash-tree meadow."

ASHLIN — Old English. "One who lives near the ash-tree pool."

ASHTON — Old English. "One who lives at the ash-tree farm."

ASHUR — Hebrew. "Warlike."

ASWAD — Arabic. "Black."

ASWIN — Old English. "Protector with spears."

ATHERON — Old English. "Dweller at the spring farm."

ATHMORE — Old English. "From the moor."

ATLEY — Old English. "Dweller at the meadow."

ATWATER — Old English. "From the water."

ATWELL — Old English. "Dweller by the spring."

ATWORTH — Old English. "At the farmstead."

AUBERT — The French form of Albert.

AUBIN — Latin. "Fair and blond."

AUBREY — Old French. "Ruler of the elves."

AUBYN — A variation of Aubin.

AUDRIC — The French form of Aldrich.

AUDWIN — Old German. "Prosperous friend."

AUGUST — A variation of Augustus.

AUGUSTE — The French form of Augustus.

AUGUSTIN — A variation of Augustine.

AUGUSTINE — A variation of Augustus. The teachings of St. Augustine (354-430) are rudimentary to the Catholic Church.

AUGUSTO — The Spanish form of Augustus.

AUGUSTUS — Latin. "The exalted and sacred." A title of dignity given to the first Roman emperor, Augustus Caesar.

AURICK — A variation of Warrick.

AUSTEN — A variation of Augustine.

AUSTIN — A variation of Augustine.

AVENALL — Old French. "Dweller at the vatfield."

AVENELL — A variation of Avenall.

AVERY — Old English. "Leader of the elves." The little people of ancient times were thought to have great power to affect human events.

AXEL — A variation of Absalom.

AXTON — Old English. "Sword-sharpening stone."

AYLMAR — Old English. "Awe-inspiring."

AYLMER — A variation of Aylmar. Also a variation of Elmer.

AYLSWORTH — Old English. "Of awe-inspiring value."

AYLWARD — Old English. "Revered guardian."

AYLWIN — Old English. "Renowned friend."

AYLWORTH — A variation of Aylsworth.

BAILBY — The French form of Balbo.

BAILEY — Old French. "Bailiff or steward." A trusted public servant.

BAILIE — A variation of Bailey.

BAILY — A variation of Bailey.

BAINBRIDGE — Old English. "Dweller at the bridge over the clear stream."

BAIRD — Gaelic. "Minstrel." A man of song and entertainment.

BALBI — The Italian form of Balbo.

BALBO — Latin. "Inarticulate."

BALDASSARE — The Italian form of Balthazar.

BALDEMAR — Old German. "Bold and famous."

BALDER — Old English. "Bold force." Or from the Old Norse for "God of light." In Norse mythology, Balder was the son of Odin, the god of wisdom and war.

BALDOVINO — The Italian form of Baldwin.

BALDRIC — Old German. Princely ruler."

BALDUIN — The German and Scandinavian form of Baldwin.

BALDUR — A Scandinavian variation of Balder.

BALDWIN — Old German. "Bold or friendly prince."

BALFOUR — Gaelic. "From the pastureland."

BALI — Hindu. "Mighty warrior." In mythology, the name of the tyrannical monkey king.

BALLARD — Old German. "Bold, strong."

BALTASAR — The German and Scandinavian form of Balthazar.

BALTHAZAR — Greek. "Owner of treasure." One of the three Magi who followed the star to the baby Jesus.

BANCROFT — Old English. "From the beanfield." A residence name.

BANNING — Gaelic. "Blond child."

BARCLAY — Old English. "Dweller at the birch-tree meadow." A residence name.

BARD — A variation of Baird.

BARDE — The French form of Baird.

BARDEN — Old English. "Dweller near the boar's den."

BARDO — A Danish form of Bartholomew.

BARDOLF — Old English. "Axe-wolf." A fierce competitor.

BARDOLPH — A variation of Bardolf.

BARDOUL — A French form of Bardolph.

BARDRICK — Old English. "Axe-ruler."

BARDULF — A variation of Bardolph.

BARDULPH — A variation of Bardolph.

BARLOW — Old English. "Dweller on the hill," or "on the boar's hill."

BARNABA — The Italian form of Barnabas.

BARNABAS — Greek. "Son of prophecy." St. Barnabas accompanied the aspostle Paul on his missionary work.

BARNABE — The French form of Barnabas.

BARNABY — A variation of Barnabas.

BARNARD — The French form of Bernard.

BARNEBAS — A Spanish form of Barnabas.

BARNETT — Old English. "Noblemen."

BARNEY — A nickname for Barnabas.

BARNUM — Old English. "Nobleman's home."

BARNY — A nickname for Barnabas.

BARON — Old English. "Nobleman."

BARR — Old English. "Gateway." Also possibly from the German for "bear."

BARRET — Old German. "Bearlike."

BARRETT — A variation of Barret.

BARRIE — A variation of Barry.

BARRIS — A variation of Barry.

BARRY — Old French. "One who resides at the barrier." Also from the Gaelic for "Spearlike."

BART — A nickname for Bartholomew.

BARTH — A nickname for Bartholomew. Also used as an independent name.

BARTHEL — A German form of Bartholomew.

BARTHÉLEMY — A French form of Bartholomew.

BARTHOLOMAUS — A German form of Bartholomew.

BARTHOLOMÉ — A French form of Bartholomew.

BARTHOLOMEUS — A Scandinavian form of Bartholomew.

BARTHOLOMEW — Hebrew. "Son of the farmer."

BARTHRAM — A variation of Bartram.

BARTLETT — A nickname for Bartholomew.

BARTLEY — A nickname for Bartholomew.

BARTOLOME — A Spanish form of Bartholomew.

BARTOLOMEO — An Italian form of Bartholomew.

BARTON — Old English. "From the barley farm."

BARTRAM — Old English. "Glorious raven."

BARUCH — Greek. "One who performs good deeds."

BASIL — Latin. "Magnificent and kingly."

BASILE — A French form of Basil.

BASILIO — The Italian form of Basil. Also the Portuguese and Spanish form of Basil.

BASILIUS — The German and Scandinavian form of Basil.

BAUDOIN — A French form of Baldwin.

BAUDRIC — A French form of Baldric.

BAUMER — A French form of Baldemar.

BAX — A nickname for Baxter.

BAXTER — Old English. "Baker." A name designating an occupation.

BAY — A nickname for Bayard.

BAYARD — Old English. "With reddish-brown hair."

BEACH — A nickname for Beacher.

BEACHER — Old English. "Dweller by the beach tree."

BEACHY — A nickname for Beacher.

BEAGAN — Gaelic. "Little one."

BEAL — Old French. "Handsome."

BEALE — A variation of Beal.

BEALL — A variation of Beal.

BEAMAN — Old English. "Beekeeper."

BEAMER — Old English. "Trumpeter."

BEARNARD — The Scottish form of Bernard.

BEATHAN — The Scottish form of Benjamin.

BEATIE — A variation of Beattie.

BEATTIE — Gaelic. "Food dealer."

BEATTY — A variation of Beattie.

BEATY — A variation of Beattie.

BEAU — Old French. "Handsome."

BEAUFORT — Old French. "From the architecturally attractive fort."

BEAUMONT — Old French. "From the beautiful mountain."

BEAUVAIS — The French form of Bevis.

BEAVEN — A variation of Bevan.

BECK — German. "Brook."

BEECH — A nickname for Beacher.

BEECHER — A variation of Beacher.

BEECHY — A nickname for Beacher.

BELA — Hebrew. "Holocaust."

BELDEN — Old English. "From the beautiful glen."

BELDON — A variation of Belden.

BELLAMY — Old French. "Beautiful friend."

BELSHAZZAR — The Hebrew form of Balthasar.

BEM — African. "Peace."

BEN — A nickname for names beginning with "Ben."

BENCI — A Hungarian form of Benedict.

BENDIX — A variation of Bendix.

BENEDETTO — The Italian form of Benedict.

BENEDICK — A variation of Benedict.

BENEDICT — Latin. "Blessed." The name of the founder of the Benedictine Order. A popular name with priests.

BENEDICTO — A Spanish form of Benedict.

BENEDIKT — A German and Swedish form of Benedict.

BENEDYKT — A Polish form of Benedict.

BENGT — A Swedish form of Benedict.

BENIAMINO — The Italian form of Benjamin.

BENITO — A Spanish form of Benedict.

BENJAMIN — Hebrew. "Son of the right hand." A symbol of strength. In the Bible, Benjamin was the youngest son of Abraham.

BENJIE — A nickname for Benjamin.

BENNET — A variation of Bennett.

BENNETT — French and Latin. "Little blessed one."

BENNIE — A nickname for names beginning with "Ben."

BENNY — A nickname for names beginning with "Ben."

BENOIT — A French form of Benedict.

BENSON — Hebrew and English. "Son of Benjamin."

BENTLEY — Old English. "From the moor."

BENTON — Old English. "Moor dweller." A residence name.

BERESFORD — Old English. "From the barley ford."

BERG — German. "From the mountain."

BERGER — French. "Shepherd." Or "one who lives near a mountain."

BERK — A variation of Burke.

BERKE — A variation of Burke.

BERKELEY — A variation of Barclay.

BERN — Old German. "Bear." A symbol of courage.

BERNARD — Old German. "Brave as a bear."

BERNARDO — An Italian and Spanish form of Bernard.

BERNHARD — A German and Scandinavian form of Bernard.

BERNIE — A nickname for Bernard.

BERNY — A nickname for Bernard.

BERT — Old English. "Bright." Also a nickname for names beginning with "Bert."

BERTHOLD — Old German. "Brilliant ruler."

BERTIE — A variation of Bert.

BERTIN — Spanish. "Distinguished friend."

BERTON — Old English. "From the fortified town." Also a variation of Bertram.

BERTOUD — A French form of Berthold.

BERTRAM — Old English. "Glorious raven." In ancient times, the raven was a symbol of successful warfare.

BERTRAND — The French form of Bertram.

BERTRANDO — The Italian form of Bertram.

BERTWIN — Old English. "Shining friend."

BERTY — A variation of Bert.

BERWICK — Old English. "From the barley barn."

BERWIN — Old English. "Friend of the harvest."

BEVAL — Old English. "Like the wind."

BEVAN — Welsh. "Son of the youthful warrior."

BEVEN — A variation of Bevan.

BEVIN — A variation of Bevan.

BEVIS — Old French. "Fair view."

BIAGIO — The Italian form of Blaze.

BICK — A nickname for Bickford.

BICKFORD — Old English. "From the hewer's ford."

BIMSI — American Indian. "Slippery."

BING — Old German. "From the kettle-shaped hollow."

BINK — Old English. "Dweller on the slope."

BIRCH — Old English. "At the birch tree."

BIRK — A variation of Birch.

BIRKETT — Old English. "Dweller at the birchland."

BIRKEY — Old English. "From the birch-tree island."

BIRNEY — Old English. "Dweller on the brook island."

BIRTLE — Old English. "From the bird hill."

BISHOP — Old English. "The bishop."

BJØRN — A popular Scandinavian form of Bern.

BLACK — Old English. "With dark complexion."

BLADE — Old English. "Glory."

BLAGDEN — A variation of Blagdon.

BLAGDON — Old English. "From the dark valley."

BLAINE — Gaelic. "Thin and lean."

BLAINEY — A variation of Baline.

BLAIR — Gaelic. "From the plain." A residence name.

BLAISE — A French form of Blaze.

BLAKE — Old English. "Fair-haired and fair-complected." Also could be derived from a different root meaning "dark one."

BLAKELEY — Old English. "From the black meadow."

BLANCO — Spanish. "Blond."

BLAND — Latin. "Gentle."

BLANDON — A variation of Bland.

BLANE — A variation of Blaine.

BLANFORD — Old English. "From the river crossing of the gray-haired one."

BLAS — A Spanish form of Blaze.

BLASE — A variation of Blaze.

BLASIEN — A German form of Blaze.

BLASIUS — A Swedish form of Blaze.

BLAYNE — A variation of Blaine.

BLAYZE — A variation of Blaze.

BLAZE — Latin. "Stammerer." St. Blaze was a 4th-century Armenian bishop on whose feast day the throats of Catholics throughout the world are blessed.

BOAS — A variation of Boaz.

BOAZ — Hebrew. "Swift and strong."

BOB — A nickname for Robert.

BOBBIE — A nickname for Robert.

BOBBY — A nickname for Robert.

BODEN — Old French. "Herald."

BOGART — Old French. "Bow-strong."

BOHDAN — Russian. "Given by God."

BOLTON — Old English. "Of the manor farm."

BONAMY — French. "Good friend."

BONAR — Old French. "Kind and good."

BOND — Old English. "One who tills the soil."

BONDON — A variation of Bond.

BONIFACE — Latin. "One who performs good works."

BONIFACIO — The Italian and Spanish form of Boniface.

BONIFACIUS — The Dutch, German, and Scandinavian form of Boniface.

BONNER — A variation of Bonar.

BOONE — Old French. "Good." Daniel Boone was a great American frontiersman.

BOOTH — Old English. "Dweller from the stall."

BOOTHE — A variation of Booth.

BORDEN — Old English. "From the valley of the boar."

BORG — Norse. "One who lives in the castle."

BORIS — Slavic. "Battler."

BOSWELL — Old French. "A town in the forest."

BOSWORTH — Old English. "Dweller at the wall of the castle."

BOTOLF — Old English. "Herald-wolf."

BOURKE — A variation of Burke.

BOURNE — Old English. "From the brook."

BOWDEN — A variation of Boyden.

BOWEN — Old Welsh. "Son of the nobleman."

BOWIE — Gaelic. "Blond-haired."

BOWLE — Old English. "Snail."

BOWMAN — Old English. "An archer." Appropriate name for a child born under the sign of Sagittarius, the Archer.

BOYCE — Old French. "From the woodland."

BOYD — Gaelic. "Blond."

BOYDEN — Old English. "Herald." Also means "blond."

BOYNE — Gaelic. "From the white cow river." A river in Ireland.

BOYNTON — A variation of Boyne.

BRAD — Old English. "Broad." Also a nickname for names beginning with "Brad."

BRADBURN — Old English. "From the near broad brook."

BRADEN — Old English. "From the wide valley."

BRADFORD — Old English. "Dweller on the broad meadow."

BRADSHAW — Old English. "From the broad new forest."

BRADWELL — Old English. "From the wide spring."

BRADY — Old English. "From the broad island." Also from the Gaelic meaning "spirited."

BRAHMA — Hindu. One of the gods of the Hindu trinity.

BRAINARD — Old English. "Bold raven."

BRAM — A variation of Abram.

BRAN — Old English. "Raven."

BRAND — Old English. "Fire-brand."

BRANDEIS — German. "Dweller on a burned clearing."

BRANDER — A variation of Brand.

BRANDON — Old English. "From the beacon hill."

BRANT — A variation of Brand.

BRAWLEY — Old English. "From the hilly meadow."

BREDE — Scandinavian. "Glacier."

BRENDAN — Gaelic. "Little raven." Also from the German, "a flame."

BREWSTER — Old English. "Brewer." An occupation name.

BRIAN — Celtic. "Strong, virtuous."

BRIANO — An Italian form of Brian.

BRIANT — A variation of Brian.

BRICE — Celtic. "Quick."

BRIDGER — Old English. "Dweller by the bridge."

BRIEN — A variation of Brian.

BRIGHAM — Old English. "Dweller at the bridge enclosure."

BRINTON — English. "From Brinton." A town in Norfolk, England.

BRION — A variation of Brian.

BROCK — Old English. "Badger."

BROCKLEY — Old English. "From the badger meadow."

BRODERICK — Old English. "From the broad ridge." Or from the Welsh for "son of the nobleman."

BRODIE — Gaelic. "A ditch."

BRODY — A variation of Brodie.

BROMLEY — Old English. "From the broom-covered meadow."

BRON — African. "Source." A child who is a fount of happiness.

BRONSON — Old English. "Son of the dark-skinned one."

BROOK — Old English. "From the brook."

BROOKE — A variation of Brook.

BROOKS — A variation of Brook.

BROUGHER — Old English. "From the fortress."

BROUGHTON — A variation of Brougher.

BROWN — Old English. "Dark-skinned."

BRUCE — Old French. "From the brushwood thicket."

BRUNO — Old English. "With a dark complexion."

BRYAN — A variation of Brian.

BRYANT — A variation of Brian.

BRYON — A variation of Brian.

BUCK — Old English. "Buck deer."

BUCKLEY — Old English. "From the meadow with the buck deer."

BUD — A variation of Budd.

BUDD — Old English. "Herald."

BUDDIE — A nickname for Budd.

BUDDY — A nickname for Budd.

BUNDY — Old English. "A free man."

BURBANK — Old English. "One who resides on the slope near the castle."

BURCH — Old English. "Birch tree."

BURCHARD — Old English. "Strong beyond compare."

BURCKHARDT — The German form of Burchard.

BURDETT — Old French. "Small shield."

BURDON — Old English. "One who lives near the hill of the castle."

BURFORD — Old English. "From near the ford of the castle."

BURGAUD — The French form of Burchard.

BURGESS — Old English. "One who is a citizen of the burgess."

BURK — A variation of Burke.

BURKE — Old French. "Form the fortress."

BURKETT — Old French. "From the small fortress."

BURKHARD — A German form of Burchard.

BURL — Old English. "Wine servant."

BURLEIGH — Old English. "From the meadow by the hill."

BURLEY — A variation of Burleigh.

BURN — A variation of Burne.

BURNABY — A variation of Barnabas.

BURNARD — A variation of Bernard.

BURNE — Old English. "From the brook."

BURR — Scandinavian. "Youth."

BURRELL — Old French. "Reddish-brown complexion."

BURT — A variation of Bert.

BURTON — Old English. "Dweller at the fortress."

BUSBY — Scottish. "From the village in the woodlands."

BYFORD — Old English. "From the river crossing."

BYRAM — Old English. "Dweller near the cattleyard."

BYRD — Old English. "Birdlike." Admiral Richard E. Byrd was the first American to explore Antarctica.

BYRLE — A variation of Burl.

BYRNE — A variation of Byron.

BYRON — Old French. "From the cottage."

CADBY — Old Norse. "Village of warriors."

CADDOCK — Old Welsh. "Battle ability."

CADELL — Old Welsh. "With battle spirit."

CADMAN — Old English. "Warrior."

CADMAR — Celtic. "Strong in battle."

CADMUS — Greek. "From the East." An exotic character.

CADWALLADER — Old Welsh. "Battle leader."

CAESAR — Latin. "Long-haired." Has become to mean emperor since it was assumed as a title for the Roman emperors following Julius Caesar.

CAHIL — Turkish. "Innocent."

CAIN — Hebrew. "Possessed." The biblical son of Adam and Eve who is said to have committed the first murder, that of his brother Abel.

CAL — A nickname for Calhoun, Calvert, or Calvin.

CALBERT — A variation of Calvert.

CALDER — Old English. "From the clear spring."

CALDWELL — Old English. "Dweller near the cold spring."

CALE — A variation of Caleb.

CALEB — Hebrew. "Dog." A name connoting loyalty and affection.

CALEY — Gaelic. "Lithe."

CALHOUN — Gaelic. "From the narrow patch of forest."

CALVERT — Old English. "Cattle herdsman."

CALVIN — Latin. "Bald." Calvin Coolidge was the 30th president of the United States.

CAM — A nickname for Camden, Cameron, or Campbell.

CAMDEN — Old English and Gaelic. "Dweller in the winding valley."

CAMERON — Scottish. "Crooked nose."

CAMP — A nickname for Campbell.

CAMPBELL — Scottish. "Crooked mouth." Also from the Old French for "from the fair field."

CANUTE — Old Norse. "Knot."

CARADOC — Welsh. "Beloved."

CARDEN — Celtic. "From the black fortress."

CAREW — Celtic. "From the fortress."

CAREY — Old Welsh. "Dweller near the castle." Also a variation of Carew.

CARL — Old German. "Farmer." Also a German form of Charles.

CARLETON — Old English. "From the town of the farmer."

CARLIN — Gaelic. "Little champion."

CARLING — A variation of Carlin.

CARLISLE — Old English. "From the fortified city."

CARLOS — The Spanish form of Carl.

CARLTON — A variation of Carleton.

CARLYLE — A variation of Carlisle.

CARMICHAEL — Scottish. "Friend of St. Michael." St. Michael the Archangel was triumphant over the forces of the devil in the Bible story depicting the struggle between the angels of good and evil.

CARNEY — Gaelic. "Victorious warrior."

CARNY — A variation of Carney.

CAROLLAN — Gaelic. "Little champion."

CARR — Old Norse. "From the marsh."

CARRICK — Gaelic. "Dweller on the rocky cape."

CARROLL — Gaelic. "Champion." A worthy defender.

CARSON — Old English. "Son of the family on the marsh."

CARTER — Old English. "Cart driver." An occupation name.

CARTLAND — Scottish and English. "Land between the streams."

CARVEL — A variation of Carvell.

CARVELL — Old English. "From the country estate by the marsh."

CARVER — Old English. "Wood sculptor."

CARVEY — Gaelic. "Athlete." One with agility and strength.

CARY — A variation of Carey.

CASAR — The German form of Caesar.

CASEY — Gaelic. "Valorious."

CASH — A variation of Cassius.

CASIMIR — Old Slavic. "Peacemaker."

CASIMIRO — The Spanish form of Casimir.

CASPAR — A variation of Gaspar.

CASS — The variation of Cassius.

CASSIDY — Gaelic. "Clever." A man who is shrewd and inventive.

CASSIUS — Latin. "Vain."

CASTELAR — Latin. "From the castle." A princely sort.

CASTOR — Greek. "Beaver." Industriousness characterizes this individual.

CATHMOR — Gaelic. "Outstanding warrior."

CATO — Latin. "Sagacious." The name of two great orators of ancient Rome.

CATON — A Spanish form of Cato.

CAVAN — Gaelic. "Handsome."

CAVELL — Old French. "Active." A live wire.

CAWLEY — Scottish. "One of ancestral resemblance."

CECE — A nickname for Cecil.

CECIL — Latin. "Blind."

CÉCILE — The French form of Cecil.

CECILIUS — The Dutch form of Cecil.

CEDRIC — Old English. "Chieftain."

CÉSAR — The French, Spanish, and Portuguese form of Caesar.

CESARE — The Italian form of Caesar.

CHAD — Old English. "Warlike."

CHADBURN — Old English. "From the brook of the wild cat."

CHADWICK — Old English. "From the warrior's town."

CHAIM — Hebrew. "Life."

CHALE — A Spanish variation of Carlos.

CHALMER — Old Scottish. "Lord of the manor."

CHALMERS — Old Scottish. "The son of the lord."

CHANCE — A nickname for Chancellor or Chancey.

CHANCELLOR — Old English. "Secretary to the throne."

CHANDLER — Old French "Candlemaker." A name that denotes an occupation.

CHANNING — Old French. "A cannon or bishop."

CHAPIN — Old French. "Clergyman."

CHAPMAN — Old English. "Merchant."

CHAPPEL — Old French. "From the chapel."

CHAPPELL — A variation of Chapel.

CHARLES — Old German. "Manly." Charlemagne is probably the most famous of the many Charleses who have had a role in history.

CHARLEY — A nickname for Charles.

CHARLIE — A nickname for Charles.

CHARLTON — Old English. "From the farmstead of Charles."

CHASE — Old French. "Hunter."

CHATAM — Old English. "Soldiers' land."

CHATWIN — Old English. "Friend of war."

CHAUNCE — A nickname for Chauncey.

CHAUNCEY — Middle English. "Chancellor church official."

CHE — A nickname for José.

CHEN — Chinese. "Great."

CHENEY — Old French. "From the oak forest."

CHES — A nickname for Chester.

CHESTER — Old English. "Dweller at the fortified camp."

CHESTON — A variation of Chester.

CHET — A nickname for Chester.

CHETWIN — Old English. "From the cottage on the narrow path."

CHICK — A nickname for Charles.

CHICO — A nickname for Francisco.

CHILTON — Old English. "From the farm by the spring."

CHIM — Vietnamese. "Bird."

CHRÉTIEN — A French form of Christian.

CHRIS — A nickname for Christopher or Christian.

CHRISSY — A nickname for Christopher or Christian.

CHRISTIAN — Greek. "Follower of Christ."

CHRISTIANO — The Italian and Spanish form of Christian.

CHRISTIE — A nickname for Christian.

CHRISTOFFER — The Danish form of Christopher.

CHRISTOPH — A German form of Christopher.

CHRISTOPHE — A French form of Christopher.

CHRISTOPHER — Greek. "Christbearer." St. Christopher is the patron saint of travelers because legend tells that he carried the Christ Child across a raging river.

CHRISTOPHORUS — A German form of Christopher.

CHUCK — A nickname for Charles.

CHURCHILL — Old English. "One who lives on the hill of the church."

CIAN — Gaelic. "Ancient."

CICERO — Latin. "Chickpea." A famous Roman statesman of the 1st century B.C.

CICERON — A Spanish form of Cicero.

CIPRIANO — The Spanish form of Cyprian.

CIRILLO — The Italian form of Cyril.

CIRILO — The Spanish form of Cyril.

CIRO — A Spanish form of Cyrus.

CLAIBORN — A variation of Clayborne.

CLAIR — A variation of Clare.

CLARE — Latin. "Famous."

CLARENCE — Latin. "Famous."

CLARK — Old French. "Scholar."

CLAUDE — Latin. "Lame."

CLAUDIO — The Italian and Spanish form of Claude.

CLAUDIUS — The German form of Claude.

CLAUS — A nickname for Nicholas.

CLAY — Old English. "From the earth."

CLAYBORN — A variation of Clayborne.

CLAYBORNE — Old English. "Born of the earth." An appropriate name for boys born under the earth signs of the Zodiac: Taurus, Virgo, and Capricorn.

CLAYTON — Old English. "From the town on the clay bed."

CLEARY — Gaelic. "Scholar."

CLEM — A nickname for Clement.

CLEMENCE — Latin. "Kind."

CLEMENS — A Danish form of Clement.

CLEMENT — Latin. "Merciful."

CLEMENTE — The Italian and Spanish form of Clement.

CLEMENTIUS — A Dutch form of Clement.

CLEMMY — A nickname for Clement.

CLEVE — A nickname for Cleveland.

CLEVELAND — Old English. "Cliff dweller."

CLIFF — A nickname for Clifford.

CLIFFORD — Old English. "From the cliff of the river crossing."

CLIFTON — Old English. "From the farm at the cliff."

CLINT — A nickname for Clinton.

CLINTON — Old English. "From the headland farm."

CLIVE — A variation of Cleve.

CLODOVEO — The Spanish form of Clovis.

CLOVIS — Old German. "Illustrious battler."

CLUNY — Gaelic. "From the meadow."

CLYDE — Welsh. "Heard from afar."

COBB — A nickname for Jacob.

COLAN — A variation of Colin.

COLBERT — Old English. "Outstanding seafarer." Also from the Old German for "charm."

COLBY — Old English. "From the black farm."

COLE — A nickname for Nicholas.

COLEMAN — A variation of Colum.

COLIN — Gaelic. "Child." Also a nickname for Nicholas.

COLLAYER — A variation of Collier.

COLLIER — Old English. "Miner."

COLLIS — Old English. "Son of the dark man."

COLMAN — A variation of Coleman.

COLON — A Spanish form of Colum. In Spanish, Christopher Columbus is Cristóbal Colón.

COLTER — Old English. "Colt herder."

COLTON — Old English. "From the dark town."

COLUM — Gaelic. "Dove."

COLUMBO — A variation of Columbus.

COLUMBUS — The Spanish form of Colum.

COLVER — A variation of Culver.

COMYN — Gaelic. "Crooked."

CON — A variation of Conan. Also a nickname for names beginning with "Con."

CONAN — Celtic. "Intelligent." Also from the Gaelic for "lofty." Sir Arthur Conan Doyle is the creator of the most well-known sleuth of all times, Sherlock Holmes.

CONANT — A variation of Conan.

CONDON — Celtic. "The dark-haired wise man."

CONLAN — Gaelic. "Hero."

CONLEN — A variation of Conlan.

CONLIN — A variation of Conlan.

CONN — Celtic. "Wise."

CONNIE — A nickname for names beginning with "Con."

CONRAD — Old German. "Able counselor."

CONRADE — The French form of Conrad.

CONRADO — An Italian and Spanish form of Conrad.

CONROY — Gaelic. "Wise man."

CONSTANTIN — The Danish, French, and German form of Constantine.

CONSTANTINE — Latin. "Firm and constant." Constantine was the first Christian Roman emperor. His reign in the 4th century ended imperial persecution of Christians in the Roman Empire.

CONSTANTINO — The Spanish form of Constantine.

CONSTANTINOUS — The Greek form of Constantine.

CONWAY — Gaelic. "Hound of the plain."

COOP — A nickname for Cooper.

COOPER — Old English. "Barrel-maker." An occupation name.

CORBET — A variation of Corbett.

CORBETT — Latin. "The raven." In ancient times, the raven was a symbol of valor in battle.

CORBIN — A variation of Corbett.

CORBY — A nickname for Corbett.

CORCORAN — Gaelic. "Of reddish complexion."

CORDELL — Old French. "Rope-maker."

CORMACK — A variation of Cormick.

CORMICK — Gaelic. "Chari-oteer."

CORNALL — A variation of Cornell.

CORNEL — A variation of Cornell.

CORNELIUS — Latin. "Horn." In the Roman culture, the symbol of kingly majesty was the horn.

CORNELL — Old French. "Horn-colored."

CORT — Old German. "Auda-cious." Also from the Old Norse for "short."

CORWIN — A variation of Corbin.

CORYDON — Greek. "Helmeted."

COSIMO — The Italian and Span-ish form of Cosmos.

COSMÉ — The French form of Cosmos.

COSMO — Greek. "Order." This name has come to be a term de-noting orderliness of the universe. St. Cosmos is the patron saint of physicians; he was martyred in the 3rd century.

COSTA — A nickname for Con-stantinos.

COURT — A nickname for Court-land.

COURTLAND — Old English. "Dweller in the court."

COURTNAY — A variation of Courtland.

COURTNEY — A variation of Courtland.

COVELL — Old English. "From the near cave."

COWAN — Gaelic. "From the clearing on the hillside."

COYLE — Gaelic. "A man who is happy only in battle."

CRADDOCK — A variation of Caradoc.

CRAIG — Gaelic. "One who lives near the crag."

CRANDALL — Old English. "From the valley of the cranes."

CRANDELL — A variation of Crandall.

CRANLEY — Old English. "From the crane valley."

CRANSTON — Old English. "From the town of the cranes."

CRAWFORD — Old English. "From the ford where the crow flies."

CREIGHTON — Old English. "From the town near the creek."

CRÉPIN — The French form of Crispin.

CRICHTON — A variation of Creighton.

CRIS — A nickname for Cristóbal.

CRISPIAN — A variation of Crispin.

CRISPIN — Latin. "Curly-haired."

CRISPO — The Spanish form of Crispin.

CRISPUS — The German form of Crispin.

CRISTÓBAL — The Spanish form of Christopher.

CHRISTOFORO — An Italian form of Christophor.

CROFTON — Old English. "From the enclosed farm."

CROMPTON — Old English. "Dweller at the winding farm."

CROMWELL — Old English. "From the winding spring."

CROSBEY — A variation of Crosby.

CROSBIE — A variation of Crosby.

CROSBY — Old Norse. "Dweller near the shrine of the cross."

CULBERT — A variation of Colbert.

CULLAN — A variation of Cullen.

CULLEN — Gaelic. "Handsome."

CULLEY — Gaelic. "At the forest."

CULLIN — A variation of Cullen.

CULLY — A variation of Culley.

CULVER — Old English. "Dove."

CURCIO — A Spanish form of Curtis.

CURRAN — Gaelic. "Hero." A man revered.

CURREY — A variation of Curran.

CURRIE — A nickname for Curran.

CURT — Latin. "Short." Also a nickname for Curtis.

CURTIS — Old French. "Courteous."

CUTHBERT — Old English. "Famous and brilliant."

CUTLER — Old English. "Knifemaker."

CY — A nickname for Cyrus.

CYNRIC — Old English. "With royal might."

CYPRIAN — Greek. "From the island of Cyprus."

CYRANO — Greek. "From the Cyrene." Cyrano de Bergerac was the hero of Rostand's play famous for his long nose, his dueling, and his poetic ability.

CYRIL — Greek. "Lordly."

CYRILL — A German form of Cyril.

CYRILLE — A French form of Cyril.

CYRILLUS — The Dutch and Scandinavian form of Cyril.

CYRUS — Persian. "Sun." A perfect name for a male Leo.

DAEGAL — Scandinavian. "Dawn."

DAGAN — East Semitic. "Earth." A Babylonian god of the earth and its cultivation.

DAGON — A variation of Dagan.

DAGWOOD — Old English. "Forest of the brilliant one." Dagwood Bumstead is a well-known comic-strip character.

DAIN — A variation of Dane.

DALBERT — Old English. "Shining valley." Possibly also from the Old English for "proud and glorious."

DALLAS — Old English. "From the waterfall."

DALSTON — Old English. "Dweller in the town to the east."

DALTON — Old English. "Dweller in the town in the valley."

DALY — Gaelic. "Advisor."

DAMIAN — The German form of Damon.

DAMIANO — An Italian form of Damon.

DAMIEN — A French form of Damon.

DAMON — Greek. "Tamer."

DAN — Hebrew. "Judge." Also a nickname for Daniel.

DANA — A variation of Dane.

DANE — Scandinavian. "A man from Denmark." Also the Dutch form of Daniel.

DANIEL — Hebrew. "God is my judge." A major biblical prophet who is believed to have returned unharmed from the lions' den.

DANIELLE — The French form of Daniel.

DANLADI — African. "A child born on Sunday."

DANNEL — A variation of Daniel.

DANTE — A variation of Durante. Dante Alighieri, the 13-century poet, is famous for his *Divine Comedy*, especially the *Inferno* section.

DANYA — A nickname for Bohdan.

DAR — Hebrew. "Pearl."

DARBY — Gaelic. "Freeman." Also from the Old Norse for "deer park."

DAREN — African. "Born at night."

DARIO — A Spanish form of Darius.

DARIUS — Greek. "Weathly."

DARNALL — A variation of Darnell.

DARNELL — Old English. "From the hidden niche."

DARREL — Old English. "Beloved."

DARREN — Gaelic. "Great."

DARRICK — A variation of Derrick.

DARYL — A variation of Darrel.

DAUDI — African. "Beloved."

DAVE — A nickname for David.

DAVEN — A variation of Davin.

DAVID — Hebrew. "Beloved." Biblical king of Israel who was believed to have authored the *Psalms.*

DAVIDDE — The Italian form of David.

DAVIDE — A French form of David.

DAVIE — A nickname for David.

DAVIN — Scandinavian. "Brilliance of the Finns."

DAVIS — Old Scottish. "Son of the beloved."

DAVY — A nickname for David.

DEAN — Old English. "From the valley."

DEANE — A variation of Dean.

DEARBORN — Old English. "Beloved child." Or "from the brook where the deer water themselves."

DECIMUS — Latin. "Tenth." A birth-order name.

DECKER — Belgian. "Roofer." An occupation name.

DEDRIC — A nickname for Theodoric.

DEDRICK — A variation of Dedric.

DEEMS — Old English. "Son of the judge."

DEKEL — Arabic. "Palm tree."

DEL — A nickname for names beginning with "Del."

DELANO — Gaelic. "Healthy black man." Or from the Old French for "dweller near the nut trees."

DELBERT — A variation of Dalbert.

DELLING — Old English. "Shining."

DELMAR — A variation of Delmer.

DELMER — Old French. "From the sea."

DELWIN — Old English. "Friend from the valley," or "proud friend."

DELWYN — A variation of Delwin.

DEMAS — Greek. "Popular."

DEMÉTRE — A French form of Demetrius.

DEMETRIO — The Italian form of Demetrius.

DEMETRIUS — Greek. "Belonging to Demeter." Demeter was the Greek goddess of fertility.

DEMOS — Greek. "The people." A supporter of the common man.

DEMPSEY — Gaelic. "Proud."

DEMPSTER — Old English. "The judge."

DENBY — Old Norse. "From the settlement of the Danes."

DENIS — The Irish form of Dennis.

DENLEY — Old English. "From the valley meadow."

DENMAN — Old English. "Valley dweller."

DENNIS — Greek. "God of wine." Dionysus was the god of wine and revelry. St. Dennis was the patron saint of France.

DENNISON — Old English. "Son of Dennis."

DENTON — Old English. "From the valley estate."

DENVER — Old English. "From the edge of the valley."

DENYS — The Russian form of Dennis.

DERBY — A variation of Darby.

DEREK — A nickname for Theodoric.

DERMOT — Gaelic. "Free from envy."

DERMOTT — A variation of Dermot.

DERRICK — A nickname for Theodoric.

DERRY — Gaelic. "The red-haired one." The image of an Irishman with blue eyes and fiery red locks.

DERWARD — Old English. "Gamer warden."

DERWIN — Old English. "Friend of the wild game." A naturalist.

DESMOND — Old English. "Kindly protector." Also from the Gaelic for "man from South

Munster." South Munster was a kingdom in Southern Ireland.

DEVERELL — Old Welsh and English. "From the river bank."

DEVIN — Gaelic. "Poet." One blessed with a knowledge of the music of language.

DEVLIN — Gaelic.

DEWEY — Old Welsh. "Cherished."

DE WITT — Old Flemish. "Blond."

DEX — A nickname for Dexter.

DEXTER — Latin. "Skillful."

DICKSON — Old English. "Son of the powerful ruler."

DIEGO — A Spanish form of James.

DIGBY — Old Norse. "From the dike settlement."

DILLON — Gaelic. "Faithful."

DIMITRY — A Russian form of Demetrius.

DINOS — A nickname for Constantinos.

DINSMORE — Celtic. "From the fortified hill."

DION — A nickname for Dennis and Dionysus. Also used as an independent name.

DIONISIO — The Italian and Spanish form of Dennis.

DIONYSUS — Greek. God of wine in Greek mythology. The Greek and German form of Dennis.

DIRK — A nickname for Theodoric.

DIXON — A variation of Dickson.

DMITRI — A Russian form of Demetrius.

DOANE — Celtic. "Black."

DOLAN — Gaelic. "Black hair."

DOM — A nickname for Dominick.

DOMENICO — An Italian form of Domanick.

DOMINGO — A Spanish form of Dominick.

DOMINIC — Latin. "Belonging to the Lord." Appropriate for a child born on a Sunday.

DOMINICK — A variation of Dominic.

DOMINIK — A Slavic form of Dominic.

DOMINIQUE — A French form of Dominic.

DON — Latin. "Lord." Also from the Celtic for "dark." A nickname for Donald.

DONAHUE — Gaelic. "Dark warrior."

DONALD — Celtic. "Mighty ruler," or "dark-haired."

DONALT — A Norwegian form of Donald.

DONAT — A variation of Donato.

DONATELLO — An Italian form of Donato.

DONATI — An Italian form of Donato.

DONATO — Latin. "Gift."

DONNELLY — Celtic. "Brave black man."

DONOHUE — A variation of Donahue.

DONOVAN — Celtic. "Dark warrior."

DOOLEY — Gaelic. "Dark hero."

DORAN — Celtic. "Stranger."

DORIAN — Greek. "Child of the sea." The Dorians were a people in ancient Greece known for their rugged simplicity. Dorian Gray is a famous literary character created by Oscar Wilde.

DORON — Hebrew. "Gift."

DORRAN — A variation of Doran.

DORY — French. "Golden-locked."

DOUG — A nickname for Douglas.

DOUGAL — Gaelic. "Black stranger."

DOUGIE — A nickname for Douglas.

DOUGLAS — Gaelic. "Dweller from the black stream."

DOUGLASS — A variation of Douglas.

DOW — Gaelic. "Raven."

DOYLE — Gaelic. "Dark stranger."

DREW — Old French. "Sturdy." Also from the Old Welsh for "wise," or from the Old German for "vision." In addition, a nickname for Andrew.

DRISCOLL — Celtic. "Interpreter."

DRU — A variation of Drew.

DRUCE — Celtic. "Wise man."

DRURY — Old French. "Darling."

DRYDEN — Old English. "From the dry valley." John Dryden was a 17th-century English poet.

DUANE — A variation of Dwayne.

DUC — Old French. "Leader."

DUD — A nickname for Dudley.

DUDLEY — Old English. "From the meadow of the people."

DUER — Celtic. "Heroic."

DUFF — Gaelic. "Dark-skinned."

DUFFY — A variation of Duff.

DUGALD — A variation of Dugan.

DUKE — A variation of Duc.

DUNC — A nickname for Duncan.

DUNCAN — Gaelic. "Dark-skinned warrior." Macbeth and his wife executed the murder of Duncan, King of Scotland, in 1040.

DUNHAM — Gaelic. "Dark man."

DUNLEY — Old English. "From the hill of the meadow."

DUNMORE — Gaelic. "From the great fortress on the hill."

DUNN — Old English. "One of the dark-skinned."

DUNSTAN — Old English. "From the brown rock quarry."

DUNTON — Old English. "From the town on the hill."

DURAND — Latin. "Enduring."

DURANT — A variation of Durand.

DURANTE — An Italian form of Durand.

DURWARD — Old English. "Keeper of the gate."

DURWIN — Old English. "Beloved friend."

DUSTIN — Old German. "Valiant fighter."

DUTCH — German. "The German."

DWAYNE — Gaelic. "Little dark one."

DWIGHT — Old Dutch. "Blond." A name made famous by Dwight D. Eisenhower.

DYAMI — American Indian. "Eagle."

DYLAN — Old Welsh. "From the sea." Dylan was the Welsh god of the sea. Dylan Thomas was a famous Welsh poet who lived in the first half of the 20th century.

EACHAN — Gaelic. "Little horse." A boy as playful as a pony.

EAMON — The Irish form of Edmund.

EARL — Old English. "Chief and nobleman." Also from the Gaelic for "pledge."

EARLE — A variation of Earl.

EATON — Old English. "From the town on the river bank."

EBEN — Hebrew. "Rock." A nickname for Ebenezer.

EBENEZER — Hebrew. "Rock of help." A 17th-century Puritan name.

EBERHARD — The German form of Everard.

EBNER — A variation of Abner.

ED — A nickname for names beginning with "Ed."

EDAN — Celtic. "Fiery." An appropriate name for a child born under the fire signs of the Zodiac: Aires, Leo, and Sagittarius.

EDBERT — Old English. "Successful."

EDDIE — A nickname for names beginning with "Ed."

EDDY — A variation of Eddie.

EDEL — Old German. "Noble."

EDELMAR — Old English. "Famous."

EDEN — Hebrew. "Delight." Eden was Adam and Eve's garden of delight. A name popularized by the Puritans.

EDGAR — Old English. "Prosperous spearman."

EDGARD — The French form of Edgar.

EDGARDO — The Italian form of Edgar.

EDIK — A Russian form of Edward.

EDLIN — A variation of Edwin.

EDMOND — The French and Dutch form of Edmund.

EDMUND — Old English. "Prosperous protector."

EDMUNDO — The Spanish form of Edmund.

EDOLF — Old English. "Prosperous wolf."

EDOUARD — The French form of Edward.

EDRIC — Old English. "Prosperous ruler."

EDSEL — Old English. "From the rich man's estate."

EDISON — Old English. "Son of the prosperous guardian." Thomas A. Edison was a famous American inventor.

EDSON — A variation of Edison.

EDUARD — The Dutch, German, and Slavic form of Edward.

EDUARDO — The Italian, Portuguese, and Spanish form of Edward.

EDUINO — The Italian and Spanish form of Edwin.

EDVARD — The Scandinavian form of Edward.

EDWALD — Old English. "Prosperous ruler."

EDWARD — Old English. "Prosperous guardian." There have been eight King Edwards of England.

EDWIN — Old English. "Prosperous friend."

EGAN — Gaelic. "Ardent." Also from the Old English for "all-powerful."

EGBERT — Old English. "Sword-bright."

EGERTON — Old English. "From the town on the ridge."

EGIDE — A French form of Giles.

EGIDIO — An Italian form of Giles.

EGIDIUS — The German and Dutch form of Giles.

EGON — A variation of Egan.

EGOR — The Russian form of George.

EHREN — Old German. "Honorable." A well-respected man.

EINAR — Old Norse. "Leader in battle."

EJNAR — A Danish form of Einar.

ELBERT — A variation of Albert.

ELDEN — Old English. "Valley of the elves." Also a variation of Alden.

ELDER — Old English. "Dweller at the elder tree."

ELDIN — A variation of Alden.

ELDON — A variation of Elden.

ELDRED — Old English. "Wise counselor."

ELDRID — A variation of Eldred.

ELDRIDGE — Old German. "Aged counselor."

ELDWIN — A variation of Aldwin.

ELEAZAR — Hebrew. "The Lord hath helped."

ELAZARO — The Spanish form of Eleazar.

ELI — Hebrew. "The highest." A name for Jehovah.

ELIA — The Italian form of Elijah.

ELIAS — The Dutch and German form of Elijah.

ELIE — The French form of Elijah.

ELIHU — Hebrew. "Jehovah is God."

ELIJAH — Hebrew. "Jehovah is God." A 9th-century B.C. prophet of Israel who, according to the Bible, was taken to heaven in a fiery chariot.

ELIOT — A variation of Elliot.

ELISÉE — A French form of Elisha.

ELISEO — The Italian and Spanish form of Elisha.

ELISHA — Hebrew. "God is salvation." A man who possesses great faith in the will of the Lord.

ELKAN — Hebrew. "He belongs to God." A child dedicated to the Almighty.

ELLARD — Old English. "Nobly brave." Also "sacred."

ELLARY — A variation of Ellery.

ELLERY — Old English. "One who lives near the alder tree." A popular fictional detective is Ellery Queen.

ELLIOT — Hebrew and French. "Jehovah is my God." A name re-affirming one's faith.

ELLIOTT — A variation of Elliot.

ELLIS — A variation of Elijah.

ELLISON — Hebrew and English. "Son of Elijah."

ELLWOOD — A variation of El-wood.

ELMAR — A variation of Elmer.

ELMER — Old English. "Of famed dignity."

ELMO — Italian. "Protection."

ELOY — Latin. "Worthy choice." St. Eloy is the patron saint of metallurgists.

ELRAD — Hebrew. "God is the ruler."

ELROY — Latin. "Royal."

ELSDON — Old English. "From the hill of the noble."

ELSON — A variation of Ellison.

ELSTON — Old English. "From the town of the nobleman."

ELSWORTH — Old English. "Dweller at the noble estate."

ELTON — Old English. "From the old estate."

ELVIN — A variation of Elwin.

ELVIS — Old Norse. "All-wise."

ELWIN — Old English. "Friend of the elves." One whose well-being has been placed in the hands of the little people.

ELWYN — A variation of Elwin.

ELY — A variation of Eli.

EMAN — A Slovak form of Emmanuel.

EMANUEL — The German form of Emmanuel.

EMANUELE — The Italian form of Emmanuel.

EMELEN — A variation of Emlen.

EMELIN — A variation of Emlen.

EMÉRI — The French form of Emery.

EMERSON — Old German and English. "The son of the industrious leader."

EMERY — Old German. "Industrious leader."

EMIL — Latin. "Flattering." Also from the Gothic for "industrious."

ÉMILE — The French form of Emil.

EMILIO — The Spanish form of Emil.

EMLEN — Gothic. "Industrious."

EMLYN — A variation of Emlen.

EMMANUEL — Hebrew. "God is with us."

EMMERICH — The German form of Emery.

EMMET — A variation of Emmett.

EMMETT — Old German. "Hard-working and strong."

EMMIT — A variation of Emmett.

EMMOTT — A variation of Emmett.

EMORY — A variation of Emery.

ENEAS — The Spanish form of Aeneas.

ENNE — The French form of Aeneas.

ENNIS — Gaelic. "Choice." Also derived from the Greek for "ninth."

ENOCH — Hebrew. "Dedicated." A popular name among the Puritans.

ENOS — Hebrew. "Mortal." A man conscious of his humanity.

ENRICO — The Italian form of Henry.

ENRIQUE — The Spanish form of Henry.

EPHRAIM — Hebrew. "Fruitful." An Old Testament name revived by the Puritans.

EPHREM — A variation of Ephraim.

ERASME — The French form of Erasmus.

ERASMUS — Greek. "Amiable." One who is worthy of love. A Dutch philospher of the 16th century.

ERASTE — The French form of Erastus.

ERASTUS — Greek. "Beloved."

ERIC — Old Norse. "All-powerful." Eric the Red was a Viking hero who possibly headed the first expedition to North America.

ERICH — The German form of Eric.

ERIK — A Scandinavian form of Eric.

ERLAND — Old English. "From the land of the nobleman." Also means "stranger."

ERLE — A variation of Earl.

ERLING — Old English. "Son of the noble."

ERMANNO — An Italian form of Herman.

ERNALD — Old English. "Mighty eagle."

ERNEST — Old English. "Serious in intent."

ERNESTO — The Italian and Spanish form of Ernest.

ERNESTUS — The Dutch form of Ernest.

ERNST — The German form of Ernest.

ERROL — A variation of Earl.

ERSKINE — Gaelic. "Dweller at the top of the cliff."

ERVIN — A variation of Erwin.

ERWIN — Old English. "Lover of the sea." One who is nourished by the salty spray.

ESDRAS — The French and Spanish form of Ezra.

ESMOND — Old English. "Gracious protector."

ESRA — The German form of Ezra.

ESTE — Italian. "From the east." A man with the promise of the exotic.

ESTES — A variation of Este.

ETHAN — Hebrew. "Strong, firm."

ETHELBERT — Old English. "Of majestic nobility."

ETHELRED — Old English. "Noble counsel."

ETTORE — An Italian form of Hector.

ETU — American Indian. "Sun."

EUGEN — The German form of Eugene.

EUGENE — Greek. "Well-born." Eugene O'Neill was the first great American dramatist.

EUGENIO — The Italian, Portuguese, and Spanish form of Eugene.

EUGENIUS — The Dutch form of Eugene.

EUSTACE — Greek. "Fruitful." Also from the Latin for "stable."

EUSTACHE — The French form of Eustace.

EUSTASIUS — The German form of Eustace.

EUSTAZIO — The Italian form of Eustace.

EUSTIS — A variation of Eustace.

EVALD — A variation of Ewald.

EVAN — Greek. "Well-born." Also from the Old Welsh meaning "youthful."

EVERARD — Old English. "Strong as a boar."

EVERARDO — The Italian form of Everard.

EVERED — A variation of Everard.

EVERET — A variation of Everard.

EVERETT — A variation of Everard.

EVERHART — A Dutch form of Everard.

EVERS — Old English. "Wild boar."

EVRAUD — The French form of Everard.

EWALD — Old English. "With authoritative power."

EWEN — A variation of Evan.

EWING — Old English. "A friend of authority."

EZECHIEL — The Dutch and German form of Ezekiel.

EZECHIELE — An Italian form of Ezekiel.

EZEKIEL — Hebrew. "Strength of the Lord."

EZEQUIEL — The Spanish form of Ezikiel.

EZER — Hebrew. "Strength."

EZHNO — American Indian. "Solitary."

EZRA — A variation of Ezer.

FABER — A German form of Fabian.

FABIAN — Latin. "Bean farmer." A man of the earth.

FABIANO — An Italian form of Fabian.

FABIEN — A French form of Fabian.

FABIO — An Italian form of Fabian.

FABRA — A French form of Fabron.

FABRON — Latin. "Mechanic." The Fabrici were an ancient Roman clan.

FABRONI — The Italian form of Fabron.

FADIL — Arabic. "Generous."

FAGAN — Gaelic. "Fiery."

FAGIN — A variation of Fagan. The leader of the adolescent gang of pickpockets in Dickinson's *Oliver Twist*.

FAIRFAX — Old English. "Fairhaired."

FAIRLEIGH — A variation of Farley.

FAIRLIE — A variation of Farley.

FANE — Old English. "Joy."

FARLEIGH — A variation of Farley.

FARLEY — Old English. "From the meadow of the bulls."

FARMAN — Old English. "Traveler."

FARNALL — A variation of Farnell.

FARNELL — Old English. "From the fern-covered slope."

FARNHAM — Old English. "From the field of fern."

FARNLEY — Old English. "From the meadow of fern."

FAROLD — Old English. "Powerful traveler."

FARQUHAR — Gaelic. "Friendly."

FARR — Old English. "Traveler."

FARRAND — A variation of Ferrand.

FARREL — A variation of Farrell.

FARRELL — Gaelic. "Defender." A man of valor.

FARRIS — A variation of Farrell.

FAUST — "Promising." A child of hope. The hero of Goethe's novel by the same name.

FAUSTO — The Italian form of Faust.

FAXON — Old German. "Long thick hair."

FEDOR — A Russian variation of Theodore.

FEDORE — A Slavic form of Theodore.

FELICE — The Italian form of Felix.

FELIKE — A Russian form of Felix.

FELIX — Latin. "Fortunate."

FELTON — Old English. "From the estate in the field." Residence names such as this are quite common.

FENTON — Old English. "From the marshland farm."

FERD — A nickname for Ferdinand.

FERDINAND — Old German. "World-venturing." A daring seeker of adventure and excitement.

FERGIE — A nickname for Fergus.

FERGUS — Gaelic. "With virile strength."

FERNALD — A variation of Farnald.

FERNANDO — A Spanish form of Ferdinand.

FERRAND — Old French. "Iron-gray hair."

FERRELL — A variation of Farrell.

FERRIS — A Gaelic form of Pierce.

FIDEL — Latin. "Faithful, sincere." Fidel Castro has been the premier of Cuba since 1959.

FIDÈLE — The French form of Fidel.

FIDELIO — An Italian form of Fidel.

FIELDING — Old English. "Dweller in the field."

FIL — A nickname for Filbert, Filipo, or Filmore.

FILBERT — Old English. "Brilliant."

FILBERTE — The French form of Filbert.

FILBERTO — The Italian form of Filbert.

FILIP — A Slovak form of Phillip.

FILIPO — A Spanish form of Phillip.

FILMER — Old English. "Famous."

FILMORE — A variation of Filmer.

FINDLAY — A variation of Finley.

FINDLEY — A variation of Finley.

FINEAS — A Spanish form of Phineas.

FINLAY — A variation of Finley.

FINLEY — Gaelic. "Fair-haired warrior."

FINN — Gaelic. "Fair of face and hair." Also from the Old German for "from Finland."

FIRMAN — Old English. "Fair." Also a variation of Farman.

FISK — A variation of Fiske.

FISKE — Old English. "Fish."

FITCH — Middle English. "Polecat."

FITZ — Old French. "Son."

FITZGERALD — Old English. "Son of the skillful spearman."

FITZHUGH — Old English. "Son of the man renowned for his intelligence."

FITZPATRICK — Old English. "Son of the nobleman."

FLANN — Gaelic. "Red-haired."

FLAVIUS —Latin. "Golden-haired."

FLETCHER — Middle English. "A feather of arrows."

FLINN — A variation of Flynn.

FLINT — Old English. "Stream."

FLOYD — A variation of Lloyd.

FLYNN — Gaelic. "Child of the red-haired man."

FORBES — Gaelic. "Owner of the field."

FORD — Old English. "River crossing."

FOREST — A variation of Forrest.

FORREST — Old French. "One who lives in the woods."

FORRESTER — Middle English. "Protector of the forest."

FORSTER — A variation of Forrest.

FOSS — A nickname for Forrester.

FOSTER — A variation of Forrest.

FRAN — A nickname for Francis.

FRANCESCO — An Italian form of Francis.

FRANCHOT — A French form of Francis.

FRANCIS — Latin. "Free man." Also a name for a "French man." St. Francis of Assisi, the founder of the Franciscan order of monks, is known for his gentleness and ability to communicate with the animals.

FRANCISCO — The Portuguese and Spanish form of Francis.

FRANCISKUS — A German form of Francis.

FRANCKLIN — A variation of Franklin.

FRANÇOIS — A French form of Francis.

FRANK — A nickname for Francis and Franklin.

FRANKIE — A nickname for Francis and Franklin.

FRANKLIN — Middle English. "Free landowner."

FRANKLYN — A variation of Franklin.

FRANS — The Swedish form of Francis.

FRANTS — The Danish form of Francis.

FRANZ — The German form of Francis.

FRASER — A variation of Frazer.

FRASIER — A variation of Frazer.

FRAYNE — Middle English. "Stranger." Also from the Old French for "dweller at the ash tree."

FRAZER — Old French. "Strawberry." Or from the Old English for "curly-haired."

FRAZIER — A variation of Frazer.

FRED — A nickname for Frederick.

FREDDIE — A nickname for Frederick.

FREDDY — A nickname for Frederick.

FREDEK — A Scandinavian and Slovak form of Frederick.

FRÉDÉRIC — The French form of Frederick.

FREDERICH — A German form of Frederick.

FREDERICK — Old German. "Powerful ruler."

FREDERICO — The Spanish form of Frederick.

FREDERIGO — The Italian form of Frederick.

FREDERIK — The Danish and Dutch form of Frederick.

FREDRIC — A variation of Frederick.

FREDRICK — A variation of Frederick.

FREELAND — Old English. "From the free land."

FREEMAN — Old English. "A free man." A man who has no binds.

FREMONT — Old German. "Free guardian."

FREWEN — A variation of Frewin.

FREWIN — Old English. "Freeman of dignity."

FREY — Old English. "Lord." The Scandinavian mythological god of agriculture, peace, and plenty.

FREYNE — A variation of Frayne.

FRICK — Old English. "Darling."

FRIEDRICH — A German form of Frederick.

FRITZ — A German form of Frederick.

FULLER — Middle English. "One who presses clothes."

FULTON — Old English. "Dweller at the fowl pen."

GABE — A nickname for Gabriel.

GABI — A nickname for Gabriel.

GABIE — A nickname for Gabriel.

GABLE — The Old French form of Gabriel.

GABRIEL — Hebrew. "God is my strength." According to the Gospel of St. Luke, Gabriel was the Archangel of the Annunciation.

GABRIELE — An Italian form of Gabriel.

GABRIELLO — An Italian form of Gabriel.

GABY — A nickname for Gabriel.

GADI — A nickname for Gadiel.

GADIEL — Hebrew. "God is my fortune."

GAGE — Old French. "Pledge."

GAINER — A variation of Gaynor.

GAINOR — A variation of Gaynor.

GALEN — Gaelic. "Bright." An intelligent child.

GALENO — A Spanish form of Galen.

GALLAGHER — Gaelic. "Willing helper."

GALLOWAY — Old Gaelic. "Man from the Scottish Highlands."

GALLWAY — A variation of Galloway.

GALTON — Old English. "Man who lived on rented land."

GALVIN — Gaelic. "Sparrow." An energetic man.

GALWAY — A variation of Galloway.

GAMALIEL — Hebrew. "Reward by God." One who is blessed because of his devotion to the work of the Almighty.

GANNON — Gaelic. "Fair-complected." Many Gaelic names refer to hair and complexion colors.

GARALD — The Russian form of Gerald.

GARDELL — Old English. "Watchman." One who can be trusted to care for something precious.

GARDENER — Middle English. "One who tends his garden."

GARDINER — A variation of Gardener.

GARDNER — A variation of Gardener.

GARETH — Welsh. "Gentle." A knight of the Round Table.

GAREY — A variation of Gary.

GARFIELD — Old English. "Battlefield."

GARI — A variation of Gary.

GARLAND — Old English. "From the battlefield." Also from the Old French for "wreath of flowers," a symbol of victory.

GARMAN — Old English. "Spearman." Skillful in battle.

GARMON — A variation of Garmond.

GARMOND — Old English. "One who guards with spears."

GARMUND — A variation of Garmond.

GARNER — Old French. "Army guard."

GARNET — A variation of Garnett. The dark red gem that is the birthstone for January.

GARNETT — Old English. "Active with a spear." Also from the Latin for a "pomegranate seed."

GAROLD — A variation of Gerald.

GARRARD — A variation of Garrett.

GARRAWAY — A variation of Garroway.

GARRET — A variation of Garrett.

GARRETT — Old English. "Mighty warrior."

GARRICK — Old English. "One who governs with a spear."

GARROTT — A variation of Garrett.

GARROWAY — Old English. "Spear warrior."

GARRY — A variation of Gary.

GARTH — Old Norse. "From the protected enclosure."

GARTON — Old English. "Dweller at the enclosed farmstead."

GARVEY — Gaelic. "Peace after great strife."

GARVIN — Old English. "Warrior friend."

GARWIN — A variation of Garvin.

GARWOOD — Old English. "From the forest of fir trees."

GARY — Old English. "Spearman."

GASPAR — Persian. "Treasure." One of the three Magi who followed a star to the stable birthplace of the Christ Child.

GASPARD — The French form of Gaspar.

GASPARO — The Italian form of Gaspar.

GASTON — French. "Man from Gascony," a region of France.

GAVAN — A variation of Gavin.

GAVEN — A variation of Gavin.

GAVIN — Old Welsh. "From the hawk field."

GAVRIL — Russian. "Man of God."

GAWAIN — A variation of Gavin. Knight of the Round Table.

GAWEN — A variation of Gavin.

GAYLER — A variation of Gaylord.

GAYLOR — A variation of Gaylord.

GAYLORD — Old French. "Vivacious." A child characterized by enthusiasm for life.

GAYNER — A variation of Gaynor.

GAYNOR — Gaelic. "Son of the fair-haired one."

GEARALT — An Irish form of Gerald.

GEARARD — An Irish form of Gerald.

GEAREY — A variation of Geary.

GEARY — Middle English. "Flexible." One who is adaptable to meeting new situations.

GEOFFREY — A variation of Godfrey.

GEORAS — The Scottish form of George.

GEORG — A German and Scandinavian form of George.

GEORGE — Latin. "Tiller of the soil." A name that can be used for boys born under the earth signs of the Zodiac. St. George, a Roman soldier martyred in the early 4th century, served as the symbol of chivalry in medieval times. He is also the patron saint of England.

GEORGES — A French form of George.

GEORGIE — A nickname for George.

GEORGY — The Russian form of George. Also a nickname for George.

GEPHANIA — Hebrew. "Wine," or "vineyard of the Lord."

GERAINT — Welsh. "Old." Possibly a child wise beyond his years.

GERALD — Old German. "Strong with a spear."

GÉRALD — A French form of Gerald.

GERARD — Old English. "Brave with a spear."

GERARDO — An Italian and Spanish form of Gerard.

GÉRAUD — A French form of Gerard.

GEREMIA — The Italian form of Jeremy.

GERHARD — A German form of Gerard.

GEROME — A variation of Gersham.

GERRIE — A nickname for Gerard.

GERRY — A nickname for Gerard or Gerald.

GERSHAM — Hebrew. "Exiled." A frequent plight of the Jewish people throughout their history.

GERSHOM — A variation of Gersham.

GERVASE — Old German. "Armor bearer."

GIACOBO — An Italian form of Jacob.

GIACOMO — An Italian form of Jacob.

GIAMO — An Italian form of James.

GIB — A nickname for Gibson or Gilbert.

GIBSON — Old English. "Son of the famed as a promise."

GIDEON — Hebrew. "One who fells lumber." A Puritan virtue name.

GIFF — A nickname for Gifford.

GIFFARD — A variation of Gifford.

GIFFERD — A variation of Gifford.

GIFFORD — Old English. "Magnificent gift." A child to fulfill his parents' hopes.

GIFFY — A nickname for Gifford.

GIL — A nickname for names beginning with "Gil."

GILAD — Arabic. "Camel hump." A name that connotes height.

GILBERT — Old English. "A man famed for his promise."

GILBERTO — The Italian and Spanish form of Gilbert.

GILBEY — A variation of Gilby.

GILBURT — A variation of Gilbert.

GILBY — Old Norse. "Home of the earnest one."

GILCHRIST — Gaelic. "Servant of Christ."

GILES — Greek. "Shield bearer."

GILFORD — Old English. "From the ford of the earnest one."

GILFRED — Old English. "Pledge of peace."

GILIBEIRT — The Irish form of Gilbert.

GILLEABART — The Scottish form of Gilbert.

GILLEASBUIG — The Scottish form of Archibald.

GILLETT — Old French. "Little one famed for his earnestness."

GILLETTE — A variation of Gillett.

GILLMORE — A variation of Gilmore.

GILMER — Old English. "Famous hostage."

GILMORE — Gaelic. "Servant of Mary the Virgin Mother."

GILMOUR — A variation of Gilmore.

GILROY — Gaelic and Latin. "Servant of the king." Also from the Gaelic for "servant of the red-haired lord."

GIORDANO — The Italian form of Jordan.

GIORGIO — The Italian form of George.

GIOVANNI — The Italian form of John.

GIRALDO — An Italian form of Gerald.

GIRAUD — A French form of Gerald.

GIRVAN — A variation of Girvin.

GIRVEN — A variation of Girvin.

GIRVIN — Gaelic. "Tempestuous." A man to be handled gently.

GIULIO — The Italian form of Julius.

GIUSEPPE — An Italian form of Joseph.

GIUSTINO — The Italian form of Justine.

GIUSTO — The Italian form of Justis.

GIVON — Hebrew. "Heights."

GLADWIN — Old English. "Cheerful friend." A good-natured child.

GLANVILLE — Old French. "From the farmstead on the land of oak trees."

GLEN — A variation of Glenn.

GLENDON — Gaelic. "From the dark valley."

GLENN — Gaelic. "Dweller in a valley." A residence name.

GLYNN — A variation of Glen.

GODARD — A variation of Goddard.

GODART — A variation of Goddard.

GODDARD — Old German. "Divinely firm."

GODDART — A variation of Goddard.

GODFREY — Old German. "Peace of God." A man with a tranquil soul.

GODOFREDO — A Spanish form of Godfrey.

GODWIN — Old English. "Friend of God."

GOFFREDO — An Italian form of Godfrey.

GOLDING — Old English. "Son of the golden-haired man."

GOLDWIN — Old English. "Golden friend."

GOODWIN — A variation of Godwin.

GORAN — A Swedish form of George.

GORDAN — A variation of Gordon.

GORDEN — A variation of Gordon.

GORDIE — A nickname for Gordon.

GORDON — Old English. "From the three-cornered hill."

GORDY — A nickname for Gordon.

GOSHEVIN — American Indian. "Great leaper."

GOTHART — A German form of Goddard.

GOTTFRIED — The Dutch and German form of Godfrey.

GOUVERNEUR — French. "Ruler."

GOWER — Old Welsh. "Pure." A man of virtue.

GOZAL — Hebrew. "Bird."

GRADY — Gaelic. "Famous."

GRAHAM — Old English. "From the gray estate."

GRANGER — Old English. "Farmer." A man who entrusts his life to the elements.

GRANT — Latin. "Great."

GRANTHAM — Old English. "From the great meadow."

GRANTLAND — Old English. "From the large plain."

GRANTLEY — A variation of Grantland.

GRANVILLE — Old French. "From the large town."

GRAYSON — Old English. "Son of the local bailiff." The bailiff was the magistrate of the medieval town.

GREG — A nickname for Gregory.

GREGG — A nickname for Gregory.

GREGOOR — A Dutch form of Gregory.

GREGOR — A German, Scandinavian, and Slovak form of Gregory.

GREGORIO — The Italian, Portuguese, and Spanish form of Gregory.

GREGORIUS — A German form of Gregory.

GREGORY — Greek. "Watchman."

GRENVILLE — A variation of Granville.

GRESHAM — Old English. "From the grassland."

GRIFFITH — Old Welsh. "Lord." Also from the Old Welsh for "ruddy."

GRISWOLD — Old German. "From the gray forest."

GROMAN — Gaelic. "Blue-eyed child."

GROSVENOR — French and Latin. "A mighty hunter.

GROVER — Old English. "From the grove of trees."

GUIDO — The German, Italian, Spanish, and Swedish form of Guy.

GUILBERT — A French form of Gwynn.

GUNNAR — Old Norse. "Battle army."

GUNNER — A variation of Gunnar.

GUNTER — A variation of Gunnar.

GUNTHER — A variation of Gunnar.

GUR — Hebrew. "Lion cub."

GURION — Hebrew. "Lion." The symbol of the zodiacal sign Leo.

GUS — A nickname for Gustave.

GUSSIE — A nickname for Gustave.

GUSTAF — A Swedish form of Gustave.

GUSTAV — A German form of Gustave.

GUSTAVE — Old Norse. "Staff of the Goths." The Goths were an ancient Germanic tribe.

HALBERT — Old English. "Bright stone."

HALDAN — Old Norse. "Half-Dane." A half-Danish and half-English adventurer of the 6th century who invaded England.

HALE — Old English. "Hero." Also meaning "one who resides at the hall." Nathan Hale was an American Revolutionary hero.

HALEY — Gaelic. "Resourceful."

HALFDAN — A variation of Haldan.

HALFORD — Old English. "From the manor near the ford."

HALL — Old English. "From the manor."

HALLAM — Old English. "From the hillside."

HALLEY — Old English. "From the meadow near the manor."

HALSEY — Old English. "From Hal's island."

HALSTEAD — Old English. "From the manor state."

HALSTED — A variation of Halstead.

HALTON — Old English. "From the estate on the hillside."

HALWARD — Old English. "Guardian of the manor."

HAMAL — Arabic. "Lamb." A gentle child.

HAMILTON — Old English. "From the beautiful estate."

HAMISH — A Scottish form of James.

HAMLET — Old French and German. "Little home." Child who is a source of comfort and solace.

HAMLIN — Old French and German. "Lover of the home."

HAMO — Old German. "House."

HAMON — A variation of Hamo.

HANAN — A Hebrew form of John.

HANFORD — Old English. "From the high ford."

HANK — A nickname for Henry.

HANLEY — Old English. "From the high meadow."

HANS — A Scandinavian form of John.

HANSEL — A German form of Hans.

HARALD — The Scandinavian form of Harold.

HARBERT — A variation of Herbert.

HARCOURT — Old French. "From the fortified dwelling."

HARDEE — A variation of Hardy.

HARDEN — Old English. "From the valley of the hares."

HARDEY — A variation of Hardy.

HARDIE — A variation of Hardy.

HARDY — Old German. "Strong and daring."

HARFORD — Old English. "From the river crossing of the hares," or "ford of the army."

HARGRAVE — A variation of Hargrove.

HARGROVE — Old English. "From the grove of the hare."

HARI — Hindu. "Amber-colored." Another name for the great god Vishnu.

HARLAN — Old English. "From the land of the hare," or "from the territory of the army."

HARLAND — A variation of Harlan.

HARLEY — Old English. "From the meadow of the hare."

HARLOW — Old English. "Dweller at the fortified hill."

HARMAN — A variation of Herman.

HARMON — A variation of Herman.

HAROLD — Old Norse. "Powerful in battle."

HARPER — Old English. "Harp player." One who plays the music of the angels.

HARRIS — Old English. "Son of the army man."

HARRISON — A variation of Harris.

HARRY — Old English. "Army man." Also a nickname for Harold.

HART — Old English. "Deer."

HARTFORD — Old English. "From the river crossing of the deer."

HARTLEY — Old English. "From the pasture of the deer."

HARTMAN — Old English. "Keeper of the deer."

HARTWELL — Old English. "From the spring of the deer."

HARTWOOD — Old English. "Dweller from the forest of the deer."

HARV — A nickname for Harvey.

HARVEY — Old French. "Worthy of battle."

HASAD — Turkish. "Harvest." Child of his parents' cultivation.

HASKEL — Hebrew. "Understanding."

HASKELL — A variation of Haskel.

HASLETT — Old English. "From the headland of the hazel tree."

HASSAN — Arabic. "Handsome."

HASTINGS — Old English. "Son of the stern man."

HAVEN — Old English. "Refuge." A child who is a source of comfort.

HAWLEY — Old English. "From the hedged meadow."

HAYDEN — Old English. "From the hedged hill."

HAYDON — A variation of Hayden.

HAYES — Old English. "From the hedged place."

HAYWARD — Old English. "Guardian of the hedged enclosed area."

HAYWOOD — Old English. "From the hedged forest."

HAZLETT — A variation of Haslett.

HEARN — A variation of Ahern.

HEARST — A variation of Hurst.

HEATH — Middle English. "From the wasteland."

HEATHCLIFF — Middle English. "From the cliff of the wasteland." Heathcliff was the lord of the manor in Emily Brontë's novel *Wuthering Heights.*

HECTOR — Greek. "Steadfast." In Greek history, Hector was reputed to be the bravest of the Trojan warriors. His story is told in Homer's *Iliad.*

HEINDRICK — A variation of Henry.

HEINRICH — A German variation of Henry.

HEINRIK — A Scandinavian form of Henry.

HENRI — A variation of Henry.

HENRY — Old German. "Ruler of an estate," or an "heir." A favored name among the royal families of England, France, and Germany.

HERANE — A variation of Ahern.

HERB — A nickname for Herbert.

HERBERT — Old German. "Glorious soldier."

HERCULES — Greek. "Glorious gift of Hera." Hera was the Queen of Mount Olympus. Her son Heracles was the famous mythological hero renowned for his Twelve Labors.

HEREWARD — Old English. "Army protection."

HERIBERTO — The Spanish form of Herbert.

HERMAN — Old German. "Warrior."

HERMANN — A Danish and German form of Herman.

HERNALDO — A Spanish form of Henry.

HERNANDO — A Spanish form of Ferdinand.

HEROLD — A variation of Harold.

HERRICK — Old German. "Army commander."

HERSCH — A variation of Hersh.

HERSH — Hebrew. "Deer." A man swift of body and mind.

HERVEY — A variation of Harvey.

HERWIN — Old German. "Friend of war." One who enjoys a good battle.

HEWETT — Old French and German. "Little intelligent one."

HEWITT — A variation of Hewett.

HEYWOOD — A variation of Haywood.

HI — A nickname for Hiatt or Hiram.

HIATT — A variation of Hyatt.

HILAIRE — The French form of Hilary.

HILARIO — The Spanish and Portuguese form of Hilary.

HILARIUS — The Dutch, German, and Scandinavian form of Hilary.

HILARY — Latin. "Cheerful."

HILDEBRAND — Old German. "Sword of battle."

HILLIARD — Old German. "Courageous in battle." One who is most serious about his role as a warrior.

HILLIER — A variation of Hilliard.

HILTON — Old English. "From the estate on the hill." One of the many residence names.

HIPPOLYTUS — Greek. "Running horse." In ancient times, the horse was the symbol of sacredness. In mythology, Hippolytus was wrongly accused of seducing his stepmother Phaedra, and his death was arranged by his father Theseus. His story is told in Euripides' *Hippolytus.*

HIRAM — Hebrew. "Noble-born." A Puritan virtue name.

HIROSHI — Japanese. "Charitable."

HIRSCH — A variation of Hersh.

HO — Chinese. "Good."

HOBART — A variation of Hubert.

HOGAN — Gaelic. "Youth." A man whose mind is always open to new ideas.

HOLBROOK — Old English. "From the brook in the dale."

HOLCOMB — Old English. "From the deep valley."

HOLDEN — Old English. "From the hollow in the valley."

HOLLIS — Old English. "From the grove of holly trees." Also from the Old Norse for "man from the island."

HOLMAN — Middle English. "From the island in the river."

HOLMES — Middle English. "Son of the man from the island in the river."

HOLT — Old English. "From the forest."

HOMER — Greek. "A pledge or security." The blind Greek poet of the 9th century B.C. who was the author of the *Iliad* and the *Odyssey.*

HOMÈRE — The French form of Homer.

HOMERUS — The German form of Homer.

HORACE — Latin. "Keeper of the hours."

HORACIO — The Spanish and Portuguese form of Horace.

HORATIO — A variation of Horace.

HORATIUS — A German form of Horace.

HORTON — Old English. "From the gray estate."

HOSEA — Hebrew. "Salvation."

HOUGHTON — Old English. "From the manor on the cliff."

HOWARD — Old English. "Heart protection."

HOWE — Old German. "Prominent." Also from the Middle English for "hill."

HOWIE — A nickname for Howard.

HOWLAND — Old English. "From the hilly land."

HUBE — A nickname for Hubert.

HUBERT — Old German. "Bright intelligence."

HUBERTO — The Spanish form of Hubert.

HUDSON — Old English. "Son of the hooded one."

HUEY — A nickname for Hugh.

HUGH — Old English. "Intelligent." A man who is well known for his keen mind.

HUGHIE — A nickname for Hugh.

HUGHY — A nickname for Hugh.

HUGIBERT — A German form of Hubert.

HUGO — The Dutch, German, Spanish, and Scandinavian form of Hugh.

HUGUES — The French form of Hugh.

HULBARD — A variation of Hubert.

HULBERT — Old German. "Outstandingly graceful." A well-coordinated young man.

HULBURD — A variation of Hubert.

HULBURT — A variation of Hubert.

HUMBERT — Old German. "Very bright" or "brilliant Hun." The Huns were a group of Mongolian horsemen whose sweep of Europe was aborted by the Romans and the Goths in 451.

HUMFREY — A variation of Humphrey.

HUMFRID — A Swedish form of Humphrey.

HUMFRIED — The Dutch and German form of Humphrey.

HUMP — A nickname for Humphrey.

HUMPHREY — Old German. "Champion of the peace." A brilliant pacifist.

HUNDREDO — The Spanish form of Humphrey.

HUNT — A variation of Hunter.

HUNTER — Old English. "A huntsman." In ancient times, hunting was a much honored profession.

HUNTINGDON — Old English. "From the hill of the hunter."

HUNTINGTON — Old English. "From the manor of the hunter."

HUNTLEY — Old English. "From the meadow of the hunter."

HURLEY — Gaelic. "Sea-tide." A child of Neptune, the Roman god of the sea.

HURST — Middle English. "Dweller in the forest."

HUSSEIN — Arabic. "Little handsome one."

HUTTON — Old English. "From the dwelling on the jutting ledge."

HUXFORD — Old English. "From the river crossing of Hugh."

HUXLEY — Old English. "From Hugh's meadow."

HYATT — Old English. "From the high gate."

HYDE — Old English. "From the hide." A hide was a specified piece of land in ancient England.

HYMAN — Hebrew. "Life." A child with a zest for living.

IAN — The Scottish form of John.

IBRAHIM — The Arabic form of Abraham.

ICHABOD — Hebrew. "The glory has departed."

IDEN — Old English. "Successful."

IDRIS — Old Welsh. "Fiery lord." A man to approach cautiously.

IFOR — A variation of Ivor.

IGASHO — American Indian. "Wanderer."

IGNACE — A French form of Ignatius.

IGNACIO — A Spanish form of Ignatius.

IGNATIUS — Latin. "Ardent, fiery."

IGNAZ — The German form of Ignatius.

IKE — A nickname for Isaac or Dwight.

ILARIO — An Italian form of Hilary.

ILLIAS — A Greek form of Elias.

IMMANUEL — A variation of Emanuel.

INGAR — A variation of Inger.

INGELBERT — Old German. "Divinely brilliant."

INGEMAR — Old Norse. "Famous son."

INGER — Old Norse. "A son's army."

INGRAM — Old Norse. "The raven of Ing." Ing was the god of fertility and crops in Norse mythology.

INNESS — A variation of Innis.

INNIS — Gaelic. "From the island."

IOKIM — The Russian form of Joakim.

IOSEP — The Irish form of Joseph.

IRA — Hebrew. "Descendant."

IRVIN — A variation of Irving.

IRVINE — A variation of Irving.

IRVING — Old Welsh. "From the white river." Also from the Old English for "friend of the sea."

IRWIN — A variation of Irving.

ISAAC — Hebrew. "He who laughs." A child of mirth. The son of the Hebrew patriach Abraham who was saved from being sacrificed by his father through God's intervention.

ISAAK — A German form of Isaac.

ISACCO — The Italian form of Isaac.

ISADORE — A variation of Isodore.

ISAIAH — Hebrew. "God is my salvation." A name signifying a reaffirmation of one's faith. A 17th-century Puritan name.

ISHAM — Old English. "From the estate of the iron-willed."

ISHMAEL — Hebrew. "God will laugh."

ISIDOR — A German form of Isidore.

ISIDORE — Greek. "Gift of Isis." Isis was the Eygptian goddess of the moon.

ISIDORO — The Italian form of Isidore.

ISIDRO — The Spanish form of Isidore.

ISRAEL — Hebrew. "Soldier of the Lord." The name of the twelve Hebrew tribes.

ISSY — A nickname for Isidore.

IVAN — A Russian form of John.

IVAR — Old Norse. "Archer." An appropriate name for a Sagittarian male child.

IVEN — Old French. "Young archer."

IVER — A variation of Ivar.

IVES — Old English. "Son of the archer."

IVOR — Old Welsh. "Lord."

IZAAK — A variation of Isaac.

IZZIE — A nickname for Isaac.

JACK — A nickname for Jacob or John.

JACKSON — Old English. "Son of Jack."

JACOB — Hebrew. "The supplanter." Jacob tricked his older brother Esau out of his birthright and the blessing of his father Isaac. Jacob went on to father the twelve men who founded the twelve tribes of Israel.

JACOBO — A Spanish form of Jacob.

JACQUES — The French form of Jacob.

JAGGER — Old English. "A teamster."

JAIME — A Spanish form of James.

JAMES — Old Spanish. "The supplanter."

JAMIE — A nickname for James.

JAMIL — Arabic. "Handsome."

JAN — A Slavic form of John.

JANOS — A Slavic form of John.

JARED — Hebrew. "Descendant."

JARMAN — Old German. "A German."

JARVIS — Old German. "Keen as a spear."

JASON — Greek. "Healer." The story of the heroic deeds of Jason in pursuit of the Golden Fleece is a well-known legend of Greek mythology.

JASPER — Old French. "Jasper stone."

JAVIER — Spanish. "Owner of the new house."

JAY — Old French. "Blue jay." Also from the Old German meaning "lively."

JAYME — A Spanish form of James.

JEAN — The French form of John. A most popular name in France.

JED — Arabic. "The hand." Also a nickname for Jedidiah.

JEDIDIAH — Hebrew. "Beloved of the Lord."

JEFF — A nickname for Jeffrey.

JEFFEREY — A variation of Jeffrey.

JEFFERSON — Old English. "Son of Jeffrey."

JEFFIE — A nickname for Jeffrey.

JEFFREY — A variation of Godfrey.

JENS — A Scandinavian form of John.

JÉRÉME — The French form of Jeremy.

JEREMIAH — Hebrew. "Appointed by Jehovah." A Hebrew prophet of the 6th century B.C.

JEREMIAS — The Spanish form of Jeremy.

JEREMY — A variation of Jeremiah.

JERMAN — A variation of Jarman.

JEROME — Greek. "Holy name."

JERRIE — A nickname for Jeremiah, Jerome, or Gerald.

JERROLD — A variation of Gerald.

JERROME — A variation of Jerome.

JERRY — A nickname for Jerome or Gerald.

JESPER — A Swedish form of Jasper.

JESS — A variation of Jesse.

JESSE — Hebrew. "Wealth of God." A popular name among the 17th-century Puritans.

JESSIE — A nickname for Jesse.

JETHRO — Hebrew. "Excellence."

JIN — Chinese. "Gold."

JO — A nickname for Joseph.

JOACHIM — Hebrew. "God will establish."

JOB — Hebrew. "Persecuted." A biblical character known for his patience.

JOCELYN — Latin. "Gay."

JOE — A nickname for Joseph.

JOEY — A nickname for Joseph.

JOHAN — A Scandinavian form of John.

JOHANN — A German form of John.

JOHANNES — A German form of John.

JOHN — Hebrew. "God is gracious."

JOHNSON — Old English. "Son of John."

JOHNSTON — A Scottish form of Johnson.

JON — A nickname for John or Jonathan. Also used as an independent name.

JONAH — Hebrew. "Dove." A symbol of peace in many cultures The well-known story of Jonah and the whale is in the Old Testament.

JONAS — A variation of Jonah.

JONATHAN — Hebrew. "Gift of the Lord." The son of Saul and the friend of David in the Bible.

JONE — The Welsh form of John.

JORDAN — Hebrew. "The descender."

JORGE — The Spanish form of George.

JORGEN — A Scandinavian form of George.

JOSÉ — The Spanish form of Joseph.

JOSEPH — Hebrew. "He shall add." St. Joseph was the husband of Mary.

JOSH — A nickname for Joshua.

JOSHUA — Hebrew. "The Lord is salvation." According to the Old Testament, Joshua led the Israelites into the Holy Land.

JOSIAH — Hebrew. "May the Lord heal."

JOURDAIN — A French form of Jordon.

JUAN — The Spanish form of John.

JUDAS — A variation of Judd.

JUDD — Hebrew. "Praised."

JUDE — A variation of Judd.

JULE — A nickname for Julius.

JULES — A French form of Julius.

JULIAN — A form of Julius.

JULIO — The Spanish form of Julius.

JULIUS — Greek. "Youthful, downy-bearded."

JUSTE — The French form of Justis.

JUSTIN — Latin. "Just, upright." A man reputed for his honesty.

JUSTINO — The Spanish form of Justin.

JUSTIS — Old French. "Justice."

JUSTO — The Spanish form of Justis.

JUSTUS — A German form of Justis.

KADIN — Arabic. "Friend."

KAIN — A variation of Kane.

KAINE — A variation of Kane.

KAISER — A German form of Caesar.

KALB — An arabic form of Caleb.

KALLE — A Scandinavian form of Karl.

KAMI — Hindu. "Loving." Kama is the Hindu god of love.

KANE — Gaelic. "Fair." Also means "warlike" and "tribute."

KANIEL — Hebrew. "Reed."

KAREL — A Slavic form of Charles.

KARIM — Arabic. "Generous."

KARL — A German form of Charles.

KARNEY — A variation of Carney.

KAROLY — A Slavic form of Charles.

KARR — A variation of Carr.

KARSTEN — A Slavic form of Charles.

KASIMIR — A German and Slavic form of Casimir.

KASPAR — The German form of Gaspar.

KAVAN — A variation of Cavan.

KAYNE — A variation of Kane.

KEAN — A variation of Keane.

KEANE — Old English. "Sharp." Also from the Gaelic for "handsome."

KEARNEY — A variation of Carney.

KEARY — A form of Kerry.

KEDAR — Arabic. "Powerful." Also from the Hindu for "mountain lord."

KEEFE — Gaelic. "Lovable and handsome." A cherished child.

KEEGAN — Gaelic. "Little fiery one."

KEELAN — Gaelic. "Little and slender."

KEEN — A variation of Keane.

KEENAN — Gaelic. "Little ancient one."

KEGAN — A variation of Keegan.

KEIR — Gaelic. "Dark complexion."

KEITH — Old Welsh. "From the forest." Also from the Gaelic for "place of battle."

KELBY — Old Norse. "From the farm by the springs."

KELCY — A variation of Kelsey.

KELL — Old Norse. "From the spring."

KELLER — Gaelic. "Little companion."

KELSEY — Old Norse. "Dweller by the water."

KELVAN — A variation of Kelvin.

KELVEN — A variation of Kelvin.

KELVIN — Gaelic. "From the narrow river."

KELWIN — A variation of Kelvin.

KEMP — Middle English. "Champion."

KEN — A nickname for names beginning with "Ken."

KENDAL — A variation of Kendall.

KENDALL — Old English. "From the bright valley."

KENDELL — A variation of Kendall.

KENDRICK — Gaelic. "Son of Henry." Also from the Old English for "princely ruler."

KENELM — Old English. "Brave helmet."

KENLEY — Old English. "Dweller at the king's meadow."

KENN — Old Welsh. "Clear water." An appropriate name for a child born under the water signs of the Zodiac: Cancer, Scorpio, and Pisces.

KENNEDY — Gaelic. "Helmeted chief."

KENNETH — Gaelic. "Handsome." Also from the Old English for the "oath of the king."

KENNIE — A nickname for names beginning with "Ken."

KENNY — A nickname for names beginning with "Ken."

KENRIC — Old English. "Bold and princely."

KENRICK — A variation of Kenric.

KENT — Old Welsh. "White and bright."

KENTON — Old English. "From the estate of the king."

KENWARD — Old English. "Bold guardian of the king."

KENWAY — Old English. "Bold warrior of the king."

KENYON — Gaelic. "Blond-haired."

KERBY — A variation of Kirby.

KEREL — African. "Youth."

KERMIT — Gaelic. "Free."

KERN — Gaelic. "Dark." A Child with Celtic coal-black hair.

KERR — Gaelic. "Dark" and "spear." Also a variation of Carr.

KERRY — Gaelic. "Son of the dark one."

KERWEN — A variation of Kerwin.

KERWIN — Gaelic. "Little dark-skinned one."

KESTER — Latin. "From the camp of the Roman army." Also a nickname for Christopher.

KEY — Gaelic. "Son of the fiery one."

KHALIL — Arabic. "Friend."

KIENAN — A variation of Keenan.

KIERNAN — Gaelic. "Dark-skinned." Names denoting coloring were common among the early Irish.

KILBY — A variation of Kelby.

KILIAN — A variation of Killian.

KILLIAN — Gaelic. "Warlike."

KIMBALL — Old English. "Bold warrior."

KIMBELL — A variation of Kimball.

KIMBLE — A variation of Kimball.

KING — Old English. "Ruler."

KINGDON — Old English. "From the hill of the king."

KINGSLEY — Old English. "From the meadow of the king."

KINGSTON — Old English. "From the estate of the king."

KINGSWELL — Old English. "Dweller at the well of the king."

KINNARD — Gaelic. "From the top of the hill."

KINNELL — Gaelic. "Dweller at the head of the cliff."

KINSEY — Old English. "Victorious prince."

KIPP — Old English. "Dweller at the pointed hill."

KIRBY — Old Norse. "From the village of the church."

KIRK — Old Norse. "Dweller by the church." Also Scottish for "the church."

KIRKWOOD — Old English. "From the woodland of the church."

KIRWIN — A variation of Kerwin.

KIT — A nickname for Christopher.

KLEMENS — A German form of Clement.

KLEMENT — A Hungarian form of Clement.

KLIMENT — A Russian form of Clement.

KNIGHT — Middle English. In medieval times, knights were the soldiers of the king, brave, chivalrous, and daring.

KNOX — Old English. "From the hills."

KNUD — Danish. "Kind."

KNUT — A nickname for Canute.

KOENRAAD — A dutch form of Conrad.

KONRAD — A German form of Conrad.

KONSTANDINOS — A Greek form of Constantine.

KORT — A German form of Conrad.

KOSTAS — A nickname for Konstandinos.

KRIPSIN — A Slavic form of Cripin.

KRISTIAN — A Scandinavian form of Christian.

KRISTO — A nickname for Christoforos.

KURT — A German form of Conrad.

KWAME — African. "Child born on Sunday."

KWSIND — American Indian. "Strongman." A man strong in both mind and body.

KYLE — Gaelic. "From the strait."

KYNE — Old English. "Princely."

LANCE — A nickname for Lancelot or Lawrence. Also used as an independent name.

LANCELOT — Old French. "Attendant." According to the legends of King Arthur, Sir Lancelot failed in his mission to recover the Holy Grail because of his love for Arthur's queen, Guinevere.

LANDER — Old French. "From the grassy plain."

LANDERS — A variation of Lander.

LANDIS — A variation of Lander.

LANDON — A variation of Langdon.

LANDRY — Old English. "Lord of the manor."

LANE — Old English. "From the narrow road."

LANG — Old Norse. "Tall men."

LANGDON — Old English. "From the long hill."

LANGLEY — Old English. "From the long meadow."

LANGSTON — Old English. "From the tall man's estate."

LANGUNDO — American Indian. "Peaceful." A tranquil soul.

LANGWORTH — Old English. "From the long enclosed area."

LARRY — A nickname for Lawrence.

LARS — A Scandinavian form of Lawrence.

LARSON — Scandinavian. "Son of Lars."

LATHAM — Old Norse. "From the barns."

LATHROP — Old English. "From the barns on the estate."

LATIMER — Middle English. "Interpreter of Latin."

LAUNCELOT — A variation of Lancelot.

LAURENCE — A variation of Lawrence.

LAURENS — The Dutch form of Lawrence.

LAURENT — The French form of Lawrence.

LAURIE — A nickname for Lawrence.

LAURITZ — A Danish form of Lawrence.

LAVI — Hebrew. "Lion."

LAWFORD — Old English. "From the ford on a hill."

LAWLER — Gaelic. "Softspoken." An even-tempered lad.

LAWLEY — Old English. "From the meadow on the hill."

LAWRENCE — Latin. "Laurel-crowned." The laurel wreath was a symbol of victory in ancient Greece.

LAWRY — A nickname for Lawrence.

LAWSON — Old English. "Son of the victorious one."

LAWTON — Old English. "From the estate on the hill."

LAZARE — The French form of Lazarus.

LAZARO — The Italian and Spanish form of Lazarus.

LAZARUS — Hebrew. "God will help." An affirmation of faith.

LEAL — Old French and Latin. "Faithful." A loyal friend.

LEANDER — Greek. "Lion-like." A man of courage.

LEANDRE — A French form of Leander.

LEANDRO — The Italian and Spanish form of Leander.

LEAROYD — Old French. "From the empty meadow."

LEDYARD — Old French. "Guardian of the nation."

LEE — Latin. "Lion." Also from the Old English for "from the meadow." or Gaelic meaning "poetic."

LEGGETT — Old French. "Delegate."

LEGGITT — A variation of Leggett.

LEICESTER — A variation of Lester.

LEIF — Old Norse. "Beloved." A child of adoration.

LEIGH — A variation of Lee.

LEIGHTON — Old English. "From the meadow farm."

LEITH — Gaelic. "Wide." The river Leith is in Scotland.

LELAND — Old English. "From the meadowland."

LEM — A nickname for Lemuel.

LEMUEL — Hebrew. "Consecrated to God." A child dedicated to God.

LEN — A nickname for Leonard.

LENARD — A variation of Leonard.

LENCI — A Slavic form of Lawrence.

LENNIE — A nickname for Leonard.

LENNON — Gaelic. "Little cape." A protective child.

LENNOX — Gaelic. "From the field of elm trees."

LENNY — A nickname for Leonard.

LEO — Latin. "Lion." The lion in ancient times was a symbol of pride. A name chosen by thirteen Popes.

LEON — French and Latin. "Lion-like."

LEONARD — Old French. "Brave as a lion."

LEONARDO — An Italian and Spanish form of Leonard.

LEONERD — A variation of Leonard.

LEONHARD — The German form of Leonard.

LEOPOLD — Old German. "Patriot." A man of the people.

LEOPOLDO — The Italian and Spanish form of Leonard.

LEROY — Old French and Latin. "King." A man of power and influence.

LES — A nickname for Lester.

LESTER — Latin. "From the camp of the legion."

LEUPOLD — A German form of Leopold.

LEV — The Russian form of Leo. Also a nickname for Leverett.

LEVERETT — Old French. "Young rabbit." An active energetic youth.

LEVI — Hebrew. "United." A man at one with God.

LEW — A nickname for Lewis.

LEWIS — A variation of Louis.

LIAM — An Irish form of William.

LIANG — Chinese. "God."

LIEF — A variation of Leif.

LIN — A variation of Lynn.

LINC — A nickname for Lincoln.

LINCOLN — Old English. "From the settlement by the pool." Abraham Lincoln, the great American statesman.

LIND — Old English. "Dweller at the linden tree."

LINDBERGH — Old German. "From the hill of the linden tree." Charles A. Lindbergh made the first transatlantic flight.

LINDELL — Old English. "From the valley of the linden trees."

LINDEN — A variation of Lind.

LINDLEY — Old English. "From the meadow of the linden trees."

LINDON — A variation of Lyndon.

LINFORD — Old English. "From the river crossing of the linden trees."

LINK — Old English. "From the ridge."

LINLEY — Old English. "From the field of flax."

LINN — A variation of Lynn.

LINTON — Old English. "From the enclosed field of flax."

LINUS — Greek. "Flax-colored hair." A blond lad.

LIONEL — Old French. "Lion cub." A young man of courage.

LIONELLO — The Italian and Portuguese form of Lionel.

LISLE — A variation of Lyle.

LITTON — Old English. "From the estate on the hill."

LIU — African. "Voice."

LIVINGSTON — Old English. "From the place of the beloved son."

LLEWELLYN — Old Welsh. "Lion-like."

LLOYD — Old Welsh. "Gray-haired."

LLYWELLYN — A variation of Llewellyn.

LOCK — A variation of Locke.

LOCKE — Old English. "Dweller by the forest."

LOCKWOOD — Old English. "From the enclosed wood."

LOGAN — Gaelic. "From the hollow."

LOMBARD — Latin. "Long-bearded."

LON — Gaelic. "Fierce." Also a nickname for Lawrence.

LONNIE — A nickname for Lawrence or Lorens.

LONNY — A nickname for Lawrence or Lorens.

LORANT — A Slavic form of Lawrence.

LOREN — A nickname for Lorens, Lorenz, or Lorenzo.

LORENS — A Scandinavian form of Lawrence.

LORENZ — A German form of Lawrence.

LORENZO — The Spanish and Italian form of Lawrence.

LORIMER — Latin. "Harness-maker."

LORIN — A nickname for Lawrence.

LORING — Old German. "Son of the battle-famous."

LORRIMER — A variation of Lorimer.

LOT — Hebrew. "Veiled." A biblical name.

LOTARIO — An Italian form of Luther.

LOTHAIRE — A French form of Luther.

LOU — A nickname for Louis.

LOUIE — A nickname for Louis.

LOUIS — Old German. "Famous in battle." This name was used by 18 French kings.

LOVELL — Old English. "Little beloved one." Or from the Old French for "little wolf." In ancient times, the wolf was admired for his cunning.

LOWELL — A variation of Lovell.

LOYAL — Old French. "Faithful."

LUC — The French form of Luke. Also a nickname for Lucas.

LUCA — An Italian form of Lucius.

LUCAIS — The Scottish form of Lucius.

LUCAS — The Danish, Dutch, German, and Irish forms of Lucius.

LUCE — A French form of Lucius.

LUCIAN — A variation of Lucius.

LUCIANO — An Italian form of Lucius.

LUCIAS — A variation of Lucius.

LUCIEN — A French form of Lucius.

LUCIO — A Spanish form of Lucius.

LUCIUS — Latin. "Bearer of light" or "knowledge."

LUCK — A nickname for Luke.

LUDLOW — Old English. "From the hill of the prince."

LUDVIG — A German form of Louis.

LUDWIG — A German form of Louis.

LUIGI — An Italian form of Louis.

LUIS — A Spanish form of Louis.

LUKAS — A Swedish form of Lucius.

LUKE — A variation of Lucius. St. Luke is credited with the authorship of one of the four gospels of the New Testament. He is the patron saint of physicians.

LUKYAN — A Russian form of Lucius.

LUNDY — Scottish. "From the grove on the island." Also from the French for "born on Monday." According to the nursery rhyme, "Monday's child is fair of face."

LUNG — Chinese. "Dragon."

LUNN — A variation of Lon.

LUNT — Old Norse. "From the grove." The image is that of a house shaded by fruit trees.

LUTERO — A Spanish form of Luther.

LUTHER — Old German. "Famous warrior." Martin Luther is credited with the initiation of the Reformation by his public listings of grievances against the Catholic Church.

LYDELL — A variation of Lyle.

LYLE — Old French. "From the island."

LYMAN — Old English. "A man from the meadow."

LYNDON — Old English. "Dweller at the hill of the linden tree."

LYNN — Old Welsh. "From the waterfall."

LYSANDER — Greek. "Liberator." An ancient Greek hero.

MAC — A nickname for the various names beginning with "Mac."

MACDONALD — Gaelic. "Son of the world-mighty."

MACKLIN — Gaelic. "Son of the red-haired one."

MACMURRAY — Gaelic. "Son of the mariner."

MACNAIR — Gaelic. "Son of the hero."

MADDOCK — Old Welsh. "Beneficient." A child of good fortune.

MADDOX — A variation of Maddock.

MADISON — Old English. "Son of the mighty warrior."

MADUC — A variation of Maddock.

MAGEE — Gaelic. "Son of the fiery one." A family known for its ardent ambition.

MAGNUS — Latin. "Great." An outstanding one.

MAIMUN — Arabic. "Fortunate."

MAITLAND — Old English. "From the meadowland.

MAJOR — Latin. "Greater." A man who can compare with the best in all endeavors.

MAL — A nickname for names starting with "Mal."

MALACHI — Hebrew. "Angel." A divine messenger.

MALCOLM — Gaelic. "Follower of St. Columba." St. Columba was an early Scottish saint.

MALLORY — Old German. "Council of war." Also from the Old French for "unfortunate."

MALONEY — Gaelic. "Church worshipper."

MALVIN — Gaelic. "Polished chief." Also from the Old English for "friend of the sword."

MANDEL — German. "Almond."

MANDO — A nickname for Armando.

MANFRED — Old English. "Man of peace." A man with a calming nature.

MANLEY — Old English. "Brave," independent."

MANNING — Old English. "Son of the hero."

MANNY — A nickname for Manuel.

MANUS — An Irish form of Magnus.

MANVIL — A variation of Manville.

MANVILLE — Old French. "From the grand estate." A man known for his riches.

MARC — The French form of Mark.

MARCEL — The French form of Marcellus.

MARCELLO — The Italian form of Marcel.

MARCELLUS — Latin. "Little warlike one."

MARCELO — The Spanish form of Marcel.

MARCO — The Italian form of Mark.

MARCOS — A Spanish form of Mark.

MARCUS — The original Latin form of Mark.

MARDEN — Old English. "From the valley with the pool."

MARDON — A variation of Marden.

MARIO — The Portuguese and Spanish form of Mark.

MARIUS — A variation of Mark.

MARK — Latin. "Warlike."

MARKOS — A Greek form of Mark.

MARKUS — A German form of Mark.

MARLAND — Old English. "From the periphery."

MARLIN — A variation of Marlon.

MARLON — Old French. "Little hawk."

MARLOW — Old English. "From the hill by the lake."

MARLOWE — A variation of Marlow.

MARMADUKE — Gaelic. "The servant of Madoc."

MARMION — Old French. "Very small."

MARNIN — Hebrew. "One who brings joy." A happy child.

MARS — Latin. "Belligerent warrior." In Roman mythology, Mars was the god of war.

MARSDEN — Old English. "From the marsh valley."

MARSDON — Old English. A variation of Marsden.

MARSH — Old English. "Dweller at the marsh."

MARSHAL — Old French. "Official in charge of the horses."

MARSHALL — A variation of Marshal.

MARSTON — Old English. "From the farm on the lake."

MART — A nickname for Martin.

MARTAINN — A Scottish form of Martin.

MARTEN — A variation of Martin.

MARTIE — A nickname for Martin.

MARTIJN — The Dutch form of Martin.

MARTIN — Latin. "Bellicose."

MARTINO — The Italian and Spanish form of Martin.

MARTY — A nickname for Martin.

MARV — A nickname for Marvin.

MARVIN — Old English. "Famous friend" or "friend of the sea."

MARWIN — A variation of Marvin.

MASON — Old French. "Stoneworker." A trade name.

MASSIMILIANO — The Italian form of Maximilian.

MATA — The Scottish form of Matthew.

MATEO — The Spanish form of Matthew.

MATHER — Old English. "Strong army."

MATHIAS — A variation of Matthew.

MATIAS — A Spanish form of Matthew.

MATT — A nickname for Matthew.

MATTEO — An Italian form of Matthew.

MATTHAEUS — The Danish form of Matthew.

MATTHAUS — The German form of Matthew.

MATTHEUS — The Dutch and Scandinavian form of Matthew.

MATTHEW — Hebrew. "Gift of Jehovah."

MATTHIEU — A French form of Matthew.

MATTIE — A nickname for Matthew.

MATTY — A nickname for Matthew.

MATU — American Indian. "Brave."

MAURICE — Latin. "A Moor" or "dark-skinned."

MAURICIO — The Spanish form of Maurice.

MAURIE — A nickname for Maurice.

MAURITS — The Dutch form of Maurice.

MAURIZIO — The Italian form of Maurice.

MAURY — A nickname for Maurice.

MAX — A nickname for Maximilian. Also used as an independent name.

MAXIE — A nickname for Maximilian.

MAXIM — A nickname for Maximilian.

MAXIMILIAN — Latin."Greatest." Comparable to known.

MAXIMILIANUS — The Dutch form of Maximilian.

MAXILMILIEN — The French form of Maximilian.

MAXIMO — A Spanish form of Maximilian.

MAXWELL — Old English. "From the spring of the great man."

MAYER — Latin. "Greatest." Also a variation of Meyer.

MAYHEW — Old French. "Gift."

MAYNARD — Old German. "Brave and powerful." A man of force.

MEAD — Old English. "From the meadow."

MEDWIN — Old English. "Powerful friend." A man of influence.

MELBOURNE — Old English. "From the millstream."

MELBURN — A variation of Melbourne.

MELDON — Old English. "From the hill of the meadow."

MELVILLE — Old French. "From the estate of the hard-working king."

MELVIN — Gaelic. "Polished chief." Also from the Old English for "sword friend."

MELVYN — A variation of Melvin.

MENDEL — East Semitic. "Knowledge."

MERCER — French and Latin. "Merchant."

MERLIN — Middle English. "Falcon." In the Arthurian legends, Merlin was a wizard who advised the king.

MERREL — A variation of Merrill.

MERRICK — Old French. "Industrious ruler."

MERRILL — Old French. "Famous."

MERRITT — Old English. "Famous."

MERTON — Old English. "From the estate."

MERVIN — Old English. "Lover of the sea." A man who is nourished by the salt air. Appropriate for a child born under the water signs of the Zodiac: Cancer, Scorpio, and Pisces.

MERVYN — A variation of Mervin.

MERWIN — A variation of Mervin.

MERWYN — A variation of Mervin.

MEYER — German. "Farmer." A man of the soil.

MICAH — A Hebrew form of Michael.

MICHAEL — Hebrew. "Like unto the Lord." Michael was the archangel of God.

MICHAL — A Slavic form of Michael.

MICHEIL — The Scottish form of Michael.

MICHEL — The French form of Michael.

MICHELE — The Italian form of Michael.

MICKIE — A nickname for Michael.

MICKY — A nickname for Michael.

MIGUEL — A Spanish form of Michael.

MIKAEL — A Swedish form of Michael.

MIKE — A nickname for Michael.

MIKKEL — A Danish form of Michael.

MILBURN — Old English. "From the mill stream."

MILES — Latin. "Soldier." Also from the Greek for "mill." Miles Standish was an early leader in the colony of Massachusetts.

MILLER — Latin. "One who grinds the grain." A name designating a trade.

MILLMAN — Old English. "Man of the mill."

MILTON — Old English. "Dweller at the farmstead of the mill."

MILWARD — Old English. "Keeper of the mill."

MINER — Latin. "Youth." Also Old French for "a miner."

MISCHA — A Slavic form of Michael.

MITCH — A nickname for Mitchell.

MITCHELL — A variation of Michael.

MOE — A nickname for Moses.

MOISE — The French and Italian form of Moses.

MOISÈS — The Spanish form of Moses.

MONRO — A variation of Monroe.

MONROE — Gaelic. "From the red swamp."

MONTAGUE — Latin and French. "Dweller at the peaked hill."

MONTE — A nickname for Montgomery.

MONTGOMERY — Old French. "From the mountain of the rich one."

MOORE — Old French. "Dark-complected."

MOREL — A variation of Morrell.

MORELAND — Old English. "From the moor," or "from the land of the Moor."

MORELY — Old English. "From the meadow of the moor."

MORIE — A nickname for Maurice.

MORITZ — The German form of Maurice.

MORRELL — Latin. "Dark-skinned."

MORRIS — A variation of Maurice.

MORSE — Old English. "Son of the dark-skinned one."

MORT — A nickname for Mortimer.

MORTIE — A nickname for Mortimer.

MORTIMER — French and Latin. "From the still water."

MOSE — A nickname for Moses.

MOSES — Greek. "Drawn from the water." Moses, the great prophetic leader and lawgiver of the Hebrew people, was found in a basket on the Nile by the daughter of the Pharaoh. He had been placed in a basket on the Nile by his mother to save him from the wrath of the Pharaoh.

MOSHE — A Hebrew form of Moses.

MOSI — African. "First-born."

MOULTON — Old English. "Dweller at the mule farm."

MOZES — The Dutch form of Moses.

MUHAMMAD — Arabic. "Praised." Muhammed is the Savior of the Muslim people.

MUIR — Gaelic. "From the moor."

MUNGO — Gaelic. "Beloved."

MUNNEPUSKA — American Indian. "Fearless."

MUNRO — A variation of Monroe.

MURACO — American Indian. "White moon." Image of a beautiful moonlit evening. Those born under the sign of Cancer are the moon children of the Zodiac.

MURDOCK — Gaelic. "Wealthy mariner."

MURRAY — Gaelic. "Mariner."

MURRY — A variation of Murray.

MYLES — A variation of Miles.

MYRON — Greek. "Fragrant essence."

NABIL — Arabic. "Well-born."

NAHUM — Hebrew. "Comforter." A biblical name.

NALDO — A nickname for Reginald.

NAMID — American Indian. "Star dancer."

NARAIN — Hindu. Another name for the god Vishnu.

NASSAR — Arabic. "Successful in battle."

NAT — A nickname for Nathan or Nathaniel.

NATANAEL — A Spanish form of Nathaniel.

NATANIEL — A Spanish form of Nathaniel.

NATE — A nickname for Nathan or Nathaniel.

NATHAN — A nickname for Nathaniel. Also used as an independent name.

NATHANIEL — Hebrew. "Gift of God." A child who answers his parents' prayers.

NEAL — Gaelic. "Champion." A leader.

NEALON — A variation of Neal.

NEALSON — A variation of Nelson.

NEEL — A variation of Neal.

NEHEMIAH — Hebrew. "Comforted by the Lord." One who is given divine solace.

NEHRU — East Indian. "From the canal."

NEIL — A variation of Neal.

NEILS — A variation of Neal.

NEKIME — American Indian. "Thunder." Possibly a child who is born during a fierce storm.

NELSON — English. "The champion's son." A child who will follow in his father's footsteps.

NEMO — Greek. "From the glen." Captain Nemo was a fictional hero in Jules Verne's novels.

NESTOR — Greek. "Traveler." Also signifying "wisdom" since Nestor was a Greek leader who served as an adviser during the Trojan War.

NEVIL — A variation of Neville.

NEVILLE — Latin and French. "From the new town."

NEVIN — Gaelic and Old German. "Nephew."

NEWLIN — Old Welsh. "Dweller at the new spring."

NEWLYN — A variation of Newlin.

NEWMAN — Old English. "Newcomer."

NEWTON — Old English. "From the new estate."

NIAL — A variation of Neal.

NICCOLO — An Italian form of Nicholas.

NICHOLAS — Greek. "Victory of the people." St. Nicholas is the patron saint of children and is the bearer of Christmas presents.

NICK — A nickname for Nicholas.

NICKIE — A nickname for Nicholas.

NICKOLAUS — The German form of Nicholas.

NICKY — A nickname for Nicholas.

NICODEMUS — Greek. "Victorious for the people." A hero.

NICOL — A nickname for Nicholas.

NICOLAI — A Norwegian form of Nicholas.

NICOLAS — A Spanish form of Nicholas.

NIELS — A Scandinavian form of Neal.

NIGEL — Latin. "Dark"

NIK — A nickname for Nicholas.

NIKITA — A Slavic form of Nicholas.

NIKKI — A nickname for Nicholas.

NIKOLAI — A Russian form of Nicholas.

NIKOLAS — A Slavic form of Nicholas.

NIKOLAUS — A German form of Nicholas.

NIKOLOS — A Greek form of Nicholas.

NIL — A variation of Neal.

NILES — A Finnish form of Nicholas.

NILS — A Scandinavian form of Nicholas.

NINIAN — Latin. "Ninth." St. Ninian was a 5th-century Scottish saint.

NIXON — Old English. "Son of the victorious one."

NOACH — A Dutch form of Noah.

NOAH — Hebrew. "Rest." The biblical descendant of Adam, who, at God's command, built the Ark to save his family and selected pairs of animals from the flood.

NOAK — A Scandinavian form of Noah.

NOBLE — Latin. "Well-born." A young aristocrat.

NODIN — American Indian. "Wind." A handsome nature name.

NOÉ — The French and Spanish form of Noah.

NOLAN — Gaelic. "Famous and noble."

NOLAND — A variation of Nolan.

NORBERT — Old Norse. "Brilliance of Njord." In Norse mythology, Njord was the god who influenced the lives of seamen.

NORM — A nickname for Norman.

NORMAN — Old French. "Man from the north, a Norseman."

NORMIE — A nickname for Norman.

NORMY — A nickname for Norman.

NORRIS — Old French. "Man from the north."

NORTHROP — Old English. "Dweller on the north farm."

NORTHRUP — A variation of Northrop.

NORTON — Old English. "From the north estate."

NORVIN — Old English. "Friend from the north."

NORWARD — Old English. "Guard of the north gate."

NORWELL — Old English. "From the north spring."

NORWIN — A variation of Norvin.

NORWOOD — Old English. "From the north forest."

NORWYN — A variation of Norvin.

NYE — Middle English. "Islander."

OAKES — Old English. "One who resides by the oak tree."

OAKLEY — Old English. "From the meadow of the oak tree."

OBADIAH — Hebrew. "Servant of God." A biblical name.

OBERT — Old German. "Wealthy one."

OBINKARAM — African. "My heart is strong." A child who survives a difficult birth.

OCTAVIUS — Latin. "Eighth." A birth-order name.

OCTAVUS — A variation of Octavius.

ODELL — Old Norse. "Man of wealth." Also from the Old English for "from the valley."

ODIN — Old Norse. The chief god of Norse mythology.

ODOLF — Old German. "Prosperous wolf." In ancient times, the wolf was the symbol of cunning.

OGDEN — Old English. "From the valley of the oak trees."

OGILVIE — Scottish. "From the high peak."

OLAF — Old Norse. "Relic of an ancient ancestor." King Olaf was the first Christian monarch of Norway.

OLAV — A variation of Olaf.

OLEN — A variation of Olaf.

OLIN — A variation of Olaf.

OLIVER — Latin. "The olive." The olive branch has been a token of peace since ancient times.

OLIVERIO — The Spanish form of Oliver.

OLIVIER — The French form of Oliver.

OLIVIERO — The Italian form of Oliver.

OLLEY — A nickname for Oliver.

OLLIE — A nickname for Oliver.

OLLY — A nickname for Oliver.

OLNEY — Old English. "From the town of Olney." The meaning of the town name is undetermined.

OLVAN — A variation of Oliver.

OMAR — Arabic. "Follower of the Prophet, first son, highest and richest."

OMER — A variation of Omar.

OMERO — An Italian form of Homer.

ONFRÉ — The Spanish form of Humphrey.

ONFROI — The French form of Humphrey.

ONOFREDO — The Italian form of Humphrey.

ONSLOW — Old English. "From the hill of the ardent one."

ORAM — Old English. "From the enclosed area of the river bank."

ORAN — Gaelic. "Pale."

ORAZIO — The Italian form of Horace.

ORDWAY — Old English. "Spear-warrior."

OREN — A variation of Oran.

ORESTES — Greek. "Mountain man." In mythology, Orestes was the son of Agamemnon and the brother of Electra.

ORFORD — Old English. "From the river crossing of the cattle."

ORIN — A variation of Oran.

ORION — Greek. "Son of fire." A mythological hunter.

ORLAN — Old English. "From the land of the famous one."

ORLAND — A variation of Orlan.

ORLANDO — A variation of Orlan.

ORMAN — Old English. "Spearman" or "sailor."

ORMUND — Old English. "Spear protector" or "ship protector."

ORO — Spanish. "Golden." A precious child.

ORREN — A variation of Oran.

ORRICK — Old English.

ORRIN — A variation of Oran.

ORSON — Old French. "Son of the bear." A bear symbolizes strength.

ORTON — Old English. "From the town on the shore."

ORVAL — Old English. "Spear-strong."

ORVILLE — Old French. "From the estate of the golden fields."

ORVIN — Old English. "Courageous friend."

OSBERT — Old English. "Divinely brilliant."

OSBORN — Old English. "Warrior of God." Also from the Old Norse for "divine bear." The bear was the symbol of strength.

OSCAR — Old Norse. "Divine spearman."

OSGOOD — Old Norse. "Divine creator."

OSMOND — Old English. "Divine protector."

OSMUND — A varition of Osmond.

OSRIC — Old English. "Divine ruler."

OSWALD — Old English. "With power from God."

OSWELL — A variation of Oswald.

OTHMAN — Old German. "Prosperous man."

OTIS — Old German. "Prosperous." Also from the Greek for "with acute hearing."

OTTO — Old German. "Prosperous, wealthy." A popular name for German emperors.

OTWAY — Old German. "Fortunate in battle."

OUTRAM — Old German. "Prospering raven."

OWEN — Greek. "Noble." Also from the Old Welsh for "young warrior."

OXFORD — Old English. "From the river crossing of the oxen."

OXTON — Old English. "Dweller near the oxen pen."

PABLO — The Spanish form of Paul.

PADDY — A nickname for Patrick.
PADGET — A variation of Padgett.
PADGETT — French. "Attendant." A willing assistant.
PADRAIC — An Irish form of Patrick.
PADRAIG — An Irish form of Patrick.
PAGE — French. "Youthful attendant." In medieval Europe, the early stage of knighthood.
PAGET — A variation of Padgett.
PAINE — Latin. "Man from the country." A rustic soul.
PALL — A Scandinavian form of Paul.
PALMER — Old English. "Palm-bearer." It was once a custom for pilgrims to return from the Holy Land with a palm branch.
PANCHO — A variation of Francisco.
PAOLO — The Italian form of Paul.
PARK — Old English. "From the park."
PARKE — A variation of Park.
PARKER — Old English. "Guardian of the park."
PARKIN — Old English. "Little Peter."
PARLE — Old French. "Little Peter."
PARNELL — Old French. "Little Peter."
PARRISH — Middle English. "A dweller near the churchyard."
PARRY — Old Welsh. "Son of Harry." Son of the army man.
PARSIFAL — A variation of Percival.
PASCAL — Hebrew. "Pass over." A name appropriate for a child born during the Jewish holiday of Passover and the coinciding Christian Eastertime.
PAT — A nickname for Patrick.
PATON — A variation of Patton.
PATRICE — A French form of Patrick.
PATRICIO — A Spanish form of Patrick.

PATRICK — Latin. "Nobleman." St. Patrick, the patron saint of Ireland, was a 5th-century missionary. His name was not conferred on children until the 17th century because it was considered too sacred.
PATRIZIO — The Italian form of Patrick.
PATRIZIUS — The German form of Patrick.
PATTEN — A variation of Patton.
PATTIE — A nickname for Patrick.
PATTIN — A variation of Patton.
PATTON — Old English. "From the estate of the warrior."
PATTY — A nickname for Patrick.
PAUL — Latin. "Little." St. Paul was a fervent early Christian missionary.
PAVEL — A Russian form of Paul.
PAX — A nickname for Paxton.
PAXON — A variation of Paxton.
PAXTON — Old English. "From the estate of the warrior."
PAYNE — A variation of Paine.
PAYTON — Old English. "From the estate of the warrior."
PEADAR — The Irish form of Peter.
PEARCE — An Anglo-French form of Peter.
PEARSON — A variation of Pierson.
PEDER — A Scandinavian form of Peter.
PEDRO — The Spanish form of Peter.
PEIRCE — An Anglo-French form of Peter.
PELL — Old English. "Scarf."
PELTON — Old English. "From the estate by a pool."
PEMBROKE — Old Welsh. "From the cape."
PENN — Old English. "Enclosure." Also from the Old German for "commander."
PENROD — Old German. "Famous commander." Booth Tarkington wrote the stories of the adventures

of a young Midwesterner by this name.

PEPI — A variation of Pepin.

PEPIN — Old German. "One who seeks favors."

PEPPI — A variation of Pepin.

PERC — A nickname for Percival.

PERCE — A nickname for Percival.

PERCEVAL — A variation of Percival.

PERCIVAL — Old French. "Valley piercer." Sir Percival was a knight of the Round Table.

PERCY — A nickname for Percival. Percy Bysshe Shelley was an 18th-century Romantic poet.

PEREGRINE — Latin. "Traveler."

PERKIN — Old English. "Little Peter."

PERREN — Old French. "Little Peter."

PERRIN — A variation of Pierre.

PERRY — Middle English. "From the pear tree." Also a variation of Pierre.

PERRYN — A variation of Pierre.

PETE — A nickname for Peter.

PETER — Greek. "Rock." St. Peter was the leader of the Apostles, chosen by Christ to be the founder of his church.

PETERUS — A German form of Peter.

PETEY — A nickname for Peter.

PEYTON — A variation of Payton.

PHELAN — Gaelic. "Little wolf." In ancient times, the wolf was honored for his courage.

PHELPS — Old English. "Son of Philip."

PHIL — A nickname for Philip.

PHILANDER — Greek. "Lover of mankind." A man with a generous and kind nature.

PHILBERT — A variation of Filbert.

PHILIP — Greek. "Lover of horses." Horses were revered in ancient times as the transporters of the gods.

PHILIPP — A German form of Philip.

PHILIPPE — A French form of Philip.

PHILIPS — Old English. "Son of Philip."

PHILLIP — A variation of Philip.

PHILO — Greek. "Loving."

PHINEAS — Greek. "Mouth of brass."

PICKFORD — Old English. "From the ford at the peak."

PIERO — An Italian form of Peter.

PIERPONT — French and Latin. "From the stone bridge."

PIERRE — The French form of Peter.

PIERREPONT — A variation of Pierpont.

PIERSON — French and English. "Son of Peter."

PIETER — The Dutch form of Peter.

PIETREK — A Polish form of Peter.

PILIB — An Irish form of Philip.

PITNEY — Old English. "Island of the determined one."

PLATO — Greek. "Broad-shouldered." The name of probably the most famous philosopher.

PLATT — Old French. "From the flat land."

POLLOCK — Old English. "Little Paul."

POMEROY — Old French. "From the apple orchard."

PORTER — Latin. "Keeper of the gate."

POUL — The Danish form of Paul.

POWELL — Old Welsh. "Son of Howel." Howel was an ancient king of Wales.

PRENTICE — Middle English. "An apprentice."

PRESCOTT — Old English. "From the dwelling of the priest."

PRESTON — Old English. "From the domain of the priest."

PRICE — Old Welsh. "Son of the ardent one."

PRIMO — Italian. "First." A birth-order name.

PRIOR — A variation of Pryor.

PROCTER — A variation of Proctor.

PROCTOR — Latin. "Manager." An occupation name.

PROKTER — A variation of Proctor.

PRYOR — Latin. "Head of the monastery."

PURDY — Hindu. "Secluded."

PUTMAN — Old English. "From near the mill pond."

QUENBY — A variation of Quimby.

QUENNEL — Old French. "From the small oak tree."

QUENTIN — A variation of Quinton.

QUIGLEY — Gaelic. "Distaff." A most necessary part of the spinning wheel.

QUILLAN — Gaelic. "Cub." An appropriate name for a Leo child.

QUIMBY — Old Norse. "From the estate of the woman."

QUINBY — A variation of Quimby.

QUINCY — Old French and Latin. "From the estate of the fifth son."

QUINLAN — Gaelic. "One of physical prowess."

QUINN — Gaelic. "Wise."

QUINTON — Latin. "Fifth child." Also from the Old English for "from the estate of the queen."

RAD — Old English. "Counselor." One to turn to for advice.

RADBERT — Old English. "Counselor with outstanding ability."

RADBORNE — Old English. "From the red stream."

RADBOURN — A variation of Radborne.

RADBURN — A variation of Radborne.

RADCLIFF — Old English. "Red cliff."

RADCLIFFE — A variation of Radcliff.

RADFORD — Old English. "From the red ford."

RADLEY — Old English. "From the red meadow."

RAFAEL — The Spanish form of Raphael.

RAFAELLO — An Italian form of Raphael.

RAFFERTY — Gaelic. "Rich and prosperous." A man of influence.

RAGNAR — A Scandinavian form of Rainer.

RAHMAN — Arabic. "Compassionate." One of the qualities assigned to God in the Koran.

RAIMONDO — An Italian form of Raymond.

RAIMUND — A German form of Raymond.

RAIMUNDO — A Spanish form of Raymond.

RAINER — A German form of Raynor.

RAINGER — A variation of Ranger.

RALEIGH — Old English. "From the meadow of the roe-deer."

RALF — A variation of Ralph.

RALPH — Old Norse. "Counsel wolf." A man of courage and wisdom.

RALSTON — Old English. "From Ralph's estate."

RAMON — A Spanish form of Raymond.

RAMSAY — Old English. "From the island of the ram," or "the raven" or "the strong."

RAMSDEN — Old English. "From the valley of the ram," or "raven" or "the strong."

RAMSEY — A variation of Ramsay.

RAND — A nickname for Randolph.

RANDAL — A variation of Randolph.

RANDALL — A variation of Randolph.

RANDELL — A variation of Randolph.

RANDOLF — A variation of Randolph.

RANDOLPH — Old English. "Shield-wolf."

RANDY — A nickname for Randolph.

RANEN — Hebrew. "Joyous." A child of bliss.

RANGER — Old French. "Guardian of the forest."

RANKIN — Old English. "Little shield."

RANSFORD — Old English. "From the raven's ford."

RANSOM — Old English. "Son of the shield." A protected child.

RAOUL — The French form of Ralph.

RAPHAEL — Hebrew. "God has healed." Raphael was one of the great Italian Renaissance painters.

RAS — A nickname for Erasmus.

RASMUS — A variation of Erasmus.

RAVI — Hindu. "Benevolent." One of the names for the sun god.

RAWLEY — A variation of Raleigh.

RAY — Old French. "Kingly." Also a nickname for Raymond.

RAYBURN — Old English. "From the brook of the roe-deer."

RAYMOND — Old German. "Mighty or wise protector."

RAYMUND — A variation of Raymond.

RAYNOR — Old Norse. "Mighty army."

RAZIEL — Hebrew. "Secret of God."

READ — Old English. "Red-haired" or "red-complected."

READING — Old English. "Son of the red-haired one."

REAGAN — A variation of Regan.

REAGEN — A variation of Regan.

REAMONN — An Irish form of Raymond.

REAVE — A variation of Reeve.

RED — A variation of Read.

REDDING — A variation of Read.

REDDY — A variation of Read.

REDFORD — Old English. "From the red ford."

REDLEY — Old English. "From the red meadow."

REDMAN — Old English. "Counsellor" or "horseman."

REDMOND — Old English. "Protecting adviser." A well-respected man.

REDMUND — A variation of Redmond.

REECE — A variation of Rhys.

REED — A variation of Read.

REESE — A variation of Rhys.

REEVE — Middle English. "Bailiff."

REG — A nickname for Reginald.

REGAN — Gaelic. "Little king." The small majestic one.

REGEN — A variation of Regan.

REGINALD — Old English. "Powerful and mighty." A man of strength.

REGINAULD — A French form of Reginald.

REID — A variation of Read.

REILLY — A variation of Riley.

REINALD — A German form of Reginald.

REINALDO — A Spanish form of Reginald.

REINALDOS — A Spanish form of Reginald.

REINHARD — A German form of Reynard.

REINHOLD — A Scandinavian form of Reginald.

REINOLD — A Dutch form of Reginald.

REINWALD — A German form of Reginald.

REMINGTON — Old English. "From the estate of the raven."

REMUS — Latin. "Fast-moving." A man of quick body.

RENALDO — A Spanish form of Ronald.

RENARD — A French form of Reynard.

RENATO — A Spanish form of Reynard.

RENAUD — A French form of Reynard.

RENAULT — A French form of Reginald.

RENE — A nickname for Reginald.

RENÉ — A French form of Reginald.

RENEFRED — Old French. "Strong but peace-loving." A man who prefers not to have to show his strength.

RENNY — Gaelic. "Small but mighty."

RENTON — Old English. "From the estate of the roe-deer."

RENWICK — Old English. "From the place where the ravens roost."

REUBEN — Hebrew. "Behold, a son." In the Bible, a founder of one of the tribes of Israel.

REX — Latin. "King." The majestic one.

REXFORD — Old English. "From the ford of the king."

REY — A Spanish form of Rex.

REYNARD — Old French. "The fox."

REYNOLD — A variation of Reginald.

REYNOLDS — A variation of Reginald.

RHODES — Greek. "Place of the roses."

RHYS — Old Welsh. "Rash, ardent."

RICARD — A variation of Richard.

RICARDO — A Spanish form of Richard.

RICCARDO — An Italian form of Richard.

RICE — A variation of Rhys.

RICH — A nickname for Richard.

RICHARD — Old German. "Powerful ruler." A popular name among the royal families of England, Richard the Lionhearted being its most famous bearer.

RICHART — A Dutch form of Richard.

RICHIE — A nickname for Richard.

RICHMAN — Old English. "Powerful man."

RICHMOND — Old German. "Powerful protector."

RICK — A nickname for Richard.

RICKER — Old English. "Powerful army."

RICKERT — A variation of Richard.

RICKIE — A nickname for Richard.

RICKY — A nickname for Richard.

RICO — A Spanish form of Richard.

RIDER — Old English. "Horseman."

RIDGE — Old English. "From the ridge."

RIDGLEY — Old English. "From the ridge meadow."

RIDLEY — Old English. "From the red meadow."

RIGBY — Old English. "From the valley of the ruler."

RIGG — Old English. "From the ridge."

RILEY — Gaelic. "Valiant." A brave little one.

RINALDO — An Italian form of Reginald.

RIOBARD — The Irish form of Robert.

RIOCARD — The Irish form of Richard.

RIORDAN — Gaelic. "Bard of the king." A court entertainer.

RIPLEY — Old English. "From the meadow of the shouter."

RISLEY — Old English. "From the meadow of the brush wood."

RITCHIE — A nickname for Richard.

RITTER — Old German. "Knight."

ROALD — Old German. "Famous ruler."

ROAN — Old English. "Dweller by the rowan tree."

ROARKE — Gaelic. "Outstanding ruler."

ROB — A nickname for Robert.

ROBBY — A nickname for Robert.

ROBERS — A French form of Robert.

ROBERT — Old German. "Bright or shining fame." A popular masculine name used in eight languages.

ROBERTO — The Italian and Spanish form of Robert.

ROBERTSON — Old English. "Son of Robert."

ROBIN — A nickname for Robert.

ROBINSON — A variation of Robertson.

ROCHESTER — Old English. "From the fortress of stone." A dweller in a well-fortified town.

ROCK — Old English. "From the rock."

ROCKWELL — Old English. "From the rocky spring."

ROD — A nickname for names beginning with "Rod."

RODAS — A Spanish form of Rhodes.

RODDIE — A nickname for names beginning with "Rod."

RODDY — A nickname for names beginning with "Rod."

RODEN — Old English. "From the reed valley."

RODERIC — A variation of Roderick.

RODERICH — A German form of Roderick.

RODERICK — Old German. "Famous ruler."

RODGER — A variation of Roger.

RODMAN — Old English. "Measurer of the land," or "from by the road."

RODMOND — Old German. "Famous protector."

RODMUND — A variation of Rodmond.

RODNEY — Old English. "From the island of the famous one."

RODOLFO — A Spanish form of Rudolph.

RODOLPH — A form of Rudolph.

RODOLPHE — A French form of Rudolph.

RODRIGO — A Spanish and Italian form of Roderick.

RODRIQUE — The French form of Roderick.

ROE — Middle English. "Roe-deer." An agile man.

ROELAND — Middle English. "From the land of the roe-deer."

ROGAN — Gaelic. "Red-haired."

ROGER — Old German. "Famous spearman." A skillful warrior.

ROGERIO — The Spanish form of Roger.

ROHAN — Hindu. "Sandalwood."

ROI — A French form of Roy.

ROLAND — Old German. "From the famous land."

ROLANDO — A Spanish form of Roland.

ROLDAN — A Spanish form of Roland.

ROLF — A nickname for Rudolph.

ROLFE — A nickname for Rudolph.

ROLLINS — A variation of Roland.

ROLLO — A nickname for Rudolph.

ROLPH — A nickname for Rudolph.

ROMEO — Italian. "Pilgrim of Rome." The tragic romantic hero of Shakespeare's *Romeo and Juliet.*

ROMNEY — Old Welsh. "From the curving river." Also from the Latin for "a Roman."

RON — A nickname for Ronald.

RONALD — Old Norse. "Powerful and mighty." Also a variation of Reginald.

RONAN — Gaelic. "Signet."

RONNIE — A nickname for Ronald.

RONNY — A nickname for Ronald.

RONSON — Old English. "Son of the powerful and mighty one."

ROONEY — Gaelic. "Red." A lad with fiery red hair.

ROPER — Old English. "Rope-maker." A trade name.

RORKE — A variation of Roarke.

ROSCOE — Old Norse. "From the forest of the roe-deer."

ROSLIN — Old French. "Little red-haired one."

ROSS — Gaelic. "From the island." Also from the Old German for "horse."

ROSSLYN — A variation of Roslin.

ROSWALD — Old German. "Mighty one on a horse."

ROSWELL — A variation of Roswald.

ROTH — German. "Red-haired."

ROURKE — A variation of Roarke.

ROUVIN — A Greek form of Ruben.

ROVER — Middle English. "Wanderer." A restless traveler.

ROWAN — Gaelic. "Red-haired."

ROWE — A variation of Rowan.

ROWEN — A variation of Rowan.

ROWLAND — A variation of Roland.

ROXBURY — Old English. "From the rook's fortress."

ROY — Old French. "King."

ROYAL — Old French and Latin. "Regal."

ROYCE — Old English. "Song of the king."

ROYD — Old Norse. "From the clearing in the forest."

ROYDEN — French and Old English. "From the king's hill," or "from the hill of rye."

RUBE — A nickname for Ruben.

RUBÉN — The Spanish form of Reuben.

RUDD — Old English. "Ruddy-complected."

RUDIE — A nickname for Rudolph.

RUDOLF — The German, Dutch, and Scandinavian form of Rudolph.

RUDOLFO — The Italian form of Rudolph.

RUDOLPH — Old German. "Famous wolf." A man recognized for his courage.

RUDYARD — Old English. "From the red enclosure."

RUFF — French. "Red-haired."

RUFORD — Old English. "From the red ford."

RUFUS — Latin. "Red-haired."

RUGGIERO — The Italian form of Roger.

RUPERT — A variation of Robert.

RUPERTO — An Italian and Spanish form of Rupert.

RUPRECHT — The original Old German form of Robert.

RURIK — A slavic form of Roderick.

RUS — A nickname for Russell.

RUSH — French. "Red-haired." Also a nickname for Russell.

RUSKIN — Old French and German. "Red-haired."

RUSS — A nickname for Russell.

RUSSELL — Old French. "Red-haired." Also from the Old English for "red fox."

RUST — Old French. "Red-haired."

RUSTY — A nickname for Rust.

RUTGER — A Dutch form of Roger.

RUTHERFORD — Old English. "From the cattle ford."

RUTLEDGE — Old English. "From the red pool."

RYAN — Gaelic. "Little king."

RYDER — A variation of Rider.

RYE — Old French. "From the river bank."

SABER — French. "A sword."

SAFFORD — Old English. "From the willow ford."

SALIM — Arabic. "Good."

SALOMO — The German and Dutch form of Solomon.

SALOMON — The French and Spanish form of Solomon.

SALOMONE — The Italian form of Solomon.

SALVADOR — Spanish. "The Savior."

SALVATORE — The Italian form of Salvador.

SAM — Hebrew. "To hear." Also a nickname for Samson or Samuel.

SAMMIE — A nickname for Sam, Samuel, or Sampson.

SAMMY — A nickname for Sam, Samuel, or Sampson.

SAMPSON — Hebrew. "Child of the sun." In the Bible, Sampson, an Israeli judge, was rendered helpless after his hair, the symbol of his strength, was cut by Delilah. An appropriate name for a child born under the sign of Leo.

SAMSON — The Dutch, French, and Scandinavian form of Sampson.

SAMUEL — Hebrew. "Asked of God." A major prophet of the Old Testament.

SANAT — Hindu. "Ancient." A name honoring the Hindu god Brahma.

SANBORN — Old English. "From the sandy brook."

SANCHO — Latin. "Holy."

SANDERS — Greek and Middle English. "Son of Alexander."

SANDERSON — A variation of Sanders.

SANDIE — A nickname for Alexander, Sanders, or Sanford.

SANDY — A nickname for Alexander, Sanders, or Sanford.

SANFORD — Old English. "From the sandy ford."

SANSOM — A variation of Sampson.

SANSÓN — The Spanish form of Sampson.

SANSONE — The Italian form of Sampson.

SANTO — Spanish. "Saintly." A model of virtue.

SARAD — Hindu. "Child born in Autumn."

SARGE — A nickname for Sargent.

SARGENT — Old French and Latin. "An officer or military attendant."

SAUL — Hebrew. "Asked for." The name of the first king of Israel and the original name of St. Paul the Apostle.

SAUNDERS — A variation of Sanders.

SAUNDERSON — A variation of Sanders.

SAUVEUR — The French form of Salvador.

SAVILL — Old French and Latin. "From the estate of the willow trees."

SAVILLE — A variation of Savill.

SAWYER — Middle English. "A sawer of timber."

SAX — A nickname for Saxon.

SAXE — A nickname for Saxon.

SAXON — Old English. "Of the Saxons" or "swordsmen." The Saxons were a Germanic tribe who invaded England in the 5th century.

SAYER — Old Welsh. "Carpenter." A trade name.

SAYERS — A variation of Sayer.

SAYRE — A variation of Sayer.

SAYRES — A variation of Sayer.

SCHUYLER — Dutch. "A shelter." A man who provides a refuge for his loved ones.

SCOT — A variation of Scott.

SCOTT — Old English. "From Scotland."

SCOTTIE — A nickname for Scott.

SCOTTY — A nickname for Scott.

SCULLY — Gaelic. "Town crier."

SEABERT — "Sea hero."

SEABRIGHT — A variation of Seabert.

SEABROOKE — Old English. "From the brook by the sea."

SEADON — Old English. "From the hill by the sea."

SEAGER — A variation of Seger.

SEAMUS — An Irish form of James.

SEAN — An Irish form of John.

SEARLE — Old German. "Armored one."

SEATON — Old English. "From the place by the sea."

SEBASTIAN — Latin. "Venerable." A most honorable man.

SEBASTIANO — The Italian form of Sebastian.

SÉBASTIEN — The French form of Sebastian.

SEALEY — A variation of Seeley.

SEELEY — Old English. "Happy." A jolly young man.

SEELYE — A variation of Seeley.

SEFTON — Old English. "From the place in the rushes."

SEGEL — Hebrew. "Treasure."

SEGER — Old English. "Sea warrior" or "victorious army."

SEIKO — Japanese. "Sacred torch."

SELBY — Old English. "From the farmstead."

SELDEN — A variation of Seldon.

SELDON — Old English. "From the valley of the willow tree."

SELIG — Old German. "Blessed."

SELWIN — A variation of Selwyn.

SELWYN — Old English. "Good friend from the palace."

SENNETT — French. "Wise."

SEPTIMUS — Latin. "Seventh." A birth-order name.

SERENO — Latin. "Calm." An even-tempered soul.

SERGE — Latin. "Attendant."

SERGEANT— A variation of Sargent.

SERGENT — A variation of Sargent.

SERGIO — An Italian form of Serge.

SERLE — A variation of Searle.

SETH — Hebrew. "Appointed." The third son of Adam.

SETON — A variation of Seaton.

SEVERIN — A variation of Severn.

SEVERN — Old English. "Boundary."

SEWALD — A variation of Sewell.

SEWALL — A variation of Sewell.

SEWARD — Old English. "Guardian of the sea."

SEWELL — Old English. "Sea-powerful."

SEXTON — Middle English. "Church official."

SEXTUS — Latin. "Sixth." A birth-order name.

SEYMOUR — Old French. A name derived from St. Maur, a French saint. Also from the Old English for "tailor."

SHAMUS — An Irish form of James.

SHANAHAN — Gaelic. "Wise."

SHANDY — Old English. "Rambunctious." A child with an exuberant personality.

SHANLEY — Gaelic. "Wise hero."

SHAW — Old English. "From the shady grove."

SHAWN — An Irish form of John.

SHEA — Gaelic. "Ingenious, courteous, and regal."

SHEEHAN — Gaelic. "Peaceful."

SHEFFIELD — Old English. "From the crooked field."

SHELBY — Old English. "From the ledge estate."

SHELDON — Old English. "From the hill on the ledge."

SHELLEY — Old English. "From the meadow of the ledge."

SHELTON — Old English. "From the farm on the ledge."

SHEP — A nickname for Shepherd.

SHEPARD — A variation of Shepherd.

SHEPHERD — Old English. "Herder of sheep."

SHEPLEY — Old English. "From the sheep meadow."

SHEPPARD — A variation of Shepherd.

SHERARD — Old English. "Of outstanding courage."

SHERBORNE — Old English. "From the clear brook.

SHERBOURN — A variation of Sherborne.

SHERBOURNE — A variation of Sherborne.

SHERBURNE — A variation of Sherborne.

SHERIDAN — Gaelic. "Wild man."

SHERLOCK — Old English. "Fair-haired."

SHERMAN — Old English. "Wood cutter."

SHERWIN — Middle English. "Swift runner," or "an outstanding friend."

SHERWOOD — Old English. "From the bright forest." Sherwood Forest was the legendary home of Robin Hood.

SHING — Chinese. "Victory."

SHIPLEY — Old English. "From the sheep meadow."

SHIPTON — Old English. "From the sheep farm."

SIDDELL — Old English. "From the wide valley."

SIEGFRIED — Old German. "Victorious peace." In the Nibelungenlied legends of ancient Germany, Siegfried was a prince of the lower Rhine, who captured gold, killed a dragon, and won Brünnhilde for King Gunther.

SIFFRE — A French form of Siegfried.

SIGFRID — A German form of Siegfried.

SIGISMONDO — The Italian form of Sigmund.

SIGISMUND — A German form of Sigmund.

SIGISMUNDO — The Spanish form of Sigmund.

SIGISMUNDUS — The Dutch form of Sigmund.

SIGMUND — Old German. "Victorious protector."

SIGSMOND — A French form of Sigmund.

SIGURD — Old Norse. "Victorious guardian."

SIGVARD — A variation of Sigwald.

SILAS — A variation of Silvanus.

SILVAIN — A variation of Silvanus.

SILVANO — An Italian and Spanish form of Silvanus.

SILVANUS — Latin. "Forest dweller." The Roman god of the forests.

SILVESTER — Latin. "From the forest."

SILVESTRE — The French and Spanish form of Silvester.

SILVESTRO — The Italian form of Silvester.

SILVIO — The Italian and Spanish form of Silvanus.

SIM — The Scottish form of Simon.

SIMEON — The French form of Simon.

SIMON — Hebrew. "Heard." A child who is an answer from God. The name of the first bishop of Rome was Simon Peter, the Apostle designated by Christ to be the founder of his Church.

SIMONE — An Italian form of Simon.

SIMPSON — Hebrew and English. "Son of Simon."

SIMSON — A variation of Simpson and a Scandinavian form of Sampson.

SINCLAIR — French. A variation of St. Claire.

SIVA — Hindu. The Indian god of destruction.

SIYOLO — African. "One who brings happiness."

SKELLY — Gaelic. "Storyteller."

SKELTON — Old English. "From the estate on the ledge."

SKIP — Old Norse. "Ship master." A man who makes a living from the sea.

SKIPP — A variation of Skip.

SKIPPER — A variation of Skip.

SKIPPY — A nickname for Skip.

SLADE — Old English. "From the valley."

SLEVIN — Gaelic. "Mountaineer."

SLOAN — Gaelic. "Warrior."

SLOANE — A variation of Sloan.

SNOWDEN — Old English. "From the snowy hill."

SOEM — Hindu. "Emerald." A precious one.

SOFIAN — Arabic. "Devoted."

SOL — Latin. "The sun." In mythology, the Roman sun god. An appropriate name for a Leo child. Also a nickname for Solomon.

SOLLY — A nickname for Sol or Solomon.

SOLOMON — Hebrew. "Man of peace." The biblical king known for his wisdom.

SOLON — Greek. "Sagacious."

SOMERSET — Old English. "From the place of the summer settlers." Somerset Maugham is a famous 20th-century English writer.

SOMERVILLE — Old English. "From the summer estate."

SORRELL — Old French. "With reddish-brown hair."

SPALDING — A variation of Spaulding.

SPANGLER — Old German. "Tinsmith."

SPARK — Middle English. "Gay."

SPAULDING — Old English. "From the meadow divided by the river."

SPEAR — Old English. "Spearman."

SPEED — Old English. "Success."

SPENCER — Middle English. "Dispenser of provisions." An important town official.

SPENSER — A variation of Spencer.

SPRAGUE — Old French. "Lively."

SPROULE — Middle English. "Vivacious."

SPROWLE — A variation of Sproule.

SQUIRE — Middle English. "Knight's attendant."

STAFFORD — Old English. "From the landing ford."

STAN — A nickname for names beginning with "Stan."

STANCIO — A nickname for Constancio.

STANDISH — Old English. "From the rocky park."

STANFIELD — Old English. "From the rocky field."

STANFORD — Old English. "From the stony ford."

STANISLAS — A French form of Stanislaus.

STANISLAUS — Slavic. "Glory of the camp."

STANISLAV — A German form of Stanislaus.

STANLEIGH — A variation of Stanley.

STANLEY — Old English. "From the stony field."

STANLY — A variation of Stanley.

STANTON — Old English. "From the stony estate."

STANWAY — Old English. "One who lives by the stone roadway."

STANWICK — Old English. "From the rocky village."

STANWOOD — Old English. "From the rocky forest."

STARLING — Old English. "The starling bird."

STARR — Middle English. "Star."

STEADMAN — A variation of Stedman.

STEDMAN — Old English. "Owner of the farmstead."

STEFAN — A German and Scandinavian form of Stephen.

STEFANO — An Italian form of Stefan.

STEIN — German. "Stone."

STEPHANUS — A Scandinavian form of Stephen.

STEPHEN — Greek. "Crown." St. Stephen was the first Christian martyr.

STERLING — Old English. "Of value."

STERN — A variation of Sterne.

STERNE — Middle English. "Austere."

STEVE — A nickname for Stephen.

STEVEN — A variation of Stephen.

STEVENSON — Greek and English. "Son of Steven."

STEVIE — A nickname for Stephen.

STEW — A nickname for Stewart.

STEWARD — A variation of Stewart.

STEWART — Old English. "Stewart of the manor." An occupation name.

STILLMAN — Old English. "Quiet man."

STILWELL — Old English. "From the quiet spring."

STINSON — Old English. "Son of stone."

STIRLING — A variation of Sterling.

STOCKLEY — Old English. "From the meadow of the tree stumps."

STOCKTON — Old English. "From the tree stump estate."

STOCKWELL — Old English. "From the spring by the tree stump."

STODDARD — Old English. "Keeper of the horses."

STOKE — Middle English. "Village."

STORM — Old English. "Tempest."

STORR — Old Norse. "Great man."

STOWE — Old English. "From the place for assembly."

STRAHAN — Gaelic. "Poet." A man of verse.

STRATFORD — Old English. "From the street by the river ford."

STROUD — Old English. "From the thicket."

STRUTHERS — Gaelic. "From the stream."

STU — A nickname for Stewart or Stuart.

STUART — A variation of Stewart.

STYLES — Old English. "Dweller near the stiles."

SUFFIELD — Old English. "From the south field."

SULLIE — A nickname for Sullivan.

SULLIVAN — Gaelic. "Black-eyed lad."

SULLY — Old English. "From the south meadow." Also a nickname for Sullivan.

SUMNER — Old French and Latin. "Summoner." An official of the court.

SUTHERLAND — Old Norse. "From the south land."

SUTTON — Old English. "From the south village."

SVEN — Old Norse. "Youth."

SVEND — A variation of Sven.

SWAIN — Middle English. "Herdsman." Also a variation of Sven.

SWEENEY — Gaelic. "Little hero."

SYLVANUS — A variation of Silvanus.

SYLVESTER — A variation of Silvester.

TAB — Middle English. "Drummer." Also from the Old German for "outstanding among others."

TABBY — A nickname for Tab or Taber.

TABER — Old French. "Drummer." An occupation name.

TAD — A nickname for Thaddeus.

TADD — A nickname for Thaddeus.

TADDEO — The Italian form of Thaddeus.

TADEO — The Spanish form of Thaddeus.

TAFFY — Old Welsh. "Beloved."

TAGGART — Gaelic. "Son of the church official."

TAIT — Scandinavian. "Cheerful."

TALBOT — Old French. "Ravager." Also from the Old English for a breed of dog.

TALES — A variation of Thales.

TAM — A nickname for Thomas.

TAMAS — A Slavic form of Thomas.

TAMMY — A nickname for Thomas.

TANCRED — Old German. "Think counsel."

TANI — Japanese. "Valley."

TANNER — Old English. "Leather worker."

TANTON — Old English. "From the town on the quiet river."

TARN — Middle English. "From the lake in the mountain."

TARRANT — Old Welsh. "Thunder." A man with a turbulent nature.

TATE — American Indian. "Windy." Also a variation of Tait.

TAVIS — Gaelic. "Twin."

TAVISH — A variation of Tavis.

TEAGUE — Gaelic. "Bard" or "poet."

TEARLE — Old English. "Stern." One who adheres to rules.

TED — A nickname for Edward or Theodore.

TEDDIE — A nickname for Theodore.

TEDDY — A nickname for Theodore.

TEDMAN — A variation of Theodmund.

TEDMOND — A variation of Theodmund.

TEDMUND — A variation of Theodmund.

TELFOR — Old French. "Ironworker."

TELFORD — A variation of Telfor.

TELFOUR — A variation of Telfor.

TEMPLETON — Old English. "From the town of the temple."

TEOBALDO — The Italian and Spanish form of Theobald.

TEODORICO — The Spanish form of Theodoric.

TEODORO — The Italian and Spanish form of Theodore.

TERENCE — Latin. "Smooth." Or from the Gaelic for "towering."

TERRELL — Old English. "One who rules like Thor," or "thunder."

TERRENCE — A variation of Terence.

TERRIS — Old English. "Son of Terrell or Terence."

TERRISS — A variation of Terris.

TERTIUS — Latin. "Third." A birth-order name.

TEVIS — A variation of Tavis.

THACHER — A variation of Thatcher.

THAD — A nickname for Thaddeus.

THADDAUS — A German form of Thaddeus.

THADDEUS — Greek. "Courageous." Also from the Hebrew for "praised."

THAINE — A variation of Thane.

THALES — Greek. "Flourishing." An ancient Greek philosopher.

THANE — Old English. "Attendant."

THANOS — A Greek form of Arthur.

THATCH — A nickname for Thatcher.

THATCHER — Old English. "Roof thatcher." A trade name.

THAXTER — A variation of Thatcher.

THAYER — Old French. "From the nation's army."

THEBAULT — A French form of Theobald.

THEOBALD — Old German. "Patriotic."

THEODMUND — Old German. "Protector of the nation."

THEODOR — A German and Scandinavian form of Theodore.

THEODORE — Greek. "Gift of God."

THEODORIC — Old German. "Ruler of the people."

THEON — Greek. "Godly."

THEOPHILUS — Greek. "Loved of God."

THERON — Greek. "Hunter."

THIBAUD — A French form of Theobald.

THIBAUT — A German form of Theobald.

THOMA — A German form of Thomas.

THOMAS — Greek. "A twin." St. Thomas, one of the original Twelve Apostles, refused to believe in Christ's resurrection until he was able to touch his wounds; thus the phrase "Doubting Thomas."

THOR — Old Norse. "Thunder." The mythological god of thunder.

THORALD — Old Norse. "Thunder ruler."

THORBERT — Old Norse. "Thunder-bright."

THORBURN — Old Norse. "Thunder-bear."

THORLEY — Old English. "From Thor's meadow."

THORMOND — Old English. "Protected by Thor."

THORMUND — A variation of Thormond.

THORNTON — Old English. "From the thorn estate."

THOROLD — A variation of Thorald.

THORPE — Old English. "From the village."

THUMAS — A French form of Thomas.

THURLOW — Old English. "From the hill of Thor."

THURMAN — A variation of Thormond.

THURSTAN — Old English. "Thor's stone."

THURSTON — A variation of Thurstan.

TIBOLD — A German form of Theobald.

TIEBOUT — A Dutch form of Theobald.

TIERNAN — Gaelic. "Master."

TIERNEY — Gaelic. "Lordly one."

TILDEN — Old English. "From the productive valley."

TILFORD — Old English. "From the fertile ford."

TIM — A nickname for Timothy.

TIMMIE — A nickname for Timothy.

TIMOFEI — A Russian form of Timothy.

TIMON — Greek. "Reward."

TIMOTEO — The Italian and Spanish form of Timothy.

TIMOTHÉE — The French form of Timothy.

TIMOTHEUS — A German form of Timothy.

TIMOTHY — Greek. "Honoring God." A child dedicated to God.

TINO — A nickname for Augustino or Constantino.

TIOBOID — The Irish form of Theobald.

TIOMOID — The Irish form of Timothy.

TIRRELL — A variation of Terrell.

TITO — The Italian and Spanish form of Titus.

TITUS — Greek. "Of the giants."

TIYO — African. "Wise one."

TOBE — A nickname for Tobias.

TOBIA — The Italian form of Tobias.

TOBIAS — Hebrew. "Goodness of God."

TOBIE — A nickname for Tobias.

TOBIN — A variation of Tobias.

TODD — Middle English. "Fox."

TOLAND — Old English. "From the taxed land."

TOM — A nickname for Thomas.

TOMAS — The Irish and Spanish form of Thomas.

TOMASO — An Italian form of Thomas.

TOME — A Portuguese form of Thomas.

TOMKIN — Old English. "Little Tom."

TOMLIN — A variation of Tomkin.

TOMMIE — A nickname for Thomas.

TOMMY — A nickname for Thomas.

TONY — A nickname for Anthony.

TOR — A variation of Tor or Torr.

TORALD — A variation of Thorald.

TORBERT — A variation of Thorbert.

TOREY — A nickname for Torrance.

TORLEY — A variation of Thorley.

TORR — Old English. "From the tower."

TORREY — A variation of Torr.

TORRY — A variation of Torr.

TOV — Hebrew. "Good."

TOWNLEY — Old English. "From the town's meadow."

TOWNSEND — Old English. "From the end of the town."

TRACEY — Greek. "Harvester." Also from the Latin for "Courageous."

TRACY — A variation of Tracey.

TRAHERN — Old Welsh. "Strong as iron."

TRAVER — A variation of Travers.

TRAVERS — Old French. "From the crossroads."

TRAVIS — A variation of Travers.

TREDWAY — Old English. "Powerful warrior."

TREMAIN — Old Cornish. "From the house of stone."

TREMAYNE — A variation of Tremain.

TRENT — Latin. "From the torrent stream."

TREVOR — Gaelic. "Prudent." Man of a cautious nature.

TRISTAN — Old Welsh. "Tumultuous." Sir Tristan was a knight of the Round Table.

TRISTRAM — Welsh. Also Latin. "Sorrowful."

TROY — Gaelic. "Son of a foot soldier."

TRUMAN — Old English. "Faithful man." A man upon whom his loved ones can rely.

TUCKER — Old English. "One who fulled, teased, and burled cloth."

TUDOR — A Welsh form of Theodore.

TULLY — Gaelic. "One who lives with the peace of God." A tranquil soul.

TURLOUGH — Gaelic. "Thorlike."

TURNER — Latin. "Latheworker." A trade name.

TWAIN — Middle English. "Separated into two sections."

TYBALT — A variation of Theobald.

TYLER — Old English. "Maker of tiles and bricks."

TYMON — A Slavic form of Timothy.

TYNAN — Gaelic. "Dark." A name referring to hair or skin color.

TYRONE — Greek. "Sovereign."

TYSON — Old French. "Firebrand."

UDALE — A variation of Udell.

UDALL — A variation of Udell.

UDELL — Old English. "From the valley of the yew tree."

UDOLF — Old English. "Successful wolf."

UGO — The Italian form of Hugo.

UILLIOC — The Irish form of Ulysses.

ULAND — Old English. "From the land of the noble."

ULFRED — Old English. "Wolf-peace."

ULGER — Old English. "Wolf-spear."

ULISES — A Spanish form of Ulysses.

ULMAR — A variation of Ulmer.

ULMER — Old Norse. "Wolf-famous."

ULRIC — A variation of Alaric.

ULRICK — A variation of Alarick.

ULYSSES — Greek. "Wrathful." Ulysses is Homer's hero in the *Odyssey*.

UMBERTO — The Italian form of Humbert.

UPTON — Old English. "From the high town."

UPWEKE — African. "Independent."

UPWOOD — Old English. "From the upper forest."

URBAIN — A French form of Urban.

URBAN — Latin. "From the city." A man who is expected to be more sophisticated than his country cousin.

URBANO — The Italian and Spanish form of Urban.

URBANUS — The German form of Urban.

URIAH — Hebrew. "God is my light." One who turns to God for direction.

URIAN — Greek. "From heaven."

URSON — A variation of Orson.

VACHEL — Old French. "Little cow."

VAIL — Old French. "From the valley."

VALDEMAR — Old German. "Famous leader."

VALDIS — Old German. "Active in battle." A willing soldier.

VALE — A variation of Vail.

VALENTIN — The French, German, Scandinavian, and Spanish form of Valentine.

VALENTINE — Latin. "Strong and healthy." St. Valentine, a Roman martyr, is the patron saint of lovers.

VALENTINO — The Italian form of Valentine.

VALERIAN — Latin. "Powerful and healthy."

VALLIS — Old German. "Welshman."

VAN — Dutch. "Of" or "from." Sometimes found as a first name, but more often used with another name as a last name.

VANCE — Middle English. "From the grain fan."

VARDEN — Old French. "From the green hill."

VARDON — A variation of Varden.

VARECK — A variation of Warrick.

VARIAN — Latin. "Changeable." A man with a flexible nature.

VARICK — A variation of Warrick.

VARNEY — Old French. "From the alder grove."

VASILIS — A Greek form of Basil.

VASSILY — A Russian form of William.

VAUGHAN — A variation of Vaughn.

VAUGHN — Old Welsh. "Small one."

VERDON — A variation of Verden.

VERGE — A nickname for Virgil.

VERGIL — A variation of Virgil, the well-known Roman epic poet.

VERNE — Latin. "Spring-like."

VERNER — A variation of Werner.

VERNEY — A variation of Varney.

VERNON — Latin. "Springlike, flourishing."

VIC — A nickname for Victor.

VICENTE — The Spanish form of Vincent.

VICK — A nickname for Victor.

VICTOR — Latin. "Conquering."

VIN — A nickname for Vincent."

VINCE — A nickname for Vincent.

VINCENT — Latin. "Conquering."

VINCENTE — The Italian form of Vincent.

VINCENTIUS — The Dutch form of Vincent.

VINCENTY — A Slavic form of Vincent.

VINCENZ — The German form of Vincent.

VIRGE — A variation of Virgil.

VIRGIL — Latin. "Staff-bearer."

VIRGILIO — The Italian and Spanish form of Virgil.

VISHNU — Hindu. The major god of good forces.

VITO — Latin. "Alive." An animated young man.

VITTORIO — The Italian form of Victor.

VIVIEN — Latin. "Vivacious."

VLADIMIR — Old Slavic. "Powerful warrior."

VLADISLAV — Old Slavic. "Glory of the ruler."

VOLNEY — Old German. "Of the people."

WACE — Old English. "Feudal peasant." A man who worked the land for a lord.

WADE — Old English. "One who moves forward."

WADLEY — Old English. "From the meadow of the man who moves forward."

WADSWORTH — Old English. "From the farm of the one who moves forward."

WAGNER — German. "Wagonmaker." A trade name.

WAINWRIGHT — Old English. "Wagonmaker."

WAITE — Middle English. "Guard."

WAKEFIELD — Old English. "From the wet field."

WAKELEY — Old English. "From the wet meadow."

WALBRIDGE — Old English. "Dweller near the walled bridge."

WALBY — Old English. "From the walled place."

WALCOT — A variation of Walcott.

WALCOTT — Old English. "Dweller in the walled cottage."

WALD — Old English. "Dweller in the grove."

WALDEMAR — Old German. "Powerful and mighty."

WALDEN — Old English. "From the forest valley." Or from the Old German for "ruler."

WALDO — Old English. "Mighty." Also from the Old German for "ruler."

WALDON — Old English. "From the forest hill."

WALDRON — Old German. "Powerful raven."

WALFORD — Old English. "From the Welshman's ford."

WALFRED — Old German. "Peaceful ruler."

WALKER — Old English. "A thickener of cloth."

WALLACE — Old English. "Welshman."

WALLACHE — A German form of Wallace.

WALLIS — A variation of Wallace.

WALLY — A nickname for Walter.

WALMOND — Old German. "Mighty protector."

WALSH — A variation of Wallace.

WALT — A nickname for Walter.

WALTER — Old German. "Powerful warrior."

WALTHER — A German form of Walter.

WALTON — Old English. "From the walled town."

WARD — Old English. "Guardian." Names such as this derived from a trade are quite common.

WARDE — A variation of Ward.

WARDELL — Old English. "From the hill of the guard."

WARDEN — A variation of Ward.

WARDLEY — Old English. "From the guardian's meadow."

WARE — Old German. "Defender." Also from the Old English for "astute, prudent, and wary."

WARFIELD — Old English. "Dweller in the field by the dam."

WARFORD — Old English. "Dweller in the ford by the dam."

WARING — A variation of Warren.

WARNER — Old German. "Armed defender." A man prepared to protect his home and his loved ones.

WARREN — Old German. "Defender." Also from the Middle English meaning game warden.

WARRICK — A variation of Warwick.

WARTON — Old English. "From the estate by the dam."

WARWICK — Old English. "From the fortress of the defender."

WASHBURN — Old English. "Dweller near the overflowing brook."

WASHINGTON — Old English. "From the town of the one known for his astuteness." George Washington was the first president of the United States and is called the "Father of his Country."

WATKINS — Old English. "Son of Walter."

WATSON — Old English. "Son of Walter."

WAVERLY — Old English. "From the meadow of the quaking aspen trees."

WAYLAND — Old English. "From the land by the road."

WAYNE — A variation of Wainwright.

WEBB — Old English. "Weaver."

WEBER — A German form of Webb.

WEBSTER — Old English. "Weaver."

WEDDEL — Old English. "From the hill of the one moving forward."

WELBORNE — Old English. "From the spring fed brook."

WELBY — Old English. "From the farm by the spring."

WELDON — Old English. "From the hill by the spring."

WELFORD — Old English. "From the spring ford."

WELLINGTON — Old English. "From the estate of the prosperous one."

WELLS — Old English. "From the springs."

WELSH — A variation of Wallace.

WENCESLAUS — Old Slavic. "Crown of Glory." The Good King Wenceslaus of the Christmas carol was a 10th-century Duke of Bohemia who was converted to Christianity

WENDEL — A variation of Wendell.

WENDELL — Old German. "Wanderer." Also from the Old English for "one who lives near the boundary."

WENTWORTH — Old English. "From the blond one's estate."

WERNER — A German form of Warner.

WESLEY — Old English. "From the west meadow." John Wesley was the founder of the Methodist Church.

WEST — Old English. "Man from the west."

WESTBROOK — Old English. "From the west brook."

WESTCOTT — Old English. "From the west cottage."

WESTLEIGH — A variation of Wesley.

WESTLEY — A variation of Wesley.

WESTON — Old English. "From the west farmstead."

WETHERLY — Old English. "From the sheep meadow."

WHARTON — Old English. "From the estate at the hollow."

WHEATLEY — Old English. "From the wheat meadow."

WHEATON — Old English. "From the wheat farm."

WHEELER — Old English. "Wheelmaker."

WHISTLER — Old English. "Piper." An entertainer.

WHITBY — Scandinavian. "From the settlement of white dwellings."

WHITCOMB — Old English. "From the white hollow."

WHITEFIELD — Old English. "From the white field."

WHITELAW — Old English. "From the white hill."

WHITFORD — Old English. "From the white ford."

WHITLEY — Old English. "From the white meadow."

WHITMAN — Old English. "White-haired man."

WHITMORE — Old English. "Dweller on the white moor."

WHITTAKER — Old English. "From the white field."

WIATT — A variation of Wyatt.

WICENT — A Polish form of Vincent.

WICKHAM — Old English. "From the village meadow."

WILBUR — Old German. "Resolute protection." Also from the Old English for "well-fortified stronghold." Wilbur Wright and his brother Orville flew the first successful airplane.

WILDON — Old English. "From the wooded hill."

WILEK — A Polish form of William.

WILEY — A variation of William.

WILFORD — Old English. "Dweller near the willow trees by the ford."

WILFRED — Old German. "Resolute for peace."

WILFRID — A variation of Wilfred.

WILHELM — A German, Polish, and Swedish form of William.

WILL — Old English. "Determined, firm." Also a nickname for William.

WILLARD — Old English. "Resolutely brave."

WILLEM — A Dutch form of William.

WILLIAM — Old German. "Determined protector."

WILLIAMSON — Old German. "Son of William."

WILLIE — A nickname for William.

WILLIS — A variation of William.

WILLOUGHBY — Old English. "From the willow farm."

WILLY — A nickname for William.

WILMAR — A variation of Wilmer.

WILMER — Old German. "Determined and famous."

WILMOT — Old German. "With determined spirit.

WILSON — A variation of Williamson.

WILTON — Old English. "From the farm by the spring."

WINCHELL — Old English. "Dweller near the bend in the road."

WINDSOR — Old English. "From the bank on the river." This name was chosen by the royal family of England when it changed its German last name during the First World War.

WINFIELD — Old English. "From the friend's field."

WINFRED — Old English. "Friend of peace."

WINFRID — A variation of Winfred.

WINGATE — Old English. "Divine protection."

WINIFRED — A variation of Winfred.

WINN — A variation of Wynn.

WINSLOW — Old English. "From the friend's hill."

WINSOR — A variation of Windsor.

WINSTON — Old English. "From the friend's town." Winston Churchill was the famous English statesman who was prime minister during World War II.

WINTHROP — Old English. "Dweller at the friend's village."

WINTON — Old English. "From the estate of the friend."

WIRT — Old English. "Worthy." Also from the Old German for "master."

WITT — Old English. "Wise."

WOLCOTT — Old English. "From the wolf's courage."

WOLF — Old English. "Wolf." In ancient times, an animal honored for its courage and cunning.

WOLFE — A variation of Wolf.

WOLFGANG — Old German. "Advancing wolf." A predator.

WOODLEY — Old English. "From the wooded meadow."

WOODMAN — Old English. "Hunter, forester."

WOODROW — Old English. "From the hedge by the forest."

WOODWARD — Old English. "Forester."

WOODY — A nickname for names beginning with "Wood." Also used as an independent name.

WOOLCOTT — A variation of Wolcott.

WOOLSEY — Old English. "Victorious wolf."

WORDEN — A variation of Warden.

WORDSWORTH — Old English. "From the farm of the wolflike guardian."

WORTH — Old English. "From the farmstead."

WORTHINGTON — Old English. "From the farmstead on the riverside."

WORTON — Old English. "From near the vegetable garden."

WRAY — Old Norse. "From the corner property."

WREN — Old Welsh. "Chief." Also from the English for the bird of that name.

WRIGHT — Old English. "Carpenter."

WYATT — An Old French form of Guy.

WYBORN — Old Norse. "Bear of war." A brave man.

WYCLIFF — Old English. "From the white cliff."

WYLIE — Old English. "Charming."

WYMAN — Old English. "Warrior."

WYMER — Old English. "Battle-famous."

WYNDHAM — Old English. "From the enclosure with the winding path."

WYNN — Old Welsh. "Fair."

WYNONO — American Indian. "First-born."

WYTHE — Middle English. "One who resides near a willow tree."

XAVIER — Arabic. "Bright." A Spanish name honoring St. Francis Xavier, a 16th-century Jesuit missionary.

XENOPHON — Greek. "Strange voice." A Greek historian.

XENOS — Greek. "Stranger."

XERXES — Persian. "Ruler." A world-famous conqueror of 5th century B.C.

XEVER — A variation of Xavier

XYLON — Greek. "From the forest."

YALE — Old English. "From the corner of the land."

YANCY — American Indian. "Englishman."

YANNIS — A Greek form of John.

YARDLEY — Old English. "From the enclosed meadow."

YATES — Middle English. "One who resides by the city gates."

YEHUDI — Hebrew. "The lord praises."

YEMON — Japanese. "Guardian."

YEOMAN — Middle English. "A feudal tenant." A man who owed service to the lord of the manor.

YOEL — The Hebrew form of Joel.

YORK — Old English. "Estate of the boar." Also from the Old Celtic for "from the farm near the yew trees."

YUMA — American Indian. "Son of the chief."

YUSEF — A German and Scandinavian form of Joseph.

YVES — A French form of Ives.

ZACARIAS — The Spanish form of Zachariah.

ZACCARIA — An Italian form of Zachariah.

ZACHARIAH — Hebrew. "Memory of the lord." A biblical name popularized by the Puritans.

ZACHARIAS — The German form of Zachariah.

ZACHARIE — The French form of Zachary.

ZACHARY — A variation of Zachariah.

ZADOC — A French form of Zadok.

ZADOK — Hebrew. "Righteous." A forthright man.

ZAHUR — African. "Flower."

ZAK — A nickname for Zachariah.

ZAKARIAS — A Scandinavian form of Zachariah.

ZANE — A variation of John.

ZARED — Hebrew. "Ambush."

ZEBABIAH — Hebrew. "Gift of God." A child sent from heaven. A biblical name.

ZEBULON — Hebrew. "Dwelling place." One of the sons of the biblical Jacob.

ZECHARIAH — A variation of Zachariah.

ZEDEKIAH — Hebrew. "Justice from God." A biblical name.

ZEEMAN — Dutch. "Mariner." A man of the sea.

ZEKE — A nickname for Zechariah.

ZELOTES — Greek. "Zealous." A man of passionate enthusiasm.

ZENAS — Greek. "Living."

ZENON — Greek and Spanish. "Life given by Zeus."

ZEUS — Greek. "Living one." In ancient Greece, Zeus was the chief god, father of man, and ruler of Mount Olympus.

ZIV — Old Slavic. "Living vigorous."

ZIVEN — A variation of Ziv.

ZORYA - Russian. "Star." A child blessed with a sparkling personality.

ZURIEL — Hebrew. "God, the foundation."

(8) Names for Boys and Girls

ALAULA — Hawaiian. "Dawn." Most Hawaiian names are used for a child of either sex.

ALEXIS — Greek. "Defender of mankind." A variation of Alexander.

ALI — A nickname for Alison. Also used as an independent name.

ALISON — Old English. "Child of a noble."

ALLISON — A variation of Alison.

ALOHA — Hawaiian. Name implying affection. Used as a greeting.

ANG — A nickname for Angel.

ANGEL — Greek. "Messenger of God." One who brings glad tidings.

ANGELL — A variation of Angel.

ANGIE — A nickname for Angel.

ARIES — Latin. "Ram." Appropriate astrological name for a child born between March 21 and April 19.

AVERELL — A variation of Averil.

AVERIL — Old English. "Boar warrior." Also from the Middle English for "born in April."

AVERILL — A variation of Averil.

BERYL — Greek. "Green jewel." A precious child.

BEVERLEY — Old English. "From the meadow of the beavers."

BEVERLY — A variation of Beverley.

BILLIE — A nickname for Wilhelmina or William.

BLISS — Old English. "Joyful."

BLITHE — A variation of Blythe.

BLY — American Indian. "Tall." Also used in Africa to mean "cheerful."

BLYTHE — Old English. "Merry."

BOBBIE — A nickname for Robert, Roberta, or Robin.

BOBBY — A nickname for Robert, Roberta, or Robin.

BRET — Celtic. "A Briton."

BRETT — A variation of Bret.

BROOK — Middle English. "One who resides near a brook."

BROOKE — A variation of Brook.

CAREY — Old Welsh. "From the castle."

CARY — A variation of Carey.

CHRISTIAN — Latin. "A follower of Christ."

CHRISTMAS — Middle English. The holiday commemorating the birth of Christ. An appropriate name for a child born during this festive time of year.

COLUMBA — Latin. "Dove." The symbol of peace.

COREY — Gaelic. "Dweller by the misty pool."

CORY — A variation of Corey.

DACEY — Gaelic. "Southerner."

DACY — A variation of Dacey.

DAGMAR — Old Norse. "Glory of the Danes."

DALE — Old English. "From the valley."

DANA — Old English. "A Dane."

DARCIE — A variation of Darcy.
DARCY — Old French. "From the fortress." Also from the Gaelic for "dark."
DARRYL — A variation of Daryl.
DARSEY — A variation of Darcy.
DARYL — Old French. "Beloved." A child who is the target of great love and affection.
DONNIE — A nickname for various names beginning with "Don."
DONNY — A nickname for various names beginning with "Don."
DORY — French. "With golden locks."

EASTER — Old English. "The Easter holiday." Easter was a goddess of spring in ancient England.
ERIN — Gaelic. "Peace."
ESMÉ — French. "Beloved."
EVELYN — Greek. "Light." Also derived from the Old French for "ancestor."

FAITH — Middle English. "Trusting and loyal."
FAY — Gaelic. "Raven." A raven was considered the symbol of wisdom in ancient Europe.
FAYE — A variation of Fay.
FAYETTE — A variation of Fay.
FORTUNE — Latin. "Fate." Also from the Old French for "lucky."
FRAN — A nickname for Francis or Frances.
FRANKIE — A nickname for Francis or Frances.

GAIL — A variation of Gale.
GALE — Old English. "Lively."
GALYA — Hebrew. "God has redeemed."
GAYLE — A variation of Gale.
GEORGIE — A nickname for various forms of George.

HAGIA — Hebrew. "Joyful."
HALEY — Gaelic. "Inventive."

HARPER — Old English. "Harp player." One capable of producing beautiful music.
HILARY — Latin. "Cheerful."
HILLARY — A variation of Hilary.
HILLERY — A variation of Hilary.
HOKU — Hawaiian. "Star."
HOPE — Old English. "Expectation."

JAEL — Hebrew. "Mountain goat." An appropriate name for a Capricorn child.
JAMIE — Hebrew. "The supplanter." A variation of James.
JESS — A variation of Jesse.
JESSE — Hebrew. "Gift of God." A child sent from heaven.
JO — A nickname for Joseph and Josephine.
JOE — A nickname for both Josephine and Joseph.

KAI — Hawaiian. "Sea." An appropriate name for a child born under the water signs of the Zodiac: Cancer, Scorpio, and Pisces.
KAMA — Hindu. "Love." God of love, similar to the Western Cupid.
KAMALI — African. "Protection."
KANANI — Hawaiian. "The beauty."
KAPULE — Hawaiian. "Prayer."
KAY — Welsh. "Reveler." Also from the Gaelic for "Fiery." Sir Kay was one of the famous knights of the Round Table.
KEALY — A variation of Keeley.
KEELEY — Gaelic. "Handsome."
KEELY — A variation of Keeley.
KEIKI — Hawaiian. "Child."
KELLEY — A variation of Kelly.
KELLY — Gaelic. "Warrior."
KERRY — Gaelic. "Dark one."
KEVAN — A variation of Kevin.
KEVEN — A variation of Kevin.
KEVIN — Gaelic. "Gentle and lovable."

LANI — Hawaiian. "Sky."

LEE — Latin. "Lion." Also possibly from the Old English for "from the pasture meadow" or "shelter."

LEILANI — Hawaiian. "Heavenly blossom." A melodious name.

LESLEY — A variation of Leslie.

LESLIE — Gaelic. "Dweller at the gray fortress."

LINDSAY — A variation of Lindsey.

LINDSEY — Old English. "From the pool island." A residence name.

LINSAY — A variation of Lindsey.

LINSEY — A variation of Lindsey.

LUZ — Spanish. "Light."

LYNN — Old English. "A waterfall."

MALULANI — Hawaiian. "Peaceful skies."

MARION — Old French. "Little Mary." A name honoring the Virgin Mary.

MEREDITH — Old Welsh. "Protector from the sea."

MERIDITH — A variation of Meredith.

MERLE — Latin. "Blackbird." A raven-haired child.

MERRILL — Old French. "Little one of fame."

MERYL — A variation of Merle.

MICHAEL — Hebrew. "Who is like the Lord."

MICKEY — A nickname for Michael.

MIKE — A nickname for Michael.

MORGAN — Old Welsh. "Of the sea."

MORVEN — Gaelic. "Tall blond one."

NAIRNE — Gaelic. "From the alder-tree river."

NEVILLE — Old French. "From the new manor."

NEVIN — Gaelic. "Worshipper of the saint."

NOEL — French and Latin. "Born at Christmastide."

NURU — African. "Light."

PAT — A nickname for Patrick and Patricia.

PATRICE — The French form of Patrick and Patricia; from the Latin meaning "noble."

PAZ — Spanish. "Peace."

PILAR — Spanish. "Base." A name honoring the Virgin Mary as the foundation of the Roman Catholic Church.

RABI — Arabic. "Breeze."

RAY — Old French. "Regal."

REESE — Old Welsh. "Ardent."

REGAN — Gaelic. "Ardent."

RENÉ — A variation of Renée.

RENÉE — French. "Reborn."

ROBIN — Old English. "Shining fame." Robin Hood was a famous legendary hero of medieval England.

ROE — Middle English. "Roe-deer."

RORY — Gaelic. "Red."

SAL — A nickname for Sally or Salvatore.

SAM — A nickname for Samuel or Samantha.

SHALOM — Hebrew. "Peace."

SHANE — A variation of John.

SHANNON — Gaelic. "Little one of wisdom."

SHELLEY — Old English. "From the meadow on the ledge."

SID — A nickname for Sidney.

SIDNEY — A variation of Sydney.

SYDNEY — Old French. "Belonging to St. Denis." Also from the name of the ancient Phoenician city Sidon.

TAFFY — Old Welsh. "Cherished."

TALOR — Hebrew. "Morning dew."

TAYLOR — Old French and Latin. "A tailor." A trade name.

TIFFANY — Latin. "Appearance of God." In ancient Greece, Theophanias was a celebration of spring and the arrival of the sun god Apollo.

TONY — A nickname for Anthony or Antoinette.

TYE — Old English. "From the garden."

ULANI — Hawaiian. "Cheerful."

VALENTINE — Latin. "Strong and healthy."

VIVIAN — Latin. "Vivacious."

WALLACE — Old English. "Welshman."

WALLIE — A nickname for Wallace.

WALLIS — A variation of Wallace.

WHITNEY — Old English. "From the island of the blond one."

WINFRED — Old English. "Peaceful friend."

WINIFRED — A variation of Winfred.

YANCY — American Indian. "Englishman."